Pragmatic Particles

Bloomsbury Studies in Theoretical Linguistics

Bloomsbury Studies in Theoretical Linguistics publishes work at the forefront of present-day developments in the field. The series is open to studies from all branches of theoretical linguistics and to the full range of theoretical frameworks. Titles in the series present original research that makes a new and significant contribution and are aimed primarily at scholars in the field, but are clear and accessible, making them useful also to students, to new researchers and to scholars in related disciplines.

Other titles in the series:
Approaches to Predicative Possession, edited by Gréte Dalmi, Jacek Witkoś and Piotr Cegłowski
Agreement, Pronominal Clitics and Negation in Tamazight Berber, Hamid Ouali
A Neural Network Model of Lexical Organisation, Michael Fortescue
Contrastive Studies in Morphology and Syntax, edited by Michalis Georgiafentis, Giannoula Giannoulopoulou, Maria Koliopoulou and Angeliki Tsokoglou
Deviational Syntactic Structures, Hans Gotzsche
First Language Acquisition in Spanish, Gilda Socarras
Grammar of Spoken English Discourse, Gerard O'Grady
Pragmatic Syntax, Jieun Kiaer
The Semantic Representation of Natural Language, Michael Levison, Greg Lessard, Craig Thomas and Matthew Donald
The Syntax and Semantics of Discourse Markers, Miriam Urgelles-Coll
The Syntax of Mauritian Creole, Anand Syea

Pragmatic Particles
Findings from Asian Languages

Jieun Kiaer

BLOOMSBURY ACADEMIC
LONDON • NEW YORK • OXFORD • NEW DELHI • SYDNEY

BLOOMSBURY ACADEMIC
Bloomsbury Publishing Plc
50 Bedford Square, London, WC1B 3DP, UK
1385 Broadway, New York, NY 10018, USA

BLOOMSBURY, BLOOMSBURY ACADEMIC and the Diana logo are trademarks of
Bloomsbury Publishing Plc

First published in Great Britain 2021
Paperback edition published 2022

Copyright © Jieun Kiaer, 2021

Jieun Kiaer has asserted her right under the Copyright, Designs and Patents Act,
1988, to be identified as Author of this work.

For legal purposes the Acknowledgements on p. xi constitute an extension
of this copyright page.

All rights reserved. No part of this publication may be reproduced or transmitted
in any form or by any means, electronic or mechanical, including photocopying,
recording, or any information storage or retrieval system, without prior
permission in writing from the publishers.

Bloomsbury Publishing Plc does not have any control over, or responsibility for, any third-
party websites referred to or in this book. All internet addresses given in this book were
correct at the time of going to press. The author and publisher regret any inconvenience
caused if addresses have changed or sites have ceased to exist, but can accept no
responsibility for any such changes.

A catalogue record for this book is available from the British Library.

Library of Congress Cataloging-in-Publication Data
Names: Kiaer, Jieun, author.
Title: Pragmatic particles: findings from Asian languages / Jieun Kiaer.
Description: London; New York: Bloomsbury Academic, 2020. | Series: Bloomsbury
studies in theoretical linguistics | Includes bibliographical references and index.
Identifiers: LCCN 2020031003 (print) | LCCN 2020031004 (ebook) |
ISBN 9781350118461 (hardback) | ISBN 9781350191655 (paperback) |
ISBN 9781350118478 (ebook) | ISBN 9781350118485 (epub)
Subjects: LCSH: Grammar, Comparative and general–Particles. | East Asia–Languages–
Particles. | Southeast Asia–Languages–Particles. | Middle East–Languages–Particles.
Classification: LCC P283 .K53 2020 (print) | LCC P283 (ebook) | DDC 415/.5–dc23
LC record available at https://lccn.loc.gov/2020031003
LC ebook record available at https://lccn.loc.gov/2020031004

ISBN: HB: 978-1-3501-1846-1
PB: 978-1-3501-9165-5
ePDF: 978-1-3501-1847-8
eBook: 978-1-3501-1848-5

Series: Bloomsbury Studies in Theoretical Linguistics

Typeset by Deanta Global Publishing Services, Chennai, India

To find out more about our authors and books visit www.bloomsbury.com
and sign up for our newsletters.

Contents

List of illustrations	vi
Preface	ix
Acknowledgements	xi
Abbreviations and conventions	xii
1 Introduction	1
2 Modelling flexible word orders	23
3 Efficiency grammar	43
4 Multidimensional meanings	65
5 Socio-pragmatic meanings	83
6 Particles as a meaning complex	113
7 Pragmatic syntax	133
8 Constructive particles and syntactic fluidity	165
9 Expressive and attitudinal particles	177
Epilogue	211
Notes	215
Bibliography	225
Index	237

Illustrations

Figures

1.1	Syntactic structure of Japanese sentence	6
2.1	Lengthened connective particle as utterance-final particle	30
2.2	Overt verb raising: Ensuring IO DO constituency	35
2.3	*Hon-o Mary-ni* as a constituent via oblique movement	36
2.4	Baldridge's derivation of a long-distance scrambling in Turkish	41
3.1	Incremental constituency	47
3.2	Grammaticality check in a local domain	50
3.3	Structure for *Jessica rang up the boy*	56
3.4	Articulation rate (s/second) by number of syllables for both interveners and non-interveners	57
3.5	Gap in the matrix clause	59
3.6	Gap in the embedded clause	60
3.7	Syntactic structure of Korean sentence	62
3.8	Syntactic structure for dative NP versus accusative NP	63
3.9	Syntactic structure for Chinese: Ternary structure	63
4.1a	Approval with emoticon	70
4.1b	Approval without any emoticon	70
4.2a	Approval without any emoticon	71
4.2b	Approval with emoticon	71
4.3	Layers of expressive meanings	77
5.1	Hand gesture	90
5.2	Prayer or thank you	91
6.1	Subjectiveness and objectiveness scale	125
7.1	Pre-determined type-raising	138
7.2	Binary, functor-argument relation	141
7.3	Partial structure projected by the verb *iki* 'beat'	142
7.4	Persian verb ending updates the subject	144
7.5	Lao verbs: Fo(U) and Fo(V) will be updated from the context	145
7.6	Local structure building via case particle *-ka*	148
7.7	Routinized update via the accusative particle *-lul*	149

7.8	Pre-verbal constructions	153
7.9	Parsing who in (19c)	157
7.10	Anaphoric copy	158
7.11	Updating the implicit arguments from the context	159
7.12	Three motives: Efficiency, expressivity and empathy	161
8.1	Lexical macros via case particles	167
8.2	Building a sequence of LINKed structures	173
9.1	Greeting in Thai and Lao	201
9.2	Single LINK application	207
9.3	Multiple LINK application	208

Tables

1.1	Common European framework for language proficiency	3
2.1	Constructive case particles	25
4.1	Interrogative particles in Lao grammar	70
5.1	Urdu expressions sensitive to social hierarchy between speaker and hearer	100
5.2	Hindi expressions sensitive to social hierarchy between speaker and hearer	101
5.3	Bengali expressions sensitive to social hierarchy between speaker and hearer	101
5.4	Bengali verbal conjugations based on person pronouns	102
5.5	Japanese expressions sensitive to social hierarchy	102
5.6	Bengali: Pronominal	104
5.7	Second-person pronouns and address terms in Japanese	109
5.8	Second-person pronouns and address terms in Korean	110
7.1	Types in dynamic syntax	140
8.1	Constructive particles in Japanese	168
8.2	Constructive particles in Bengali	168
8.3	Constructive particles in Hindi	168
8.4	Constructive particles in Urdu	169
8.5	Constructive particles in Turkish	169
8.6	Constructive particles in Persian	169
8.7	Constructive particles in Mongolian	169
8.8	Constructive particles in Tagalog	170
8.9	Constructive particles in Tibet	170

9.1	Expressive particles in Bengali	198
9.2	Expressive particles in Hindi	198
9.3	Expressive particles in Urdu	199
9.4	Expressive particles in Vietnamese	199
9.5	Expressive particles in Lao	200
9.6	Expressive particles in Burmese	200
9.7	Expressive particles in Khmer	200
9.8	Meanings of boundary tones	202

Preface

Particles are not peripheral categories, nor are their behaviours arbitrary or accidental. They play a crucial role in unfolding structural skeletons and making syntax predictable, yet at the same time enriching socio-pragmatic, interactional meanings. Particles are observed cross-linguistically as a complex of syntactic, semantic and pragmatic primitives. However, particles, although widely observed in the languages of the world, are largely unexplored in theoretical linguistics.

Particle researchers often concentrate on only one aspect of particles, rather than grappling with their complex, multifaceted nature. Hence, some particles are called a case marker in one setting, but a discourse marker in another when it is in fact the same particle operating with dual or multiple functions. Such a fragmented view is at times unavoidable in contemporary linguistics which is, in principle, approached from a non-holistic standpoint. From an Anglo- or Euro-centric perspective, the general linguistic properties of particles are often marginalized as their roles are less crucial in English and other European languages. For instance, in English, orders and verbs provide the main combinatory information, and auxiliaries present modal meanings, although the repertoire of meanings available is much more limited than what we find in Asian languages. The starting point of this book is to observe, describe and explain particles in a logical manner, and from a position that is divorced from the traditional Euro-centric perspective. By observing the characteristics and behaviours of particles – which have so often been overlooked – I aim to show how socio-pragmatic motivations shape morphosyntactic variations through case studies of Asian languages. In doing so, I shall also show that contemporary Anglo-centric grammar formalisms are inadequate to properly observe, describe and explain the constructive roles and socio-pragmatically rich meanings that the particles in these languages project.

This book draws on data from a host of non-Western European languages. Without delving into detailed descriptions of every language, I aim to demonstrate what the commonalities shared by these languages can contribute to linguistic theory. I will also show that the paradigms set up for English and other European languages are largely inadequate for explaining phenomena seen in these Asian languages.

In this book, I highlight the necessity of researching (i) the constructive role of particles in languages which exhibit flexible word orders and (ii) the rich array of expressive and attitudinal meanings exhibited by particles, which are sensitive to sociocultural factors. I adopt Dynamic Syntax as a formal model to explain particle behaviours, which have been traditionally difficult to capture within a static linguistic framework. I also draw on Potts' expressive semantics (2005) to show how complex interpersonal relations are manifested in the morphosyntactic realization of particles and other elements of language. In formal linguistics, the effect of speaker-hearer interpersonal dynamics such as intimacy, status and kinship is considered peripheral. I take the view that these are crucial driving forces for linguistic behaviours.

Acknowledgements

This book would not have happened without inspiration from colleagues, teachers and my own students. If I had not studied Dynamic Syntax for my doctorate, I would never have pursued many of the questions discussed in this book; surrounded by wonderful specialists in Asian languages and culture at the Oriental Studies Faculty at Oxford University gave me a real appreciation and care for languages I had not previously encountered. This work is written out of a conviction that the diverse, fine-grained socio-pragmatic meanings of Asian languages deserve much more attention in contemporary linguistics.

I am very grateful to those who have provided invaluable help at the different stages of the project. Especially, I have consulted the following people for the data included in this book: Jing Yan (Chinese), Amena Nebres (Tagalog), Bihani Sarkar and Ranjamrittika Bhowmik (Bengali), Aayush Srivastava (Hindi, Urdu), Justin Watson (Burmese), Jakob Fjeldsted and Orranand Sukhasvasti (Thai and Lao), Nhung Nguyen (Vietnamese), Saera Kwak and Sahba Shaya (Persian), Lama Jabb (Tibetan), Junko Hagiwara (Japanese), Nadia Christopher (Kazakh), Nadia Jamil (Arabic) and Emine Cakir (Turkish).

Derek Driggs, Niamh Calway, Alex Kimmons and Edward Voet have also provided me with wonderful editorial help. I am also thankful to Andrew Wardell and Becky Holland from Bloomsbury for their patience and encouragement throughout this project.

I would not have begun this trajectory without the love and support of my family and friends. I would like to dedicate this book to my father, Taehoon Joe, and father-in-law, Stanley Kiaer, both of whom I dearly miss.

Abbreviations and conventions

Glossing conventions[1]

Most of the available glossing conventions are not sufficient to capture the complex and diverse nature of Asian languages' morphosyntactic and pragmatic characteristics projected by particles.[2] In this book, I propose the lexical matrix to describe and explain particles' diverse constructive, attitudinal and expressive meanings. However, for the readers' convenience, I shall provide some conventional glossing in other places.

Glossing abbreviations

ACC	accusative
ADJ	adjective
ADN	adnominal
ADV	adverb(ial)
AFTH	afterthought marker
AUX	auxiliary
CAUS	causative
CL	classifier
COM	comitative
COMP	complementizer
COND	conditional
CONJ	conjunct

COP	copula
DAT	dative
DECL	declarative
DEF	definite
EMP	empathizer
EMPH	emphatic particle added to a noun expressing empathy for the referent ('poor X')
FOC	focus
FORMAL	formal
FUT	future
GEN	genitive
HON	honorific
I	intimate
IMP	imperative
INT	interjective
INTRG	interrogative
LOC	locative
NEG	negative
NMLZ	nominalizer/nominalization
NOM	nominative
OBJ	object
OBL	oblique
ORD	ordinary
PASS	passive
PST	past
PERF	perfective

PL	plural
POL	polite
POSS	possessive
PRF	perfect
PRES	present
Q	question
REFL	reflexive
REL	relative
RETRO	retrospect
ROY	Royal suffix added to noun phrases to indicate royal referents; today also used with non-royal referents of high standing
SIP/UIP	sentence/utterance initial particle
SMP/UMP	sentence/utterance medial particle
SFP/UFP	sentence/utterance-final particle
TOP	topic
VOC	vocative
VOL	volitional

Romanization and orthography conventions

For most occasions I strive for phonetically intuitive romanization. Since many particles have homophones, whenever necessary I shall also provide the local orthography. For morphosyntactic characterizations I follow morphosyntactically suitable romanization, such as the Yale system.[3]

1

Introduction

In this chapter, I shall provide a brief overview of the status quo of research into Asian languages (1.1) and particles (1.2) and the challenges that these languages could bring to contemporary theories in linguistics. I shall introduce the target languages under discussion (1.3) and their key features (1.4) which I aim to explain in this book. I also introduce target languages (1.5).

1.1. Researching Asian languages

Modern linguistics was greatly influenced and inspired by the works of Asian linguists' grammar, such as Pāṇini's. Aṣṭādhyāyī by Pāṇini (dated c. fourth to fifth centuries BC) is the very earliest extant systematic grammar of human languages. It has inspired many pioneers of the modern linguistic science – Ferdinand de Saussure, Leonard Bloomfield and Roman Jakobson, all Sanskrit scholars. Staal (1967) notes that Pāṇini's grammar provided the formal foundation for contemporary linguistics due to its influence on Saussure and Noam Chomsky.

However, in the course of its development, the Asian touch within linguistics has been lost. Throughout the history of contemporary linguistics, in accordance with the Chomskian tradition of generative grammars, theoretical linguists have aimed to unravel universal grammars that would be applicable to all human languages. However, this search has been conducted with data taken mainly from European languages. That said, in the process of searching out and crystallizing the linguistic categories and features of world languages, mainstream Western linguists often construct their approach through the looking glass of English-like languages, implicitly assuming that the linguistic consistencies found in these languages will be applicable to all other languages with little parametric variation. This often unsaid, yet implicitly assumed, idea is prevalent in every part of contemporary linguistics.

In order to address the aforementioned lack of language diversity in linguistic discourse, this book uses data from a range of Asian languages which are relatively under-represented in theoretical linguistics. From a world languages perspective, Asian languages have never been minority languages, and their foreign speakership is growing rapidly worldwide. For instance, the 2011 UK census showed that the Asian or Asian British ethnic group category experienced one of the largest increases since 2001, comprising a third of the foreign-born population of the UK (2.4 million) (Office for National Statistics 2013). The US Census Bureau (2011) revealed that Asian and Pacific Island languages constitute a major portion of foreign languages spoken in the United States. These languages include Chinese; Korean; Japanese; Vietnamese; Hmong; Khmer; Lao; Thai; Tagalog/Filipino; the Dravidian languages of India, such as Telugu, Tamil and Malayalam; and other languages of Asia and the Pacific, including the Polynesian and Micronesian languages. Among them, Chinese, Korean and Vietnamese belong to the country's top ten most widely spoken languages. The situation is similar in other English-speaking countries such as Australia and Canada which, to use Kachru's terminology (1985), belong to the inner circle of English. In Australia, the top four foreign languages are Asian: Mandarin, Arabic, Cantonese and Vietnamese. Tagalog/Filipino, Hindi and Punjabi also appear in the top ten most spoken foreign languages. In Canada, Tagalog and Punjabi are the two fastest growing foreign languages. The growth of Asian languages is observable in other parts of the world as well.

Nevertheless, regardless of their global significance, Asian languages have been severely under-represented within contemporary linguistics. Even for mega languages like Mandarin, Standard Arabic, Hindi and Bengali/Bangla (all of which are among Ethnologue's 2019 top ten most spoken languages in the world), it is not easy to find an accessible descriptive grammar book or any handbook-like linguistic publication written for a global audience, compared to what is available for English and other Western European languages.[1] As I shall discuss later in this chapter (1.4) and in Chapter 2, most of the morphosyntactic characteristics of Asian languages, despite being found in the majority of world languages, have been largely overlooked or considered exceptional within the realm of contemporary linguistics.

General awareness of non-Western European languages is poor across the globe.[2] Asian languages in the Anglophone or Western European context have often been referred to as 'heritage' languages – implying that these are languages for Asian immigrants and their descendants only. Across universities globally, the 'Modern Languages' department frequently refers to contemporary Western

European languages: French, Italian, Spanish and German, while Asian languages are referred to as 'East Asian', 'South Asian' or 'Near Eastern' (Kiaer 2017a). Asian languages have often been classified as difficult-to-master languages for native speakers of English. According to the Foreign Service Institute, an organ of the US Federal Government, most Asian languages belong to (difficulty) categories III and IV.[3] It is noteworthy that most Western European languages – such as French, German, Dutch, Italian, Spanish and Portuguese – are considered category I languages, which shows relative easiness of learning.

From an English speaker's perspective, Asian languages tend to have a more complex socio-pragmatic system than Western European languages (see Chapter 5 for a detailed discussion). Asian languages are also often not as straightforward to romanize or gloss as English and most Western European languages. However, mere difference from the English language can justify neither the poor general awareness of, nor the lack of research on, these languages.

In fact, most available linguistic pedagogies are also based on the acquisition of European languages and cannot be applied easily to the study of Asian languages. Consider Table 1.1.

Table 1.1 shows the Common European Framework of Reference for Languages (CEFR) vocabulary profiler. Yet, even in this table, command of

Table 1.1 Common European framework for language proficiency

Level	Descriptor
C2	Has a good command of a very broad lexical repertoire including idiomatic expressions and colloquialisms; shows awareness of connotative levels of meaning.
C1	Has a good command of a broad lexical repertoire allowing gaps to be readily overcome with circumlocutions; little obvious searching for expressions or avoidance strategies. Good command of idiomatic expressions and colloquialisms.
B2	Has a good range of vocabulary for matters related to his/her field and most general topics. Can vary formulation to avoid frequent repetition, but lexical gaps can still cause hesitation and circumlocution.
B1	Has a sufficient vocabulary to express himself/herself with some circumlocutions on most topics pertinent to his/her everyday life such as family, hobbies and interests, work, travel and current events. Has sufficient vocabulary to conduct routine, everyday transactions involving familiar situations and topics.
A2	Has a sufficient vocabulary for the expression of basic communicative needs. Has a sufficient vocabulary for coping with simple survival needs.
A1	Has a basic vocabulary repertoire of isolated words and phrases related to particular concrete situations.

grammatical relations using particles, or the appropriate usage of sociocultural relation-sensitive speech, such as honorifics or sentence-final particles, is not included. Pragmatic proficiency is included briefly as 'idiomatic expressions and colloquialisms' (i.e. C2) but is a more significant concern in Asian languages in which mastering interpersonal relations is a crucial part of linguistic competence. A1-2 refers to the basic level, B1-2 refers to the intermediate level and C1-2 refers to the advanced level.

As I shall turn to in section 1.4 and Chapter 2, many key morphosyntactic features that are shared by a vast number of Asian languages have also been under-represented or overlooked, as they are analysed and understood mainly from an English-language perspective. This book aims to demonstrate the necessity of showcasing the often-overlooked properties of Asian languages that are in need of proper observation, description and explanation. These properties, as it happens, are not exclusively exhibited in Asian languages, but are observed cross-linguistically among world languages.

1.2. Particles on the fringe

The definition of the term 'particle' varies greatly, but for the purposes of this discussion, I take 'particle' to be an overarching term referring to a single or a sequence of (un)inflected grammatical morphemes which play a role as a single unit with a complexity of syntactic, semantic and (socio-)pragmatic meaning. The term 'particle' is used as an umbrella term to refer to endings, markers, suffixes, morphemes and so on in order to bring focus to the common characteristics of all these categories which fall under the wider heading of 'particle'. Particles cannot be used as standalone words, and their use is sensitive to interlocutory registers and speakers' perspectives (see Chapters 4 and 5). Particles are normally very light in terms of phonological weight. I assume that so-called dummies or clitic expressions are also kinds of particles.[4] The term 'proclitic particle' refers to a particle whose phonetic value depends on the following word, while an enclitic particle's phonetic value depends on the preceding word. I expand this discussion further and argue that prosodic breaks in certain languages also play the role of invisible – yet audible – particles.

As particles are agglutinative in nature, they differ from the inflectional morphemes found in most European languages, which require morphosyntactic agreement with the auxiliaries or main verbs. Although particle behaviours are quite relaxed compared to agreement-required morphemes, as we shall explore in this book, particle behaviours are neither arbitrary nor peripheral, but systematic and consistently motivated by socio-pragmatic needs. In particular, in Chapter 5, I show how the speaker's desire to achieve *efficiency, expressivity* and *empathy* in social communication influences particle behaviours. This is in line with Halliday's (1978) functional grammar, where interpersonal tuning matters in human communication.

In the earlier period of generative grammars, scholars such as Kuno noted the importance of particles and their two primary roles (namely, constructive and expressive/attitudinal), which are demonstrated in the following quote:

> There are two important matters that must be mentioned with respect to Japanese particles. First, particles are used not only to represent case relationships, or to represent the functions that are carried in English by prepositions and conjunctions, but also after sentence-final verbs to represent the speaker's attitude towards the content of the sentence. (Kuno 1973: 4)[5]

(1) a. *Kore   wa   hon   desu   yo.*   [Japanese]
       This   TOP   book   be   YO
       'I am telling you that this is a book.'
    b. *Kore   wa   hon   desu   ne.*
       This   TOP   book   be   NE
       '*I hope you agree that* this is a book.'
    c. *Kore   wa   hon   desu   ka.*
       This   TOP   book   be   KA
       '*I ask you* if this is a book.'
    d. *John   wa   baka   sa.*
       John   TOP   fool   SA
       '*It goes without saying that* John is a fool.'   (Kuno 1973: 5)

Despite the crucial roles which particles play in both structure building and enriching meanings, Kuno's observation has not yet been followed up in later scholarship. Many theoretical linguists, particularly those who are trained within a Chomskian framework, have mainly analysed particles from an Anglo- or Euro-centric perspective. Such analyses put forward the idea that particles are largely non-existent in syntactic representations, with only a few exceptions. In the linguistics textbooks designed for learners of Chinese, Japanese and Korean, for instance, particles seem not to play any role in the configuration of a structure. In most instances, the particle somehow evades any mention.

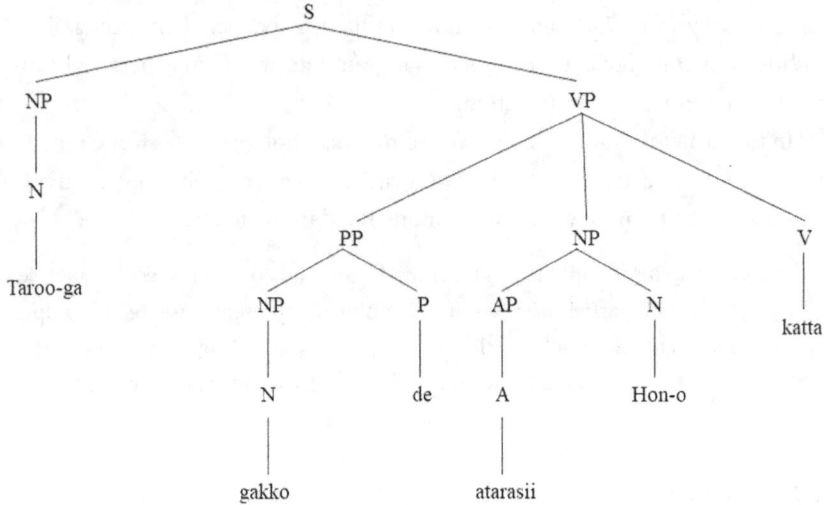

Taroo-ga gakkoo-de atarassi hon-o katta.
Taro-Nom school-at new book-Acc bought
"Taro bought a new book at school."

Figure 1.1 Syntactic structure of Japanese sentence.

Many basic syntax courses still provide analyses which assume that case particles do not exist, as seen in Figure 1.1. Tsujimura (2005: 164) provides a syntactic tree that features pre-X-bar schemata and pays no attention to case particles. The only notable difference between Japanese and English in this analysis appears to be word order. This approach of ignoring particles is not uncommon.

Particles are often referred to as grammatical or discourse markers based on their main roles in contributing to the given sentence or utterance.[6] Yet, as we shall explore in this book, the meanings and functions of particles are more complex and dynamic than is often thought. Instead of observing particles, describing them and aiming to explain their function as a grammatical entity which has multiple dimensions of information (structural, semantic and pragmatic), contemporary linguists consider them to have only a single function – mostly semantic or pragmatic. Therefore, many studies on particles are largely concentrated on their pragmatic roles (such as sentence-final particles) and do not acknowledge the dual nature which allows them to be constructive and/or expressive and contributes to the making of structural as well as semantic/pragmatic meanings.

In my view, the core problem in particle research stems from the observation stage.[7] As we shall explore in this book, the Anglo- and Euro-centric methods of observing Asian particles has led linguists to overlook their dynamic, complex and socio-pragmatically rich nature, since such particles either do not exist in English and European languages, or do not express such diverse, fine-grained interpersonal meanings.

Discussing the reliability of grammaticality judgement tests, Phillips (2009) also points out that the problem of generative linguistics is beyond the toolkit and methodological problems. I shall return to this in Chapter 3.

> I think that it would help a great deal if more linguists were to take more seriously the mentalistic commitments to which they profess. Most generative linguists would assent to the notion that their theories should be responsive to learnability considerations, yet there has been surprisingly little exploration of how to relate current understanding of cross-language variation to models of language learning. . . . <u>In sum, I agree with many of the critics cited above that some fundamental questions must be addressed (or readdressed) if generative linguistics is to again seize the initiative in the study of language</u>. The perception on the outside that mainstream linguistics is becoming irrelevant is unfortunately very real indeed. <u>However, I do not think that we should be fooled into thinking that informal judgment gathering is the root of the problem or that more formalized judgment collection will solve the problem.</u> (Philips 2009: 13; emphasis mine)

1.3. The case of Asian languages

Although many Asian languages have never been considered minority languages, they are severely under-represented in modern linguistics. Indeed, contemporary syntactic theory focuses predominantly on evidence from English and a few other European languages. One might argue against this claim, citing numerous works by theoretical linguists who worked on Asian languages. Yet, many of their studies show how they can apply the same universal theory with only minor adaptations in explaining their own languages. Very often, the works of these scholars are not accepted by home-grown, more traditional linguists. In addition, the use of highly technical terminology encouraged in the Chomskian Minimalist Program has made it almost impossible for outsiders to participate. With these barriers, non-Chomskians can only speak up against the reliability of the data, which Chomskians can easily disregard due to the belief that the data does not matter as it belongs to the realm of performance. Consider the following quote from Thomson (2012).

> Modern Bengali linguistics (from about the 1970 onwards) have taken a giant leap away from the traditional, historic, Sanskrit-oriented grammar and have adopted western formal grammar models to test the structures of Bengali. This has resulted in a considerable body of impressive work on particular features of Bengali, <u>however this work is highly technical in its language and largely inaccessible to non-linguists.</u> (Thomson 2012: 10; emphasis mine)

This chasm is seen in other disciplines, but in linguistics as it stands now, it seems almost irrecoverable. This book aims to challenge this divide. The aim of any linguistic theory is to explain the core, innate properties of human languages. In order to achieve this, unprejudiced, theory-unbound observation and description are pre-requisite.

Since Chomsky's 1957 work *Syntactic Structures*, it has been the case that categories which exist in English and Western European languages have received much attention in contemporary linguistics. However, linguistic categories and attributes that are non-existent or less relevant in these languages have been less celebrated and explored. Particles are a representative example of this. Notably, particles have failed to attract proper attention in generative grammars, which put a heavy emphasis on word orders in syntactic architecture, as will be shown in Chapter 2. The following quotes are from Enfield (2007: 10–12).

> From a modern linguistic point of view, there are a number of features of Lao not normally found in European languages which would nowadays be described on their own terms. One example is the phenomenon of serial verb constructions, a type of complex clause structure that Lao and many other languages – but not European languages like French – feature. <u>Such structures are mentioned here and there in existing Lao grammars, but (unlike early grammars of African languages) no attention is drawn to their identity as a distinct grammatical category.</u> (Enfield 2007: 11–12; emphasis mine)
>
> The two French language grammars are similar to grammars written in Lao in that their analysis of Lao follows distinctions in grammatical meaning traditionally made in European languages, such as categories of conjugation, mood and inflection of the verb. <u>But a significant difference between Lao and the average European language is that Lao lacks precisely these categories</u>. Most points of grammatical analysis of this kind are not supported with language internal arguments along lines supplied by modern standard reference grammars. <u>Rather, the grammarian is describing Lao in terms of the resources it has for expressing the grammatical distinctions one has in French or some other 'Standard Average European' grammar.</u> (Enfield 2007: 10–11; emphasis mine)

Most syntactic literature is built on the discussion of word order, often at the cost of other structural characteristics of the target languages. As I shall return to in Chapter 2, Chomsky's earlier work on transformation grammar which was set up in the process of searching for universal grammar (UG) typifies this emphasis on word order. However, according to the World Atlas of Language Structures (WALS), pragmatically driven flexibility is universally observed across languages. Instead of word order, these languages often employ particles to show word function in a sentence. Languages are said to have a 'degree of synthesis', referring to the number of morphemes that can affix to a base word. According to Balthasar Bickel and Johanna Nichols (2013), among 145 languages investigated, 140 languages had more than 2 particle categories attached to the verb. Of those, 55 languages (40 per cent) show a range of 6 to 9 particles clustered together after the verb. The whole set of meanings that particles project has not been systematically studied – in fact, particles as a whole have not been properly underpinned in linguistic theories thus far. Another problem lies in the way particles are glossed based on attributes which are primarily suitable for European languages. Some meanings of a particle and its pragmatic behaviours may be hard to gloss using the existing glossing conventions due to their interpersonal properties and complexity of socio-pragmatic meanings. I shall return to this in later chapters.

In addition to these linguistic factors, there are also some fundamental, non-linguistic factors which have pushed particle research to the fringe. For instance, the misinterpretation of modernization in East Asian academic sociology, which was understood to call for the replacement of traditional disciplines and frameworks, resulted in a tendency to bring an Anglo- or Eurocentric perspective to most academic disciplines. This process pushed out many traditional perspectives and observations and rendered them old-fashioned and outdated in common conception.

For instance, Korean and Japanese scholarship in formal, theoretical linguistics, particularly theoretical syntax, is keeping up with the complexity of the up-to-date generative framework. It is fair to suggest that a boom in this field resulted from the influx of Korean and Japanese students to the United States from the 1970s onwards, during which time many studied theoretical linguistics in accordance with the academic trend of the time which was heavily influenced by Chomskian generative grammars. To find highly technical papers on Korean syntax is quite easy, yet it is difficult to find any work that takes the roles of particles seriously and provides a more adequate explanatory account, either in scholarly research papers or in introductions to textbooks on Korean linguistics.

To date, in Korea and Japan, there have been two formats for the research of national languages: the local linguistics (國語學), or the more 'global' linguistics (語言學). US-educated scholars' approach to modernizing Korean linguistics, as was the case in other academic disciplines, was to interpret and apply Korean specificities within a modernized framework.[8] This effort led them to overlook particle studies which have been emphasized by traditional Korean linguists. The tension between the two communities is ongoing, often without any cross-border communication. Even some basic terminology and definitions remain unsettled between the groups, causing unnecessary confusion. The chasm between the two groups is well known, though rarely addressed in academic circles.

In this book, I will focus on languages spoken in Asia. What we mean when we say 'Asia' is difficult to determine, however I use the term to incorporate the regions of the Middle East, Central Asia, South Asia, Northeast Asia and Southeast Asia. The data used herein spans Arabic, Bengali, Burmese, Cantonese, Hindi, Japanese, Korean, Mandarin Chinese, Mongolian, Persian, Tagalog, Tibetan, Turkish, Urdu and Vietnamese. With the exception of a few languages such as Hindi, Japanese, Korean and Turkish, it is clear that Subject Object Verb (SOV) agglutinative Asian languages are generally significantly less studied than Western European languages within theoretical linguistics.

Based on the data I collected through consulting native speakers and descriptive grammars, I aim to shed new light on the constructive and expressive roles that particles play in natural language syntax, semantics and pragmatics. In particular, I shall show that the patterns of particles and argument realization in the target languages demonstrate that syntactic decisions are fundamentally driven by socio-pragmatic needs. I shall also show that argument and particle behaviours are neither arbitrary nor marginal, but require the consideration of multiple factors to achieve understanding.

1.4. Key features

There are a few morphosyntactic characteristics which I focus on in this book that are generally shared by every Asian language introduced in the last section. These properties have often been marginalized or under-represented in contemporary linguistics. The following key features for discussion are not shared by English and most Western European languages. The ways these key features operate are neither accidental nor arbitrary; they are systematic and pragmatic in nature, and can be explained as (socio)-pragmatically driven syntactic patterns.

1.4.1. Flexible word orders

Word orders in most Asian languages are relatively flexible with a few exceptions (these being Vietnamese, Thai and Indonesian). As I shall explore in this book, in languages with flexible word orders, particles, prosody and context play a crucial role in unfolding syntactic structures. Contemporary linguistic theories, however, have trouble explaining syntactic fluidity (such as flexible constituent formation) and various sources of structural combination (see Chapter 2).

Notably, in both synchronic and diachronic variations, we can easily see that rigid ordering is not so common in human languages, let alone Asian languages. Goddard (2005: 7) notes that generally speaking, the languages of East and Southeast Asia tend to have a more flexible and 'expressive' word order than English, and almost all languages in this region allow some variation in the constituent order of a simple sentence.

Flexible ordering is indeed not a new phenomenon; it can be found in ancient languages, for instance, Latin, Greek and Sanskrit all show flexible word orders. Examples of word-order flexibility in Latin are given in (2). One thing which the ancient languages clearly demonstrate is that structural relations are not predicted by word orders, but by the case particles which are attached to the nouns. All examples in (2) show the same propositional meanings.[9]

(2) Latin flexible word order
   a. *puer*   *canem*   *videt.*
      boyNOM   dogACC   see3sg
   b. *puer*   *videt*   *canem.*
      boyNOM   see3sg   dogACC
   c. *canem*   *puer*   *videt.*
      dogACC   boyNOM   see3sg
   d. *canem*   *videt*   *puer.*
      dogACC   see3sg   boyNOM
   e. *videt*   *puer*   *canem.*
      see3sg   boyNOM   dogACC
   f. *videt*   *canem*   *puer.*
      see3sg   dogACC   boyNOM
   'The boy sees the dog.'

Regardless of the prevalence of flexible orders in synchronic and diachronic distributions of human languages, contemporary syntactic architecture is built on the assumption of considering rigid word orders as the basic pattern over flexible word orders.

In contemporary linguistics, languages like Korean, Japanese, Turkish, Basque and German, among others, are known as scrambling languages, where scrambling is one of their main defining syntactic characteristics (see Chapter 2). The term 'scrambling', introduced by Ross (1967), was coined to refer to orders that have *scrambled* from a language's base word order. The term itself reflects the assumption within Chomskian generative grammars that every language has a basic word order which is fundamental to its sentence structure.

The term 'scrambling' as it stands imposes rather a biased view in understanding various word orders and flexibility in orderings found in these languages. Labelling a group of languages as *scrambling* suggests that they exhibit exceptional syntactic properties.

However, almost all languages exhibit flexibility in word orders to a certain extent. Even in languages known for rigid word orders, flexibility can be found; for example, in English there is great flexibility permitted between a direct object and an indirect object.

The orders in the above-mentioned so-called scrambling languages are flexible, yet not arbitrary. Most of all, the syntactic fluidity is possible because structure-building relies on multiple sources such as morphological particles or prosodic cues together with linear word orders in the process of creating meaningful communication.

However, it is noticeable in the study of natural language syntax in the last fifty years or so that fixed order and verbs have been considered as the sole important sources of syntactic architecture. Other sources – including particles, prosody and context – received little attention. More concrete discussion will follow in Chapters 2 and 8.

1.4.2. Pragmatic realization of lexical expressions and particles

In Asian languages, it is commonly observed that even the realization of subjects is pragmatically driven, and each context and register plays a crucial role in this. This echoes the Gricean maxim of quantity where one tries to be as informative as one possibly can, and gives as much information as is needed, and no more.

That is, the explicit realization of expressions depends more on context and register than on whether the expressions are morphosyntactically obligatory (i.e. argument) or optional (i.e. adjunct). For example, the decision of whether or not to have an explicit second-person subject does not depend on the verb or the propositional structure, but on the interpersonal relationship between the speaker and the hearer (see Chapters 4 and 5). Likewise, morphosyntactically, in a ditransitive construction, the verb requires three arguments (subject, direct object and indirect object). Yet in informal registers, most of the Asian target languages present one or two arguments only, and it is rare to see all three expressions phonetically realized. Kiaer (2014: 16–17) shows that even in the case of English, argument realization is influenced by multiple factors such as context and prosody.

In the generative linguistics literature, a series of terminology such as 'pro-dropness', 'deletion', 'omission' and 'ellipsis' have been somewhat casually used to describe the ways grammatical expressions are realized as shown earlier. The term 'pro-drop' was first introduced by Chomsky (1981) to refer to the phenomenon of pronoun omission. Chomsky understands pro-drop as a sort of free-omission phenomenon as shown in the following quote:

> The principle suggested is fairly general but does not apply to such languages as Japanese in which pronouns can be missing much more freely. (Chomsky 1981: 284, fn 47)

The term 'pro-drop' is also used in other frameworks in generative grammar, such as in lexical-functional grammar (LFG), but in a more general sense, 'Pro-drop is a widespread linguistic phenomenon in which, under certain conditions, a structural NP may be unexpressed, giving rise to a pronominal interpretation' (Bresnan 1982: 384).

According to WALS Chapter 101 and Dryer (2013b), among the languages attested, only 12 per cent of the world languages – that is, only eighty-two languages – showed obligatory pronouns in the subject position. Most of the Western European languages belong to this category. This means that most world languages, including our target languages, show optionality in pronominal subject realization. Nevertheless, just like *scrambling*, *pro-drop* is often used to refer to a somewhat peculiar property of a limited set of languages.

Coining an additional term such as 'pro-drop language' to refer to a vast range of languages such as Japanese, Korean, Turkish, Chinese, and Swahili, among many others, can be misleading, making readers or researchers view pragmatic realization of expression and particles as arbitrary and optional omission, where is it assumed that the unsaid expressions only lost their phonetic values yet anyhow exist there invisibly. More technically speaking, according to quite an up-to-date generative standpoint, this can be viewed as arbitrary phonetic form (PF) deletion without any clear morphosyntactic trigger; simply said, the deleted forms are there like other expressions but for some reason, they are not pronounced.

Let alone the complexity of formalisms in understanding the gist of this argument, it is rather disappointing to read this conclusion. Does this meet any one of the criteria of observational, descriptive or explanatory adequacy?

This book proposes that each needs to be rethought from observation to explanation. Not only lexical expressions but particles also show the same patterns of behaviours. Yet, often the baseline assumption was the same in that they are there or should have been there but for some reason, they are not said. Given that both particles and lexical expressions systematically operate based on their structural or semantic, pragmatic needs rather than in an arbitrary way, I think the somewhat ad hoc assumption to argue for the existence of invisible-yet-existing expressions needs to be seriously re-considered. More discussion related to this will follow in later chapters. Particles are realized and expressions are explicitly said when they are needed structurally, semantically or pragmatically. Unwanted particles, though grammatically legitimate, can make an utterance unnatural.

1.4.3. Rich socio-pragmatic and interpersonal meanings

Asian languages, though so diverse, uniformly exhibit socio-pragmatic richness, where interpersonal dynamics and other sociocultural factors play an essential role in every aspect of communication. The complexity of interpersonal meanings is far beyond what we can observe from English and Western European languages, as we shall see in Chapters 4, 5 and 9. And very often, it is through these lightweight particles that those enriched, diverse social meanings are expressed.

In this book, following Potts' (2005) expressive semantics, I consider particles as expressives. And using DS's (Kempson et al. 2001; Cann et al. 2005) logic of LINK structure, I propose that these particles project an additional structure with a socio-pragmatic meaning complex. In this way, I show how multidimensional meanings are created during the course of an utterance. I propose multimodal modulation hypothesis (MMH) to show how different layers of those meanings are modulated in tandem to make the overall utterance socio-pragmatically adequate (Chapter 5).

1.5. Target languages

The target Asian languages discussed in this book largely share a certain level of syntactic fluidity and flexibility. Word orders are relatively flexible, though preferred word orders do exist. Languages with flexible word orders tend to have richer case morphology. However, in some languages, the correct interpretation of the given syntactic structure is solely dependent on pragmatic knowledge used to retrieve relevant information from the given context.

The Indo-Aryan languages currently spoken in India, following their mother language Sanskrit, share flexible word order, with a preference for verb-final, SOV word order as the default, as well as rich case morphology. This pattern is also found in Northeast and Central Asian language families, such as Turkic and Tungusic.

According to the WALS, there are more languages which show verb-final word orders than verb-initial or medial word orders. For instance, according to Dryer (2013b), there are 713 languages which have a default object-verb (OV) ordering and 705 languages which have a default verb-object (VO) ordering. In the map shown in the WALS, it is noteworthy that most of the North and Central Asian as well as Southeast Asian languages are OV languages, whereas almost all European languages except Sorbian and Basque are VO languages.[10,11] It is worthwhile noting, as Hawkins (1994) shows, that significantly more research has been conducted in VO languages than OV languages in contemporary linguistics.

What I try to draw attention to here is that at least half of the world languages share verb-finality, often coupled with flexible orderings between constituents. Put radically, although half of the languages in the world behave like Korean, Japanese or Tibetan, these attributes have received hardly any attention and have been regarded as somewhat peculiar in terms of their linguistic attributes within mainstream contemporary theoretical linguistics.

On the other hand, varieties of Chinese, and the languages from the Indo-Chinese Peninsula (or in other words, languages from Southeast Asia) roughly share SVO ordering as a preferred word order. In these languages, pragmatic knowledge is significant in structure-building as there are no morphological indicators that could give specific guidelines for future structure-building.

Expressions are realized based on a simple pragmatic principle: 'Say what is needed, when it is needed.' I classify the target Asian languages as follows:

a) Flexible word orders with rich case particles; pragmatic realization of expressions (i.e. pro-drop); particle-rich languages:

Arabic,[12] *Korean, Japanese, Tamil, Hindi, Urdu, Bengali, Tibetan, Tagalog, Turkish, Persian, Mongolian, Sanskrit* (most of them except Standard Arabic show strong verb-finality)

b) Flexible word orders with no case particles; pragmatic realization of expression (i.e. pro-drop); particle-rich languages; mostly prefer SVO order:

Mandarin Chinese, Thai, Vietnamese, Lao

It is worth noting that none of these languages shows strictly fixed word orders. Nevertheless, under contemporary linguistic theories, it is often assumed that there is a basic fixed order, and other orders are derived from the base order by some purely grammatical operation such as movement. As I shall explore in Chapter 2 with Korean as an example, such an assumption is unfit to account for the nature of syntactic fluidity and the pragmatic motivation behind syntactic realization in an explanatorily adequate manner.

In the next section, I shall provide a brief description on the target Asian languages of this book.[13]

Languages in the Middle East

Word order in Arabic is generally VSO, but SVO is also possible. This is also the case in Hebrew. Persian and Turkish, on the other hand, exhibit OV and flexible word ordering. The major language families in the Middle East are as follows:

a) Semitic languages (Arabic, Hebrew, Aramaic/Syriac and others);
b) Iranian languages (Pashto, Persian, Baluchi, Kurdish and others);
c) Ural-Altaic languages (Turkish and other Turkic languages, such as Uzbek, Kyrgyz and Azeri/Azerbaijani).

Arabic

Arabic is a Semitic language that has a rich morphology and a flexible word order. It is common to find VSO, SVO and VOS word orders. Arabic is the sixth most spoken world language with 274 million speakers globally. It is a religiously significant language as it is the liturgical language of Islam, with the Quran and Hadith being written in Arabic. Modern Standard Arabic largely follows the grammatical standards of Classical Arabic and uses much of the same vocabulary. It is the standard language in twenty-seven nations across the Middle East and Africa, and has significant speakership elsewhere in the United Kingdom, the United States, Australia, Canada and so on.

Hebrew

Hebrew is one of the standard languages of Israel, and the liturgical language of Judaism. It has approximately 9 million speakers worldwide, is a member of the Semitic language family and is the only spoken Canaanite language. Hebrew grammar is partially inflectional and partially analytic, using prepositional particles to denote noun case.

Turkish

Turkish is the national language of Turkey and is spoken by approximately 80 million people worldwide. It is part of the Ural-Altaic language family, which also includes Uzbek and Kyrgyz. Turkish was the administrative and literary language of the Ottoman Empire; it is agglutinative and has flexible word order, but the standard order is SOV.

Persian

Persian is a language belonging to the Iranian branch of the Indo-Iranian languages. It is mainly spoken in Iran, Afghanistan and Tajikistan. It is spoken by 53 million people globally.

Languages in South Asia

India is home to a very large, diverse population which is reflected in the languages which thrive there. According to the Census of India (2001), there are 122 major languages and 1,599 other languages. There are 30 languages which are spoken by more than a million native speakers, and at least 120 languages have more than 10,000 speakers.[14]

Other than Hindi and English, which are official languages, the following languages are each spoken by more than 25 million people in India: Bengali, Telugu, Marathi, Tamil, Urdu, Gujarati, Kannada, Malayalam, Odia and Punjabi. Most of these languages share flexible SOV word orders.

Hindi

This Sanskritized and standardized register of the Hindustani language is the fourth most spoken language in the world and is the lingua franca of the so-called Hindi belt in India. It also has a significant number of speakers in the United States, the United Kingdom, South Africa, the Middle East, Uganda, New Zealand, Germany and Singapore, owing to the North Indian diaspora. Hindi is normatively SOV with free word ordering. It is an agglutinative language.

Bengali (Bangla)

The Bengali language is one of the top seven most spoken languages in the world. It is native to the region of Bengal, which comprises the Indian states West Bengal, Tripura and southern Assam and the present-day nation of Bangladesh, where it enjoys the status of the national language. Bengali is prototypically an SOV language with relatively free word ordering due to the existence of noun cases and agglutination.

Urdu

Urdu is a Persianized and standardized register of the Hindustani language. It is the national language and lingua franca of Pakistan, and an official language of five states in India. Outside of South Asia, it is spoken by large numbers of South Asian migrant workers in the major urban centres of the Persian Gulf countries, Saudi Arabia, the United Kingdom, the United States, Canada, Germany, Norway and Australia. Urdu is typically SOV, with relatively free word ordering. It is agglutinative.

Languages in Northeast Asia

Korean

Korean is the official language of the Democratic People's Republic of Korea (North Korea) and the Republic of Korea (South Korea). Korean has approximately 77 million native speakers worldwide. Korean is an SOV language with flexible word ordering.

Japanese

Japanese is the official language of Japan, and the most spoken language in the Japonic language family. It is a native language of approximately 128 million speakers. Japanese has significant speakership in the United States, Australia,

Brazil and Canada. Like Korean, it is an agglutinative language with SOV word ordering. Internal sentence constituents have flexible ordering.

Mandarin Chinese

The standard Mandarin variety is Modern Standard Mandarin (Putonghua). It is the major language of the Sinitic language family. Mandarin Chinese is an analytic language relying on word order and particles rather than agglutination. The word order is significant in determining the meaning of a sentence, and the standard word order is SVO.

Mongolian

Mongolian is a language of the Mongolic family with approximately 3.6 million native speakers. The Khalka dialect is predominant in Mongolia, while dialects in Inner Mongolia are more diverse. Mongolian belongs to the wider Altaic family. Mongolian follows an SOV word order, but word order is relatively free. It is an agglutinative language with eight to nine cases.

Burmese

Burmese belongs to the Sino-Tibetan language family and has approximately 43 million speakers worldwide. It is the native language for the majority of Myanmar people and is often spoken as a second language for those who speak another native language in this country and in neighbouring areas. While Burmese is predominantly SOV, provided the verb and its modifiers are in the final position, all other elements are somewhat freely ordered before it.

Tibetan

Standard Tibetan is a language of the Sino-Tibetan language family with approximately 1.2 million native speakers. Standard Tibetan is also known as Lhasa Tibetan. The standard word order is SOV, however, word order is flexible. Tibetan is an agglutinative language and nouns are marked by case particles.

Languages in Southeast Asia

Tagalog

Tagalog is the national language of the Philippines, with 24 million total speakers. It is part of the Austronesian language family. Tagalog has flexible word order. The standardized form of Tagalog is known as Filipino.

Thai

Thai is a language of the Kra-Dai family and has 61 million speakers worldwide. It is the national language of Thailand and is mutually intelligible with Lao and Isan. Thai has SVO word ordering.

Khmer

Khmer is the national language of Cambodia and has approximately 18 million native speakers. After Vietnamese, it is the second most spoken Austroasiatic language.

Vietnamese

Vietnamese is the most widely spoken Austroasiatic language, with 77 million native speakers worldwide. Vietnamese, like many languages in Southeast Asia, is an analytic language. Like other languages in the region, Vietnamese syntax conforms to SVO word order.

Lao

Lao is the national language of Laos and is spoken by over 4 million people there. It is also spoken by a minority in Northeast Cambodia, and a large minority (at least 10 million) in Northeast Thailand (in areas bordering lowland Laos).

1.6. Summary

Contemporary theoretical linguistics displays an undeniable bias for phenomena in English and other Western European languages. The generative framework also overlooks phenomena that are not uncommon when one considers the full spread of the world's languages. Modernist approaches to theoretical linguistics have catalysed the decay of traditional Asian linguistics, particularly the study of particles. For instance, despite the prevalence of flexible word ordering in the world's languages, theoretical analyses are often biased towards the English style of rigid word ordering. This in turn has led to the neglect of particle-based grammar languages such as Korean and Japanese, which determine grammatical relations via case particles. Additionally, non-constructive usages of particles are overlooked. Pragmatics has often been said by the generativists to belong to the realm of performance rather than competence linguistics. This claim is particularly damaging for the observation and appraisal of languages that employ expressive usages of particles, such as the ones targeted in this book. Despite the huge speakerships of Asian languages, they have been neglected in contemporary theoretical linguistics. Studying the role of particles in these languages will be particularly valuable to the field of theoretical linguistics not only through illuminating some of the key features of under-studied languages but also by challenging and dismantling exclusionary but enduring assumptions.

1.7. Outline of this book

The aim of this book is to unravel the complex nature of particles. First of all, I shall demonstrate how particles together with prosody and context build a syntactic structure, providing the source of structural combination and anticipation (Chapters 2 and 7). In explaining the pragmatic realization of expressions and particles, I shall show how different layers of meaning are displayed through particles (Chapter 4) and how interpersonal tuning/modulation takes place (Chapter 5). Chapter 6 lays out the hypothesis and grammatical framework I adopt in this book in providing analysis of the particles in the Asian target languages. In Chapters 7–9, I provide an analysis of the constructive, expressive and socio-pragmatic nature of particles.

2

Modelling flexible word orders[1]

Asian languages on the whole show flexible structures, where grammatical relations are mostly realized not through word orders but through various other sources including particles. In contemporary linguistics, however, it is typically word orders and verbs that become the foundation of syntactic architecture. Within this view, the truly flexible nature of structure building remains puzzling. As we shall explore in this chapter, it is not easy to provide an explanatorily adequate account for flexible syntax in Asian languages without postulating some exceptional, ad hoc devices in the grammar. Yet, I show in this book that the problems which we face aren't simply easy-to-repair tool kit matters but are problems which we cannot avoid within an Anglo- and Euro-centric perspective of linguistic structures. It is surprising to see how the wide range of languages in this region are under-represented in the literature and interpreted within the theoretical assumptions that are originally built for verb-initial languages with strict word orders.

There is a particular challenge in characterizing the flexible but restricted word-order phenomena in head-final languages, and these remain puzzling in both transformational (government and binding (hereafter (GB), minimalist program (MP)) and lexicalist frameworks (head-driven phrase structure grammar (HPSG), lexical-functional grammar (LFG) and combinatory categorial grammar (CCG)).

These explanations are taken purely in terms of configurational hierarchy (in the case of transformational approaches) and those in which constituency is exclusively determined from lexical specifications. Hence, they turn out not to be sufficiently rich to express the syntactic fluidity found in Asian languages.

Modelling structural flexibility is indeed a hurdle for most grammar formalisms. As we shall see, there is reason to posit a constituent made up of a sequence of more than one Noun Phrase (NP), henceforth a 'surprising constituent', following Takano (2002), where the lack of an asymmetric structural relation between lexical items within that constituent causes serious challenges for the configurational hierarchy assumed in grammar formalisms. More particularly, from the perspective of transformational paradigms (GB or MP), even if structural variation is observable within a surprising constituent, it is predicted that word-order variation should be much more restricted than what is observed. This prediction contradicts native speakers' judgements.

On the other hand, in the lexicalist tradition, the syntactic properties of a surprising constituent can only be encoded in the lexicon. Yet, given the lack of a morphological trigger to define such non-standard constituents, they remain puzzling too. Current approaches made within the lexicalist paradigm encode each surface structure as a distinct structure from any other. Hence it fails to capture the relationships displayed by the core skeleton which is shared by the various structures.

Modelling the sensitivity of syntactic structure to linear order is also a hurdle for most grammar formalisms. The phenomenon we are to turn to now is related to left-right asymmetry; across languages, the interpretation of left-peripheral expressions is relatively more flexible than that of sentence-medial or right-peripheral expressions. Right-peripheral expressions are associated with a strong locality effect, which was initially observed by Ross (1967) and named as the Right Roof Constraint.[2]

In the transformational paradigm, an asymmetry such as this is hard to capture, mainly because linear-order effects are considered marginal. In lexicalist paradigms, the only way to deal with this asymmetry is by introducing peripheral information as a lexical feature in the lexicon. Yet since word-order variation with respect to left and right peripheries is not restricted to a certain class of lexical expressions, lexical control over linear order will fail to capture the structural properties found in either left or right-peripheral position.

In the following sections, I will discuss some of the key structural properties of our target languages, by showcasing mainly Korean along with some examples from other languages. Korean and Japanese will be highlighted because these common features are comparatively well studied in contemporary linguistics of these languages – probably since Kuno (1973) and Saito's (1985) seminal work – compared to other Asian languages. Most Asian languages share the same key features; however, except for Japanese, Korean, Hindi and Turkish, studies in theoretical linguistics in many other Asian languages is relatively rare. This is not surprising as these languages see little representation in the Anglophone world in general. Hence, in the following section, I will discuss core structural properties of Korean and the transformational solutions and the non-transformational, lexicalist solutions for the given puzzles of modelling flexible word order.[3]

2.1. The core structural properties of Korean

2.1.1. Flexible word order

Although in this section Korean is used as the example language, word-order flexibility is a feature shared by most of our target Asian languages. Korean is a head-final language,[4] with a rich case morphology like many other Asian languages. Discussions in this section therefore can be further applied in those languages. Consider the core case particles, which play a crucial role in structure building (Table 2.1).

In Korean, grammatical roles such as subject or object are assigned by case markers, not by word order as in English. In English, as shown in (1), Jina becomes a subject NP when it precedes the verb as in (1a), but it becomes an object NP when it is preceded by the verb as in (1b). However, in Korean as in (2), Jina is a subject NP regardless of its surface position.

(1) a. *Jina met Mina.*
    b. *Mina met Jina.*

(2) a. *Jina-ka*   *Mina-lul*   *mannasse.* [S O V]   [Korean]
       Jina-NOM   Mina-ACC   met
       'Jina met Mina.'

    b. *Mina-lul*   *Jina-ka*   *mannasse.* [O S V]
       Mina-ACC   Jina NOM   met
       'Jina met Mina.'

Table 2.1 Constructive case particles

Case particle	Description
-ka/-i	NOM
	This particle makes the host expression a nominative NP
-ul/lul	ACC
	This particle makes the host expression a accusative NP
-ekey/hanthey	DAT
	This particle makes the host expression a dative NP
-un/nun	TOP
	This particle makes the host expression a topic-marked NP

Word order in Korean is relatively free. As seen in (2a-b), word order between lexical items in the same local structure is flexible and doesn't yield any difference in propositional meaning. This phenomenon, shifting from a so-called canonical word order into a non-canonical word order is called local or short-distance scrambling (Ross 1967; Saito 1985).

This variation is not limited to local clausal sequences, however. Expressions which are to be construed in one structure can nevertheless appear in another local structure as in (3b). In (3b), *pizza-lul* is dislocated from its local structure, contrary to (3a), in which *pizza-lul* is located in its local structure, where its theta-role and case can be assigned. This phenomenon is called non-local or long-distance scrambling (Saito 1985).

(3) a. [S2 [S1 O1 V1-COMP] V2]
    Jina-nun   Sarah-ka   pizza-lul   mekessta-ko   malhaysseyo.
    Jina-TOP   Sarah-NOM   pizza-ACC   ate-COMP   said
  b. [O1 [S2 [S1 θ V1-COMP]V2]]
    Pizza-lul   Jina-nun   Sarah-ka   θ mekessta-ko   malhaysseyo.
    pizza-ACC   Jina-TOP   Sarah-NOM   θ ate-COMP   said
    'Jina said that Sarah ate pizza.'

2.1.2. Pragmatic realization of expressions

In addition, the realization of arguments (e.g. subject or object) in Korean is optional. This is a feature shared by most of Asian languages. All given strings in (4) are grammatical and frequently used. The use of implicit or empty arguments is highly context sensitive and more frequent in colloquial than written Korean.

(4) a. O V
    pizza-lul   mekesseyo.
    pizza-ACC   ate
  b. S V
    Jina-ka   mekesseyo.
    Jina-NOM   ate
  c. V
    mekesseyo.
    ate
  d. S O V
    Jina-ka   pizza-lul   mekesseyo.
    Jina-NOM   pizza-ACC   ate
    'Jina ate pizza.'

Given these structural properties, let's now turn to the core data of interest and the theoretical treatment of the data. The ordering between a sequence of NPs is flexible not only at a mono-clausal level (5a-b) but also at a multi-clausal level (6a-b). In Korean, not only can one NP expression be dislocated across the clause boundary (i.e. long-distance scrambling) but two or more expressions can also be so dislocated as shown in (6a-b). Furthermore, as in simple clauses, the ordering variation in complex clauses as in (6a-b) does not yield any significant difference in grammaticality judgement or propositional meaning. Theta θ denotes the place where the dislocated sequence receives interpretation.

(5) Mono-clausal word-order variation: Single long-distance scrambling
   a. DO IO S V
      Pizza-lul   Mina-hanthey   Jina-ka   Pizza-Express-ese   sa-cwuessta.
      Pizza-ACC   Mina-DAT   Jina-NOM   Pizza-Express-at   buy-gave
      'Jina bought to give pizza to Mina at Pizza Express.'

   b. IO DO S V
      Mina-hanthey   Pizza-lul   Jina-ka   Pizza-Express-ese   sa-cwuessta.
      Mina-DAT   Pizza-ACC   Jina-NOM   Pizza-Express-at   buy-gave
      'Jina bought to give pizza to Mina at Pizza Express.'

(6) Multi-clausal word-order variation: Multiple long-distance scrambling
   a. [[[IO1 DO1] S2 Si θ Vi] V2]
      [[Mina-hanthey   Pizza-lul]   Sarah-nun   Jina-ka   Pizza-Express-ese θ
      Mina-DAT   Pizza-ACC   Sarah-TOP   Jina-NOM   Pizza-Express-at θ
      sa-cwuessta-ko   haysseyo.]
      buy-gave-COMP   said
      'Sarah said that Jina bought pizza to give to Mina at Pizza Express.'

   b. [[[DO1 IO1] S2 S1 θ V1] V2]
      [[Pizza lul   Mina hanthey]   Sarah nun   Jina ka   Pizza Express ese θ
      Pizza-ACC   Mina-DAT.   Sarah-TOP   Jina-NOM   Pizza-Express-at θ
      sa-cwuessta-ko   haysseyo.]
      buy-gave-COMP   said
      'Sarah said that Jina bought to give pizza to Mina at Pizza Express.'

The above data shows that word order in Korean is flexible not only at a mono-clausal level but also at a multi-clausal level. This feature is also found in many Asian languages. In Persian, multiple expressions can be dislocated from their local interpretational domain. As shown in (7), word order is flexible and both examples are grammatical.[5] Consider the examples below, taken from Karimi (2018: 165).

(7)
a. *[ketab-a-ro]₁ [be Kkmea]₂ man fekr mi-kon-am [(ke) Arezu e₁ e₂ dad]* [Persian]
b. *[be Kkmea]₂ [ketab-a-ro]₁ man fekr mi-kon-am [(ke) Arezu e₁ e₂ dad]*
'To Khmea a book I thought Areze gave.'
'A book to Khmea, I thought Arezu gave.'
Lit. I thought Arezu gave a book to Khmea.

This contradicts the prediction of current transformational approaches (GB/MP), which predict severe ungrammaticality for (6b) relative to (6a) and also (7b) relative to (7a). This is because the long-distance movement of a constituent counts as one movement as long as the canonical order is kept in that constituent. If the moved constituent has non-canonical order, it is considered as multiple occasions of movement and this subsequently causes multiple subjacency violation (see Koizumi 2000).[6] In general, lexicalist approaches do not assume the same detailed configurational hierarchy as proposed in GB/MP. However, most approaches distinguish local/mono-clausal variation from non-local/multi-clausal variation and encode such a difference in the lexicon (see Baldridge 2002). Hence, it is difficult to capture the source of the flexibility shared in mono-clausal and multi-clausal levels. More details from transformational and lexicalist paradigms will be discussed in sections 2.2 and 2.3, respectively.

2.1.3. Linear-order effect: Left-to-right asymmetry

There is also asymmetry between constituents occurring at left, medial and right positions in a sentential sequence. I will also showcase with Korean the property of resource-sensitive structure building which is seen cross-linguistically. The gist is this: expressions appearing at the left periphery can be interpreted more flexibly relative to sentence-medial expressions or right-peripheral expressions.

2.1.3.1. Freedom at left and restriction at right

In Korean, expressions at the left periphery can be interpreted more flexibly. For instance, a sentence-initial dative NP *Saca-hanthey* 'to a lion' in (8) can be interpreted in the three possible structures hosted by the verb *malhaysseyo* 'said' (=8a), *yaksokhayssta* 'promised' (=8b) or *mantule-cwuessta* 'make-give' (=8c).

(8) Dative NP can be interpreted within three different structures
Saca-hanthey   holangi-nun   penguini-ka   masissnun   cookie-lul
lion-DAT   tiger-TOP   penguin-NOM   delicious   cookie-ACC
mantule-cwuessta-ko   yaksokhayssta-ko   malhayss-eyo.
make-will.give-COMP   promised-COMP   said-DECL

(a) 'A tiger <u>said to a lion</u> that a penguin promised that he will make and give him a delicious cookie.'
(b) 'A tiger said to somebody that a penguin <u>promised to a lion</u> that he will make and give him a delicious cookie.'
(c) 'A tiger said to somebody that a penguin promised that he will make and <u>give a lion</u> a delicious cookie.'

However, the interpretation of expressions becomes gradually more restricted towards the right edge of the sentence. Before and after the final matrix verb, the dative NP can be only interpreted within the matrix clause.

2.1.3.2. Restriction at the right

(9) Dative NP can be interpreted only within matrix structures
Holangi-nun   penguini-ka   masissnun cookie-lul   mantule-cwuessta-ko
tiger-TOP   penguin-NOM   delicious   cookie-ACC   make-will.give-COMP
yaksokhayssta-ko   <u>saca-hanthey   malhayss-eyo</u>.
promised-COMP   lion-DAT said-DECL
(a) 'A tiger said to a lion that a penguin promised that he will make and give him a delicious cookie.'
(b) 'A tiger said to somebody that a penguin promised to a lion that he will make and give him a delicious cookie.' (This reading is very hard to get.)
(c) 'A tiger said to somebody that a penguin promised that he will make and give a lion a delicious cookie.' (This reading is very hard to get.)

(10) Dative NP can be interpreted only within matrix structures
Holangi-nun   penguini-ka   masissnun cookie-lul   mantule-cwukessta-ko
tiger-TOP   penguin-NOM   delicious   cookie-ACC   make-will.give-COMP
<u>*yaksokhayssta-ko   malhayss-eyo   saca hanthey*</u>
promised-COMP   said-DECL   lion-DAT
(a) 'A tiger said to a lion that a penguin promised that he will make and give him a delicious cookie.'
(b) 'A tiger said to somebody that a penguin promised to a lion that he will make and give him a delicious cookie.' (This reading is very hard to get.)
(c) 'A tiger said to somebody that a penguin promised that he will make and give a lion a delicious cookie.' (This reading is very hard to get.)

Unlike in (8) where the dative NP is at the sentence-initial, leftward position, in both (9) and (10), where the dative NP is before and after the matrix verb, (a) readings are dominant readings and (b) and (c) readings are hardly possible to Korean speakers. Note that such dominance can be observed before finishing

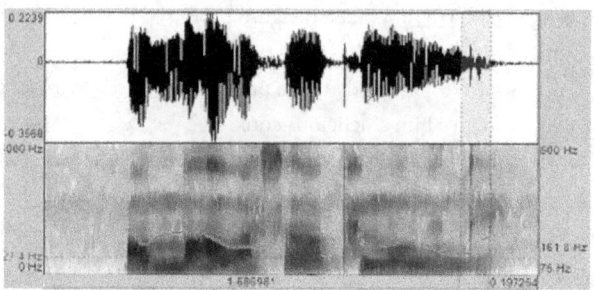

Figure 2.1 Lengthened connective particle as utterance-final particle: Evidence from Cho (2011).

the end of a sentence. This shows that structural association occurs in an incremental manner from left to right regardless of the location of a verb.

2.1.3.3. Post-verbal expression and closing-off prosody

Although Korean is regarded as a verb-final language, it is very easy to find post-verbal expressions. Such post-verbal expressions are also found in our other verb-final target languages. They are typically dependent on prosody and context, and are usually either new utterances or expressions introducing a thought that a speaker may have had mid-sentence. In those examples, the boundary tones are used to signal the end of the utterance. Consider (11) from Cho (2011): -*nuntey* is known as a connective but like many other connective particles, it can be used as an ending particle when the boundary tone (e.g. L%) follows.

In Figure 2.1, the shaded part of at the end of the prosodic input represents the unusually long end part.

(11) *emma-ka o-n-ke-ya cenhwa hallieyko ha-nuntey* (L%)
     mom-NOM come-ADN-thing-COP+DECL phone-trying.to do-CONN
     'My mum came when I was about to ring.'

Similarly, using the spoken language information lab corpus (SLILC), Kim (2010) extracted 731 examples where expressions occur after the verbal cluster. Kim found that 98 per cent of the time only one expression followed the verbal cluster at the end. Kim also found that 81.5 per cent of the time the post-verbal expression was comprised of two to four syllables. Kiaer (2007, 2014) showed how the post-verbal expression and the preceding verb tend to form one prosodic constituent. This shows that even if a verb plays a crucial role in confirming the end of a structure, prosody also plays a crucial role in confirming the completion of the structure building.

Freedom at the left periphery is in fact found cross-linguistically. For instance, in Persian, *be kimea* 'to Kimea' can be interpreted within the immediately following matrix clause as in (12a) or in the later-appearing embedded clause as in (12b). The structure where the interpretation is made is underlined.

(12)
  a. *Be kimea, (man)* ***goft-am*** *arezu un ketab-o dust dar-e*
     To Kimea (I) said-1sg arezu that book-ra likes-3sg
     'To Kimea, I said Arezu that book gave.'

  b. *Be kimea, (man) fekr kard-am (ke) arezu un ketab-o* ***dad-o***
     To Kimea (I) thought-1sg (that) arezu that book-ra gave-3sg
     'To Kimea, I thought that Arezu that book gave.'

On the other hand, *be kimea* 'to Kimea' at the right periphery, in post-verbal position as in (13) is interpreted in the closest structure, which is in the case of (13), an embedded clause.

(13)
  (man) fekr kard-am (ke) arezu un ketab-o ***dad-o*** *Be kimea,*
  (I) thought-1sg (that) arezu that book-ra gave-3sg to Kimea
  'To Kimea, I thought that Arezu that book gave.'

The right-peripheral expression cannot be interpreted in non-local structure as below.

(14)
  ???*(man) goft-am arezu un ketab-o dust dar-e* ***be kimea***
  (I) said-1sg arezu that book-ra likes-3sg to Kimea
  Intended reading: 'To Kimea said Arezu likes that book.'

2.2. Transformational approaches on word-order variation

Word-order variation in Korean and many other Asian languages with the flexible ordering property known as 'scrambling' challenges fundamental assumptions made in the Chomskian paradigm, in which syntactic explanation has to be made in structural or hierarchical terms only, without reference to time-sensitive left-to-right linear order.

Given this hierarchical point of view about natural language analysis, particular problems occur when it comes to languages such as Korean, which allow very flexible NP ordering. Most analyses in GB/MP assume that there is one basic word order and that other word orders are derived from that basic order with few exceptions (see Neeleman 1994, Bošković and Takahashi 1998, who assume scrambling is a base-generated property).

In many ways, scrambling is different from other kinds of movement. It is optional and non-feature driven. That is to say, it is not driven by the presence of any morphological trigger and is semantically vacuous (Saito 1989). Crucially, these characteristics stand strongly against the spirit of the current minimalist framework (Chomsky 1995), in which movement is regarded as a last resort operation and applied only when it is necessary, and in the presence of some morphological trigger (an expression requiring adjacency of some non-contiguous expression) to check requirements such as sub-categorization restrictions. Various solutions have been suggested to repair this problem. Grewendorf and Sabel (1999) even assumed that there is a scrambling feature as such. Miyagawa (2001, 2003, 2005) assumed that all scrambling operations are obligatory, either EPP-driven or focus-feature driven. According to them, the syntactic motivation of scrambling is to check case feature and thematic role. Yet, these solutions are clearly limited in their ability to capture the nature of flexible word-order variation as we shall see in the following section.

2.2.1. The syntactic evidence of 'surprising constituents'

First, I will show that a verb-less fragment-sequence such as [S O] or [O S] as in (15) forms in some sense is an ordinary constituent, even without a verb or its trace. The problem will then be: What can be the nature of that constituent? Clearly, we cannot even begin to tackle this problem from a verb-centred perspective; one that supposes that all combinatorial information is stored in the verb. In GB/MP frameworks, the only way to create such a constituent is by raising the verb, and then raising the entire remainder above it. This sort of a verb-less constituent which doesn't have a verb but a trace called 'a surprising constituent' (Takano 2002). It is surprising within GB/MP for two such nominal NPs to form a constituent, given that the Verb Phrase (VP) has been regarded as a core constituent in movement-based framework.

Though the current view of the phrase structure of minimalism is quite different from that in Chomsky (1965), the existence of VP as a core skeleton in minimalism is thus seen to still hold, not only in head-initial but also in head-final languages, despite considerable movement operations (see Lasnik and Saito 1992). Within this assumption, any word order which does not retain VP in the surface order is regarded as the result of some movement.

In this section, I will show first that, relative to standard criteria for constituency, nominal expressions can form a well-qualified constituent, even without postulating any verbal trace. Later, I demonstrate an example from Korean, but this can be applied to other Asian languages as well. First of all, the surprising constituent can be moved together, or, in other words, located away from its local interpretable domain. Hence, it satisfies the movement criterion of constituency.

(15)
    a. [[[S1 O1] S2 θ V1] V2]
        <u>Jina-ka</u>   <u>Pizza-lul</u>   Sarah-nun   Pizza-Express-eyse   θ mekessta-ko
        Jina-NOM   pizza-ACC   Sarah-TOP   Pizza-Express-at   θ ate-COMP
        malhaysseyo.
        said
        'Sarah said that Jina ate pizza at Pizza Express.'

    b. [[[O1 S1] S2 θ V1] V2]
        <u>Pizza-lul</u>   <u>Jina-ka</u>   Sarah-nun   Pizza-Express-eyse   θ mekessta-ko
        pizza-ACC   Jina-NOM   Sarah-TOP   Pizza-Express-at   θ ate-COMP
        malhaysseyo.
        said
        'Sarah said that Jina ate pizza at Pizza Express.'

The ordering between subject NP and object NP in (15) is flexible along with the ordering between indirect-object NP and direct-object NP as in (6), repeated in (16).

(16)
    a. [[[IO1 DO1] S2 Si θ Vi] V2]
        [[<u>Mina-hanthey Pizza-lul</u>]   Sarah-nun   Jina-ka   Pizza-Express-eyse θ
        Mina-DAT Pizza-ACC   Sarah-TOP   Jina-NOM Pizza-Express-at θ
        sa-cwuessta-ko   *haysseyo.*]
        buy-gave-COMP   said
        'Sarah said that Jina bought pizza to give to Mina at Pizza Express.'

    b. [[[DO1 IO1] S2 S1 θ V1] V2]
        [[<u>Pizza-lul</u>   <u>Mina-hanthey</u>]   Sarah-nun   Jina-ka.   Pizza-Express-ese θ
        Pizza-ACC   Mina-DAT   Sarah-TOP   Jina-NOM Pizza-Express-at θ
        sa-cwuessta-ko   *haysseyo.*]
        buy-gave-COMP   said
        'Sarah said that Jina bought pizza to give to Mina at Pizza Express.'

The grammaticality judgement for (15a-b) and (16a-b) is the same. This is also the case in the Persian example (7). All examples appear in naturalistic speech.

The surprising constituent also meets all the other criteria[7] as a constituent (see Kiaer 2007, chapter 1 for a detailed review). Hence, their constituency is legitimate, not too 'surprising'. Yet, explaining this is not so straightforward as we now turn to.

2.2.2. Syntactic accounts of surprising constituent formation

To explain the constituency of surprising constituents, Koizumi (2000) assumed that the internal arguments (i.e. objects) are generated initially within the maximal projection of a main verb (VP), which is the complement of a light verb, and the external argument (i.e. subject) is merged as Specifier (SPEC) of v (see Chomsky 1995, 1998; Larson 1988). Koizumi also adopted Nemoto's analysis (Nemoto 1993) and assumed that the external argument is raised to SPEC of intonational phrase (IP) or Tensed Phrase (TP) in overt syntax. Hence, he proposed that (17a) has an Logical Form (LF) structure given in (17b).

(17) a. *Mary-ga*   *John-ni*   *ringo-o*   *ageta.* [Japanese]
    Mary-NOM   John-DAT   apple-ACC   gave

b. $[_{CP}[_{IP} \text{Mary}_{Nom,i} [_{VP} t_i [_{VP} \text{John-to } [V' \text{ apple }_{ACC} \text{ gave}]]v]I]C]$

In explaining the configuration of (17a), Koizumi argued that two internal arguments *John-ni ringo-o* form a surface structure constituent which excludes the subject and the verb. Given the configuration as in (17b), the change Koizumi made is that the verb raises overtly to at least *v* in an 'across-the-board' manner as given in Figure 2.2. (18) shows how indirect and direct objects form a surprising constituent as underlined without an overt verb.

(18) *Mary-ga*   [*John-ni   ringo-o*]   *to*   [*Bob-ni   banana-o*]   [Japanese]
    Mary-NOM   John-to apple-ACC   and   Bob-to banana-ACC
    ageta
    gave   fact
    'Mary gave an apple to John, and bananas to Bob.'

Koizumi assumes that the surprising constituent is formed by overt verb raising as in Figure 2.2. In (18), the constituency of *John-ni ringo-o* is assured by the trace of a verb, which has been there at one point but subsequently moved. This is the so-called remnant movement analysis (i.e. verb-raising and subsequent constituent formation with the remnant NPs and verbal trace) that fits well into the X-bar schemata, as it preserves VP constituency. In this remnant movement

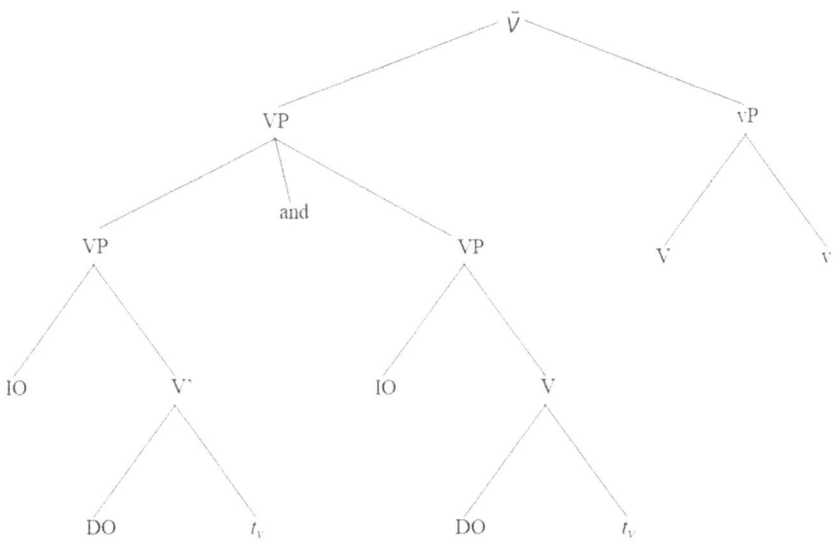

Figure 2.2 Overt verb raising: Ensuring IO DO constituency (Koizumi 2000).

analysis, a string of multiple lexical items in a 'scrambled order' is regarded as a result of multiple applications of remnant movement. On the other hand, a string of multiple lexical items in a 'canonical order' is regarded as a result of a single application of remnant movement. Hence, order-preserving is an important criterion to distinguish single/multiple long-distance scrambling. Consider Koizumi's crucial examples (19) and (20) (Koizumi 2000: 239–40).

(19) [vpHawai-de   Masami-ni   prezento-o t_v]   [John-ga   [Kiyomi-ga
     Hawai-at   Masami-DAT   present-ACC trace   John-NOM   Kiyomi-NOM
     katta$_v$-to]   omotteiru].
     bought-COMP believed
     'John thought that Kiyomi bought a present in Hawaii for Masami.'

(20) [???Prezento-o$_3$ Masami-ni$_2$ Hawai-de$_1$ John-ga   [Kiyomi-ga $t_1 t_2 t_3$
     present-ACC   Masami-DAT   Hawai-at   John-NOM   Kiyomo-NOM t $t_1 t_2 t_3$
     katta-to]   omotteiru].
     bought-COMP believed

Koizumi reported that (19) is grammatical, contrary to (20), which is highly unacceptable. This is due to a subjacency violation.[8] If two or more lexical items are scrambled out of an embedded clause, 'without' keeping the order of the original constituency, as in (20), the resulting sentence will be degraded. However, if multiple lexical items are scrambled together across the clause boundary as in (19), keeping the order of the original constituency, the grammaticality of the resulting sentence will be much improved. This prediction is however not backed up by ordinary Japanese speakers' judgements. Contrary to this judgement, ordering variation within a short or multiple long-distance scrambled sequence does not increase ungrammaticality and is frequently found in natural data of use. This is also the case in most Asian languages.

The other main recent account for verb-less constituent is given by Takano (2002). Takano adopts an adjunction-like oblique movement to analyse a surprising constituent found in Japanese cleft constructions as in (21).

(21) *John-ga   ageta   no-wa   hon-o   Mary-ni   da*
     John-NOM   gave-NM   thing-TOP   book-ACC   Mary-DAT   BE
     'It is a book to Mary that John gave.'

Takano claims that in (21), *Mary-ni* goes through an oblique movement to the sister position of *hon-o* and forms a surprising constituent, as illustrated in Figure 2.3. The crucial question for this analysis is whether the invention of a new movement as such is reasonable, because this type of movement is not ordinary. Consider (22) from Takano.

(22) Ringo-o   kinoo   Bill-ni   John-ga   [Mary-ga   ti tj   ageta-to]
      Apple-ACC   yesterday   Bill-DAT   John-NOM   Mary-NOM   ti tj   gave-COMP
      kiita
      heard
   a. 'John heard that Mary gave apples to Bill yesterday.' : Embedded reading of *kinoo*
   b. ?? John heard yesterday that Mary gave apples to Bill. : Matrix reading of *kinoo* – Not available.

According to Takano, this example can be derived as follows: first, the dative object of the embedded clause *Bill-ni* scrambles to the matrix TP, then the adjunct *kinoo* is adjoined to the matrix TP by Merge (assuming that it can be base-generated there) and finally the accusative object of the embedded clause scrambles to the matrix TP. This derivation should yield an interpretation in which *kinoo* is construed as a matrix clause modifier. However, in fact, *kinoo* is interpreted only within an embedded clause in (22a). Takano (2002: 265)

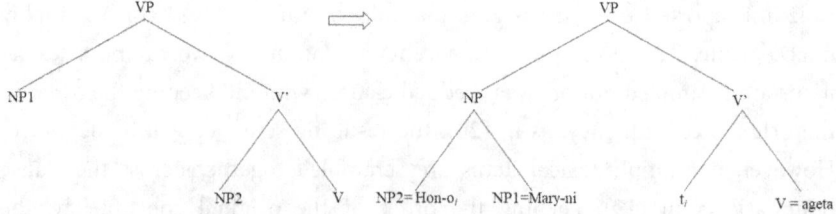

Figure 2.3 *Hon-o Mary-ni* as a constituent via oblique movement.

himself notes that the lack of relevant reading in (22) is not 'excluded by syntactic reasons, but perhaps by a processing reason as processing three pre-subject elements together seems to be much easier'.

As in Koizumi's analysis, a 'non-order preserving' surprising constituent is not assumed to easily form a constituent in Takano (2002). Instead, it is understood as multiple occasions of oblique movement. As Takano noted for the case of (22), within the pure syntactic analysis, set up in the Minimalist Program, it may be hard to capture the 'flexible' nature of the verb-less surprising constituent, since the basic core configuration assumed in the framework is not 'flexibly-built'.

Even though morphosyntactic motivation for the scrambling type of movement was regarded as very weak, within MP, it has been assumed that scrambling is an instance of feature-driven movement. Based on this assumption, further theoretical assumptions and analyses were proposed. A noticeable case is the distinct treatment between multiple *wh*-fronting and multiple NP fronting (i.e. multiple long-distance scrambling). In GB/MP, multiple *wh*-fronting and multiple NP fronting are treated as different grammatical processes, because the former is feature driven but not the latter. The latter, that is, multiple NP fronting (i.e. multiple long-distance scrambling) is considered as a result of remnant movement across a clause boundary (Koizumi 2000) or an adjunction-like oblique movement (Takano 2002).

Grewendorf (2001: 89) argued that languages like Japanese have a 'covert' cluster forming operation. He noted that the crucial difference between overt *wh*-fronting languages such as Bulgarian and Romanian and covert *wh*-fronting languages such as Japanese lies in the difference of feature strength. In the latter group of languages, the D-feature of *wh*-phrases is said to be relatively weak. Yet, as he noticed, it is not clear how minimalism can express different feature strength (see also Chomsky 2000 and Newmeyer 2005). Nevertheless, even though empirically the feature strength is not so strong at all, categorial distinctions between the two have been clearly assumed in feature-driven syntactic frameworks thus far. In the same vein, Aoshima et al. (2005) argued that parsers of Japanese can detect long-distance dependency when the fronted NP is a wh-NP contrary to the case of a referential NP (see Chapter 3).

2.3. Lexicalist frameworks

In this section, I will discuss how different lexicalist frameworks such as HPSG, LFG and (multimodal) CCG can deal with local and non-local word-order variation.

2.3.1. Head-driven phrase structure grammar

In HPSG, to explain word-order variation in relatively flexible word-order languages, an independent operation such as liberation and total/partial compaction needs to be used. In particular, there are two options in assigning order to the expression: either completely free order via liberation (Zwicky 1986) or completely frozen order via total compaction.

However, word-order variation goes beyond just this. Kathol and Pollard (1995) suggest 'partial' compaction. Intuitively, partial compaction allows designated domain objects to be liberated into a higher domain, while the remaining elements of the source domain are compacted or frozen. Yatabe (1996) and Lee (2001) analysed long-distance scrambling in Japanese and Korean via partial compaction. The rationale behind long-distance scrambling via partial compaction is as follows: liberate certain argument(s) to the higher domain and keep the rest tightly reflecting the original order. Lee noted that in general, the liberated element receives focus interpretation by accompanying pause or pitch accent.

To my knowledge, no work has been done on the trigger of liberation and subsequent partial compaction in HPSG. Lee argued that the flexibility and limitation found in scrambling phenomena can be captured by re-considering linear-order, rather than GB-sort hierarchical structure. The trigger of partial compaction used in long-distance scrambling may be found in prosody or topic/focus effects (see also Yoshimoto 2000 for similar view in Japanese). As Lee suggested at the end of her paper, more work needs to be done regarding the nature of the trigger for partial compaction. Especially, she suggested that the role of prosody and information structure needs to be further studied. Without investigating these properties, it is very hard to explain various scrambling phenomena since 'where' to liberate (if the scrambled or fronted argument has been dislocated from its non-local structure) or 'how many' constituents to liberate is hard to find out from morphosyntactic information only.

2.3.2. Lexical-functional grammar

Lexical-functional grammar is a constraint-based grammar formalism with parallel structures containing partial, localized information with no notion of movement as such. Different structures are not derived from each other, but are linked by various principles of functional correspondence. The main syntactic structures are c-(=constituent) structure and f-(=functional) structure.

c-structure models the 'surface' syntactic form of language, whereas f-structure models grammatical functions and other syntactic relations (see Bresnan 2001 for a general overview on this framework).

Within LFG, Nordlinger (1998) showed that grammatical function may be indicated by the case morphology itself, rather than from the so-called phrase structure based on Australian languages such as Warlpiri and Wambaya. Her insight on case markers is highly relevant to the claim I am pursuing in this book. Many Australian languages such as Warlpiri and Wambaya have very flexible ordering between lexical items, and there is rich morphology projected by case particles. The case of Warlpiri and Wambaya shows that functional uncertainty can be resolved by rich morphology. This principle can be applied to the Asian languages in this book too.

Consider (23) from Nordlinger (1998: 2). All the ordering of constituents is grammatical as long as the auxiliary (here *gin-a*) remains in the second position. Hence, six possible orders are available in (23):

(23) *Ngajbi gin-a   alaji   janyi-ni*   [Wambaya]
     see3SG.M.A-PST   boy.I-ACC   dog.I.ERG
     'The dog saw the boy.'

Nordlinger claimed that flexible ordering in Wambaya is evidence to show that word order cannot be used as an indicator of grammatical functions, but case particles can. Furthermore, case particles in these languages not only provide grammatical information for the nominal to which it is attached but also indicate the relation for 'higher' phrases in which they are embedded. Consider (24) from Nordlinger (1998: 5).

(24) *Karanta-ngku ka-rla   kurdu-ku   miyi   yi-nyi*
     woman-ERG PRES-3DAT   baby-DAT   food   give-NPST
     parraja-rla-ku
     coolamon-LOC-DAT
     'The woman is giving food to the baby (who is) in the coolamon.'

In (24), the locative adjunct *parraja-rla* 'coolamon-LOC' is further inflected with the dative case (*-ku*) to indicate that it is predicated of the dative argument *kurdu-ku* 'to the baby' of a higher structure. That said, (24) shows that case morphology in fact constructs a higher syntactic constituent. Nordlinger's basic intuition is that case functions should be treated as the source of constructing its context rather than treated a sort of licensing condition for the configuration.[9]

Nordlinger adopted inside-out functional uncertainty (IOFU, see Dalrymple (2001)) to capture constructive use of case within LFG.[10] However, an inside-out function itself is not sufficient to explain flexible word-order phenomena that often occurs across a clause boundary as in multiple long-distance dependency (i.e. scrambling, in particular) or linear-order effects caused by the incremental structural resolution.

Case particles invariably have the same inside-out function, but linear-order or prosody affect the interpretation. For instance, whether a certain case-marked NP is to be interpreted locally or non-locally is not decided exclusively by case, but by prosody or context. Also, whether a certain case-marked NP is to be interpreted together with the preceding NP or not is not decided by case, but by the prosody or context.

Left/right asymmetry found in the interpretation of the same lexical item also remains a puzzle in this framework as in other lexicalist frameworks. Explaining structural characteristics such as the left-to-right asymmetry effect by adopting a feature-driven account loses the explanatory power otherwise sustained in the system.

2.3.3. Combinatory categorial grammar

Of all current orthodox formalisms, categorial grammar allows highly non-standard constituents. Capturing permutativity and associativity in natural language syntax is the main goal of any categorial grammar. Flexible constituency can be easily captured in CCG via type-raising function (Steedman 2000). Hence, the constituency of a surprising constituent under our discussion can be achieved easily. In order to capture the flexible ordering in Turkish, Hoffman (1995) adopted a set-theoretical notation in the description of argument structure of a verb. Consider the following Turkish examples from Hoffman (1995).

(25) a. *Ayse*   *Kitabi*   *okuyor [S O V]*   [Turkish]
      Ayse-NOM   book-ACC   read
      'Ayse read a book.'
    b. *Kitabi*   *Ayse*   *okuyor [O S V]*   [Turkish]
      book-ACC   Ayse-NOM   read
      'Ayse read a book.'

To capture the symmetry of meaning in the example (25a-b), Hoffman unified two lexical entries for the verb *okuyor*. Two separate entries for *okyur* as in (26a-b) are unified as in (26c).

(26) a. *okuyor* ⊢ (S\ NP$_{NOM}$) NP$_{ACC}$
 b. *okuyor* ⊢ (S\ NP$_{ACC}$) NP$_{NOM}$
 c. *okuyor* ⊢ S{\NP$_{NOM}$, \NP$_{ACC}$} ⇐ set-notated category

By doing so, Hoffman tried to loosen strict directionality in CCG combinatory rules. Flexible ordering within a local clause (i.e. local scrambling) is therefore borne out not by restriction in combinatory rules but by a set-notated lexical item. Hoffman's approach is called Multi-Set CCG. Baldridge (2002) claimed, however, that the Multi-Set approach cannot capture some extraction asymmetries found in Tagalog and Toba Batak. In fact, the Multi-Set approach is also limited in explaining any non-local scrambling, since set-notated permutations between lexical items can only be possible when they are in the same local domain. In addition, Multi-Set CCG cannot capture any left-right asymmetry, since the assumption behind the set notation is that there is no asymmetry as such in scrambling languages.

The core idea of Baldridge (2002) is to redefine CCG rules to be sensitive to particular logical modalities. By doing so, he aimed to capture freedom and restriction in (relatively) free word-order languages without granting too much freedom as in Hoffman (1995). Also, by putting restriction/control in the lexicon, the same set of combinatory rules could be held across the languages. Baldridge argued that in this way CCG can capture the mildly context-sensitive nature of the grammar. Figure 2.4 is Baldridge's derivation of a long-distance scrambling in Turkish in (27). In (27), *Kitabi* 'book-ACC' is long-distance scrambled.

(27)
Kitabi   Fatma   Esránin   okudugunu   biliyor
Book-ACC Fatma-NOM Esránin-GEN read-GER-ACC   know-PROG
'As for the book, Fatma knows that Esra read it.'

Kitabi	*Fatma*	*Esra'nin*	*okudugunu*	*biliyor*
np$_a$	np$_n$	np$_g$	s$_{\vee acc}$\·{np$_g$, np$_a$}	s$_i$\·{np$_n$, np$_{\vee acc}$}

$$\text{š}_i/{\cdot}\text{š}_i\backslash\text{np}_n \quad \longrightarrow T$$

$$s_{\vee acc}\backslash\cdot\text{np}_a \quad <$$

$$s_i\backslash\cdot\text{np}_n\ \backslash\cdot\text{np}_a \quad <B$$

$$\text{š}_i\backslash\text{np}_a \quad >B_x$$

$$\text{š}_i \quad <$$

Figure 2.4 Baldridge's derivation of a long-distance scrambling in Turkish.

To derive the reading in which *Kitabi* is long-distance scrambled, the subject *Fatma* of the matrix clause, though it is a simple type as it stands, must be type-raised and go through forward cross composition into the verbal cluster. However, in reality, controlling derivation or in other words, controlling permutativity and associativity over a natural language string via modality restriction in the lexicon, can be very problematic. This is because the source of limited permutativity or associativity is often linear order, surrounding syntactic context and prosody. These factors are hard to encode in the lexicon. Furthermore, it is not easy to control these factors via modalities. Factors like syntactic position, surrounding co-argument as well as prosody all influence the interpretation of linguistic expressions. These are very hard to express within a lexical entry in an explanatorily adequate way. Also, if we try to do so, the mild context sensitivity of grammars of natural language, which CCG aims to achieve, is hard to sustain.[11]

Ultimately, capturing the appropriate balance between freedom and restrictiveness in word-order phenomena and their interpretation is hard to express within CCG, since the derivation in CCG is not sensitive to linear order at all. Hence, though the combination is procedural, CCG is not suitable to capture the incremental nature of flexible word orders.

As a last resort operation, McConville (2001) tried to reduce non-determinism and capture incrementality in CCG grammar by proposing a *ruthless reduce-first parser*. Yet, still it is hard to incorporate incrementality or left-to-right asymmetry in CCG, since the nature of derivation in CCG is not time linear.

2.4. Summary

Having now looked at all the major current frameworks, we have seen that flexible word-order phenomena remain highly controversial and poorly characterized in all major grammar formalisms. The phenomenon of variant word order is an extremely common device in Asian languages and beyond, and control of its effect on interpretation is central to the knowledge of language. Yet, accounting for all such linearity effects remains a serious challenge for all these frameworks.

This chapter has shown the fundamental problems of the Anglo- and Euro-centric syntactic framework, where linear order and verbs are regarded to carry the sole combinatory syntactic force. This may not work in particle-rich Asian languages where particles and other factors must be considered in understanding basic morphosyntactic variation.

3

Efficiency grammar

3.1. Overview

This chapter shows how natural language syntax *is* resource-sensitive, contrary to Chomsky's initial claims. In the history of contemporary theoretical linguistics, core arguments have been established around the possible and impossible structures that are distinguished using grammaticality judgements. Yet, hardly any meaningful discussion has been made on the asymmetry between possible-and-preferred structures and possible-yet-hardly preferred structures. This I refer to as *preference asymmetry* in this book. This is due to the deeply rooted generativists' assumptions of *competence* and *performance*, whereby it is believed that *competence* alone reflects the innate, universal properties of human languages and *performance* only reflects peripheral variations. The preference asymmetry in this sense belongs to the performative knowledge and hence it has received little attention. I show that even the backbones of structural architecture in the generativists' mindset, such as finding the basic unit (i.e. constituent) and grammaticality/acceptability judgements, cannot be established without considering the resource-sensitive nature of human languages, where efficiency matters in structure building.

3.2. Efficiency and linguistic competence

Linguistic competence is an innate ability that is given to every human being from birth and is responsible for one's overall syntactic behaviours. From the beginning of Chomskian linguistics, the ultimate goal of any linguistic theory has been to find the core, innate and universal properties of human language that govern the linguistic lego-building of all languages.

One of the key observations that Chomsky made is found in his famous example of *colourless green ideas*, where he showed that even very young children can make a distinction between the possible and impossible strings, despite having never been exposed to them. Any ordinary speaker of English would judge the sentence in (2a) to be grammatical, despite never having heard it before, whereas the sentence in (2b) would be deemed ungrammatical (example taken from Chomsky, 1965: 3) (* signifies ungrammaticality).

(2) a. *Colourless green ideas sleep furiously.*

b. **Furiously sleep ideas green colourless.*

For the last sixty years, theoretical linguists have explored this intuitive knowledge which allows ordinary speakers to distinguish between grammatical and ungrammatical sentences such as those in (2); consequently, they aimed to reveal the essence of human language by looking at similar patterns contrasting between possible and impossible patterns in human languages. It has been assumed that one of the core abilities of native speakers of a language is the ability to tell whether a given sequence of words is well formed or ill formed in their mother tongue. This contrast became the basis for building syntactic architecture in human language.

3.2.1. Preference asymmetry

In generative theoretical syntax, the morphosyntactic cause on possible and impossible word orders have been widely researched. Yet, precisely what causes preference asymmetry among possible orders has been overlooked or considered as mere stylistic variation which belonged to performance rather than competence or what needs to be explained in pragmatics or in the studies of information structure than in theoretical syntax (see Wasow 2002 for an overview). The following quote shows the generative mindset on the resource-sensitivity of natural language syntax.

> Linguistic theory is concerned primarily with an ideal speaker-listener, in a completely homogeneous speech-community, who knows its language perfectly and is unaffected by <u>such grammatically irrelevant conditions as memory limitations,</u> distractions, shifts of attention and interest, and errors (random or characteristic) in applying his knowledge of the language in actual performance . . . (p.3). We thus make a fundamental distinction between competence (the speaker-hearer's knowledge of his language) and performance (the actual use of language in concrete situations). (Chomsky 1965: 3f; emphasis mine)

In this section, I show how the basic building blocks are formed, assembled and assessed in an incremental, local manner – observing and maximizing the given resources. I argue that this is a natural consequence of syntax being resource-sensitive and pragmatically driven. Consider (3) from Stowe (1986) and (4) from Wasow (2002) – both show preference asymmetry (??? signifies unnaturalness).

(3) Efficiency asymmetry:
No slowdown at us:
a. *My brother wanted to know if Ruth will bring us home to mom at Christmas.*
Slowdown at us:
???b. *My brother wanted to know who Ruth will bring us home to at Christmas.*

(4) Frequency asymmetry:
Frequently observed:
a. *Pat picked up a very large mint-green hard cover book.*
Hardly observed:
???b. *Pat picked a very large mint-green hard cover book up.*

Both sentences in (3) and (4) are grammatical. Nevertheless, ordinary speakers' real-time understanding of the sentences in (3) or real usage of the sentences in (4) is very different. In the case of (3), using an online self-paced reading task, Stowe (1986) reported relatively slower reading time at the direct-object position in (3b), compared to the same position in (3a) as underlined. Such a delay or slow-down effect occurs because ordinary speakers carry a prediction or expectation for the upcoming structure. In (3b), when native speakers come across the sequence of *who Ruth*, they are most likely to interpret 'who' as the direct object of the upcoming sentence. Hence, when they realize such expectation turns out to be wrong at the time of facing *us*, they will experience some sort of delay as a 'surprising effect'. This phenomenon which Stowe originally observed is known as the Filled-Gap Effect.

Note that if there is no prediction or expectation for the future structure in the process of structure building, there should not be any such surprising effect in the middle of a sentence. The evidence for the Filled-Gap Effect, which is a proof for incremental structure building, is found cross-linguistically. The asymmetry observed in (4) is specifically due to so-called heavy NP shift. This phenomenon was observed first in Ross (1967). Though both sentences are grammatical, ordinary speakers strongly prefer to locate heavy NPs at the end of the sentence so that the verb and its accompanying particle may 'come together', as in (4a).

Timing issues, either of slowdown or facilitation, have no way of being explained in current grammar formalisms (see Phillips and Wager (2007) for an overview). The easiest solution in this case may be to regard the Filled-Gap Effect and related ancillaries as mere performance phenomena.[1] In this book, I argue, against this, that the tenet of linguistic competence has to be broadened and the evidence should be gathered not only from offline judgement tests but also from online sentence processing and moreover from big enough corpus data.[2] In particular, I assume that a grammar formalism should play a role not only in static understanding but also in the procedural, dynamic understanding of a linguistic representation.

Most grammaticality judgements used in the past are made by linguists themselves subjectively. Informants often will mark sentences which they will hardly use in real life, based on their school grammar knowledge (see Wasow 2002: 156–64). The benefit of psycholinguistic tests is that we can begin to get a handle on what is really in the human mind without even making informants conscious of what they are doing.[3] On the other hand, the interpretation of psycholinguistic results such as efficiency or complexity, expressed either as facilitation or slowdown in processing, must be carefully done in accordance with the grammar assumed.

In this book, I draw attention to the fact that ordinary speakers do not produce all the logically possible well-formed strings with equal frequency in real language use. In addition, they do not understand with similar efficiency all logically possible well-formed strings. Instead, they show a strong preference for certain well-formed strings both in understanding and in their own production. The same tendency is also found in typological variation as well as in language change. Neither diachronic nor synchronic variation displays all the logically possible alternatives, but rather a very limited set of variations. Resource-sensitivity in natural language syntax is manifested by incrementality and (prosodically sensitive) locality across the languages, regardless of verb positions. Crucially, the resource which provides structural information is not limited to verbs as I shall explore through Asian languages.

3.2.2. Domain matters: Incremental constituency

Phillips (1996, 2003) shows that the basics of syntax, such as defining a constituent, cannot be established without considering the resource-sensitive, procedural aspects of syntactic structure building. The same string of words can be diagnosed as a constituent by one constituent test, but not by another constituent test. Example (5), taken from Phillips (2003), shows a case of constituency conflict. When coordination is taken as a test for constituency, in (5a), *Gromit a biscuit* passes the coordination test and thus is regarded as a constituent. In (5b), however, *Gromit a biscuit* cannot pass the movement test and thus is not regarded as a constituent.

(5) [Gromit a biscuit] is a constituent according to the coordination test
   a. *Wallace gave [Gromit a biscuit] and [Shawn some cheese] for breakfast.*
   [Gromit a biscuit] is NOT a constituent by movement test
   b. **[VP Gromit a biscuit] Wallace gave VP* for breakfast.*

Based on the constituency shift and constituency conflict phenomena, Phillips argued for the incrementality hypothesis as described in (6).

(6) *Sentence structures are built incrementally from left to right.*

As reflected in Figure 3.1, Phillips assumed that syntactic relation must respect constituency at the point in the derivation when the relation is established. Yet, once this relation is licensed, constituency (between A and B) may change subsequently (i.e. be revised); this, he argued, was the basis for such conflict. Given that defining constituency is a crucial matter in syntax, it is striking that such a core notion is difficult to sustain without considering left-to-right growth of a structure.

3.2.3. Socio-pragmatic sensitivity in the grammaticality test

The grammaticality test has been one of the most important criteria used to attest legitimate syntactic architecture. However, as Schütze (1996) discusses in detail,

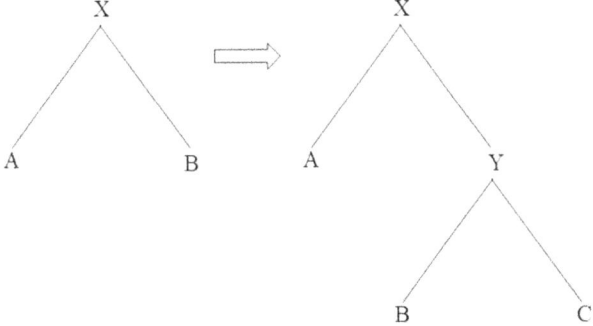

Figure 3.1 Incremental constituency (Phillips 1996, 2003).

though the concept of a grammaticality or acceptability judgement is regarded as the foremost criterion in shaping grammars, the method for defining degrees of grammaticality is not robust enough nor has solid empirical background. Phillips (2009) further questioned whether the improvement of methodology can in fact be the real solution for puzzles around grammaticality judgement tests and some other fundamental issues which generative linguists face.[4]

Grammaticality/acceptability greatly varies between speakers too, even when they have similar linguistic backgrounds. Context is also significant. In the history of generative linguistics, socio-pragmatic sensitivity was often ignored, and the examples were studied in a vacuum-like formal, written register alone. Hence, it is easy to find that the unnaturalness is caused not because of the structural oddity but because of the register or socio-pragmatic mismatch (Chapters 4 and 5).

Consider the Korean examples below. (7a) is unnatural because *-nim* is an honorific particle which predicts an honorific verbal particle. Yet, in (7a), a command-denoting ending particle *-e-la* (-어라) is used, which is typically used by a superior to their junior. Hence, the socio-pragmatic expectation is jeopardized. In contrast, (7b) shows the suffix *-ya* (-야), which is used by a superior to their junior with intimacy. However, this expectation for speaker-hearer relation is again not met when the polite *-seyyo* (-세요) ending particle appears. The unnaturalness found in (7a) and (7b) may be broadly agreed by ordinary Korean speakers. The cause of the unnaturalness is nothing to do with grammatical structures but socio-pragmatic relevance. S < H means hearer is senior to the speaker. S > H means speaker is senior to the hearer.

(7) Socio-pragmatic awkwardness/unnaturalness due to speaker-hearer relation conflict

<u>Simple clause</u>
a. S < H particle *nim*, S > H particle *e-la*
    Sensayng-nim**, pap mek-**e-la**.*   [Korean]
    teacher-HON meal eat-COM
Lit. 'Teacher, come and have a meal.'
b. S > H particle *-ya* and S < H particle *-yo*.
    Jessie-ya** pap mek-u-**seyyo**.*
    Jessie-VOC meal eat-DECL+HON+POL
Lit. 'Jessie, come and have a meal.'
<u>Complex clause</u>
c. **Sensayng-**nim**, pap mek-**e-lako** …….Mina-ka malhaysse.*
    teacher-HON meal eat-COMP Mina-NOM said

Lit. 'Mina said, "teacher, come and have a meal."'

d. *Jessie-**ya** pap mek-u-**seyo-lako** ....Mina-ka malhaysse.
Jessie-VOC meal eat-DECL+HON+POL-COMP Mina-NOM said
Lit. 'Mina said, "Jessie, come and have a meal."'

3.2.4. Incremental and local judgements

Not only structure-building, but also assessing and assigning grammaticality is done in an incremental manner within its local grammatical unit. In (7), native speakers detect the unnaturalness before finishing the whole sentence. Particularly, for (7c) and (7d), we find the socio-pragmatic unnaturalness when the underlined lexical item is heard not at the end. This shows that grammaticality or acceptability judgement is procedurally made in the process of understanding a sequence – rather than once for all at the very end of a sentence.

As such, I consider that grammaticality and acceptability judgements are made locally, rather than globally, with the unnaturalness judgement being affected by the length of the prosodic domain. That said, in spontaneous speech, if the grammaticality checking domain is too long, human parsers can easily forget to detect ungrammaticality. For instance, subject-verb mismatch in spontaneous production is frequently found in verb-final languages when the distance between the two expressions becomes too long. It is because of the limitation of resources, that is, working memory in this case.[5] In the same way, human parsers tend to resolve filler-gap dependency as soon as possible in online processing rather than some arbitrary place in order to lower the burden of the memory load (see Hawkins 2014 for cross-linguistic evidence for this claim).

Along the same line, Asudeh (2011) argues that grammaticality or well formedness in production is checked locally rather than globally – chunk by chunk. Similar claims on processing/parsing have been made by Tabor, Galantucci and Richardson (2004). Consider (8). Asudeh reports that both examples are produced and 'tolerated' – though (8b) is judged ungrammatical as shown in the diagrams due to the violation of an island condition (Figure 3.2).

(8) a. *You get a rack that the bike will sit on.*
    b. ???*You get a rack that the bike will sit on it.*

According to Asudeh (2011), the reason why both sentences are produced and tolerated by ordinary speakers is because they are 'locally legitimate'. The illegitimacy of (8b) is caused by global checking of grammaticality. Asudeh argues that, due to the incremental production that initiates local checking for grammaticality, the ungrammatical examples like (8b) are sanctioned by the

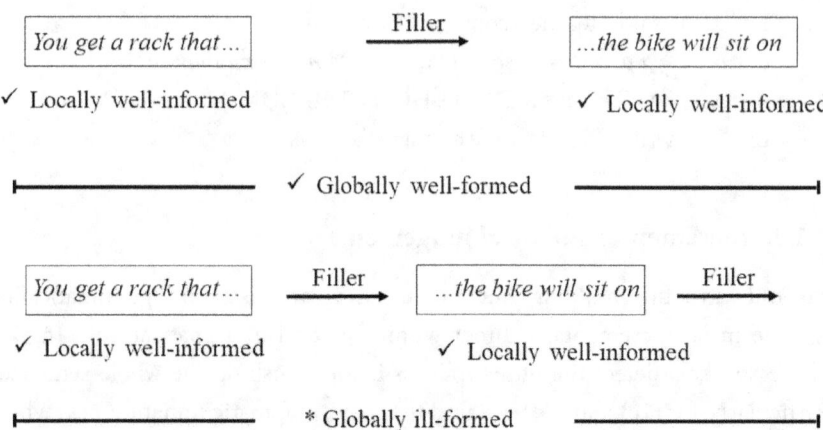

Figure 3.2 Grammaticality check in a local domain: Asudeh (2011).

grammar and indeed are often produced by ordinary speakers. Unlike local checking, global checking can be loose at times and people can and do, from time to time, turn off the checking mechanisms in using language.[6] If indeed the operating grammar is insensitive to resource, global checking, just like local checking, should cause no problem at all to human parsers.

3.2.5. Prosodically sensitive, minimal domain

The discussions on domain are further elaborated in Hawkins (1994, 2004), where he proposed the notion of minimized domain (MiD) to capture and explain resource-sensitive, efficient nature of structure building and dependency resolution. Consider the following.

(9) *Minimized Domains* (MiD):

> The human processor prefers to minimize the connected sequences of linguistic forms and their conventionally associated syntactic and semantic properties in which relations of combination and/or dependency are processed. The degree of this preference is proportional to the number of relations whose domains can be minimized in competing sequences of structures, and to the extent of the minimization difference in each domain.

The size of domain is significant because human parsers clearly have limitations in terms of working memory and physical articulation (Gick et al. 2012). Since its beginnings, the Chomskian mindset assumes the ordinary speaker's flawless and limitless ability to acquire their mother tongues. However, speaking and talking are highly resource-sensitive behaviours. It is clear, then, that speed and the length of the prosodic domain matters.

Short distance between the two functionally related lexical items is desirable for the sake of least effort. Yet, this isn't the complete story as the domain needs to be prosodically sensitive. Fodor (2002) and her colleagues argued that people use default 'prosodic' information even in silent reading. I take this insight to forefront – arguing that prosody is one of the most important driving forces for structural realization. In particular, the ideal domain is not just arbitrarily minimized but prosodically sensitive. For instance, we speak through the course of breathing. Though we want to express many things in a limited period of time, there is a clear limit in the number of syllables that we can pronounce 'within a span of time' (Gick et al. 2012).[7]

Cross-linguistically, speakers aim to attune syntactic structure to a prosodic structure through appropriate prosodic phrasing, using the right number of pauses and the correct speech rate. This tuning process finding the right combination may be universally inherent to all languages. It seems that the most efficient ways of packaging syntactic and prosodic structures tend to survive and thrive over time as patterns of speech that become default among the speech community of the language. In other words, the way in which people speak in their day-to-day life naturally reflects how structure and sound are packaged in the most efficient possible way. I shall propose in this book that survived and thrived forms are the ones that are produced within the remit of auditory-working memory and articulatory one-breadth limit – mostly close to one intonational phrase (IP).

The prosody of folk song lyrics is a good example for this claim. Most folk songs that have survived and thrived over time in a given region naturally fit within the prosodic and memory structure of the language spoken by the regional community.

3.2.6. Evidence of incremental structure building in Asian languages

Incremental, stepwise structure-building is at the heart of efficient structure-building. Yet, it is not straightforward to explain incrementality in most grammar formalisms within either transformational/derivational or lexicalist approaches. This is mainly because most grammar formalisms assume that (i) only verbs carry combinatorial information and (ii) structures are built in an 'all-at-once' manner at the end when all fragments are presented. Both assumptions make it hard to understand and explain dynamic growth of a structure. This becomes a serious problem in explaining verb-final languages, which is the case for many Asian languages. As discussed in Chapter 1, most of the North and Central Asian as well as Southeast Asian languages are OV languages, whereas almost all European languages except Sorbian and Basque are VO languages.

A verb-centred view simply predicts that speakers of verb-final languages may not be able to understand a linguistic sequence in an incremental manner, as the verb containing all the combinatorial information only comes at the very end (see Pritchett 1992, among many others). Although such a line of thinking may appear unnatural and unintuitive, this was the dominant view held for some time. However, challenging evidence started to appear in the pioneering works of Inoue and Fodor (1995) and Mazuka and Itoh (1995). Inoue and Fodor (1995) showed that in a sentence such as (10), a Japanese speaker may experience a mild surprise effect (i.e. delay) when the first verb *tabeta* ('eat') is encountered, because the parser is expecting a verb that takes all three NPs as its arguments.

(10) ???*Bob-ga*   *Mary-ni*   *ringo-wo*   *tabeta*   *inu-wo*   *ageta*.
      Bob-NOM   Mary-DAT   apple-ACC   ate   dog-ACC   gave
      'Bob gave Mary the dog that ate an apple.'

The significant slowdown that would be experienced in a reading of (10) after facing the transitive verb *tabeta* 'eat' shows that the sequence of NPs preceding the verb projects a structural template where all the NPs can be interpreted together. Simply put, the reason why native speakers of Japanese experience delay is due to the existence of *Mary-ni* because it yields a prediction for ditransitive verbs, instead of a transitive verb *tabeta* 'eat'.

Similarly, Mazuka and Itoh (1995) studied the eye movements of Japanese speakers as they parsed sentences. They demonstrated that Japanese native speakers find double centre-embedded sentences starting with a sequence as in (11a) extremely difficult to read relative to sentences starting with other case-marked NP strings as in (11b). (??? here refers to difficulties in comprehension and temporary slowdown in real-time processing.)

(11) Difficult-to-understand three consecutive *-ga*
   a. ???*Yoko-ga*   *Hiromi-ga*   *Asako-ga*
       Yoko-NOM   Hiromi-NOM   Asako-NOM   (difficult to understand)
   b. *Yoko-ga*   *Hiromi-wo*   *Asako-ni*
       Yoko-NOM   Hiromi-ACC   Asako-DAT   (easy to understand)

Mazuka and Itoh (1995) argued that the comprehension asymmetry as in (11) is caused because a -*ga* marked nominative NP constantly unfolds a new structure. The difficulty in understanding sequence (11a) is due to several 'incomplete' sentences projected by the -*ga* marked NPs. If a structure were not built incrementally, no significant difficulty should be encountered in (11a), compared to (11b), at such an early stage in structure building. In a similar vein, Ko (1997) and Kiaer (2007, 2014) among others showed incremental structure building in Korean. Özge et al. (2015) show incremental structure building in Turkish.

If it is indeed a verb alone which projects a structural skeleton, it remains as a puzzle to explain verb-less sentences that are not rare cross-linguistically. Yet, it seems that the existence of verb-less clauses occurs in language universally. Consider the Mandarin Chinese examples in (12) from Shei (2014: 106).

(12)
    a. *Zhe4   ge5   hua4ti2   hen3   re4*   [Mandarin Chinese]
       this   topic   very   hot
       'This topic (is) very hot.'
    b. *Dong1tian1   le5*
       Winter   SFP
       '(It is) winter already.'
    c. *Yi4   bai3   wan4   le5*
       One   million   SFP
       '(We have) one million already.'

Similarly, in Turkish, nominal sentences in which no explicit verbal expressions are used are common as shown in (13). (13) is from Göksel and Kerslake (2005: 160). In this example, there is no copular verb 'be'.

(13) *İstanbul büyük bir şehir.*   [Turkish]
       'Istanbul [is] a big city.'

Verb-less structures are found in Burmese too. (14) is from Jenny and Hnin Tun (2017: 248).

(14) *Di shainkɛ kəlaʔ mə-pa-bù.* [Burmese]
      this motorbike clutch NEG-included-NEG
      'This motorbike doesn't have a clutch.'

Consider the Kazakh example given in (15). This is from Muhamedowa (2015: 2).

(15) *Qazaqstanda orïstar köp.* [Kazakh]
Kazakhstan-LOC Russian-PL many
'There are many Russians in Kazakhstan.'

Such verb-less structures can be observed cross-linguistically, as discussed in greater depth by Sadler and Nordlinger (2006). Also, in the poetic genre, verbs are often unsaid and only assumed. In the case of biblical Hebrew and poetic portions of the Hebrew Bible, there are a lot of nominal sentences that do not have a verb at all. Repeated structure or other poetic tools are used in constructing a structure.

3.3. Previous approaches of explaining efficient structure building

As we have seen in Chapter 2, the verb-centred view cannot offer a satisfactory account of the nature of incremental structure-building in flexible word-order languages (often with verb-finality), which comprise more than half of the world's language. What this implies practically is that native speakers of verb-final languages do not and cannot understand what is being said before the final verb is encountered. This is hard to believe, particularly given the frequency with which verb-less utterances are encountered in everyday language use.

Originally, both dependency grammar and LFG were designed to allow an incremental update of the ongoing underspecified structure without excessive derivational complexity. Yet, as it stands, it is hard to use the LFG schemata in explaining incrementality of the not-yet-complete structures, as the target of their discussion should be only based on complete structures. In combinatory categorial grammar (CCG), which shows incremental structure building in verb-final languages, the way incrementality works is not sensitive to real-time processing; hence, the parser needs to know all the combinatory information at the start of understanding a sequence. Put simply, any analysis for an 'incomplete' linguistic sequence is in principle illegitimate. There is no syntactic theory applicable to 'not-yet-seen' structures.

This is one of the crucial reasons that left-to-right motivation hasn't been widely adopted in linguistic theories. It has been implicitly believed that the issues surrounding the incremental or partial growth of an 'incomplete' sequence is what a grammar-independent parsing theory as in Miyamoto (2002) should seek to explain, rather than a competence-based linguistic theory (see Wasow 2002 for an overview of this perspective).

3.3.1. Principle of early immediate constituent and the problem of word-counting methodology

The essence of Hawkins' (1994) claim and the works afterwards is to assume that humans build syntactic structure in the most cost-saving manner, and this is reflected in the use of language, evidenced by sufficiently sized corpora. Hawkins (1994) put forward a processing-based account of word-order phenomena, and claims that the single principle 'Principle of Early Immediate Constituent' predicts the way word orders are, reflecting rapidity and efficiency of online parsing. Consider the following example.

(16) *Early Immediate Constituents (EIC)*
 The human parser prefers linear orders that maximize the IC-to-non-IC ratios of constituent recognition domains. (Hawkins 1994: 77)

Immediate constituent (IC) is a constituent that is immediately dominated by the node in question. The definition includes two technical concepts. First, a 'constituent recognition domain' is defined as (18). To illustrate the point, consider Figure 3.3 for a sample sentence (17a).

(17) a. *Jessica rang up the boy.*
 b. *Jessica rang the boy up.* (Song 2012: 237)

(18) *Constituent Recognition Domain (CRD)*
 The CRD for a phrasal mother node M consists of the set of terminal and non-terminal nodes that must be parsed in order to recognize M and all ICs of M, proceeding from the terminal node in the parse string that constructs the first IC on the left, to the terminal node that constructs the last IC on the right, and including all intervening terminal nodes and the non-terminal nodes that they construct.

As for the above example (17a), the CRD for the phrasal mother node VP consists of the three ICs (V, Part, NP) and the four non-ICs (*rang*, *up*, Det, *the*) as in (19). Note that the node labelled N and the node decorated with *boy* are excluded in this domain; this is because the node labelled NP can be built once the determiner *the* is parsed (i.e. before parsing *boy*). The domain for VP is visually shown by the two dashed lines in Figure 3.3.

But, even in Hawkins (1994, 2004, 2014), the untouched problem is that deep down, there is an assumption that the 'verb' is the sole carrier of combinatorial information and the verb-object or verb-particle pair forms the ever-crucial

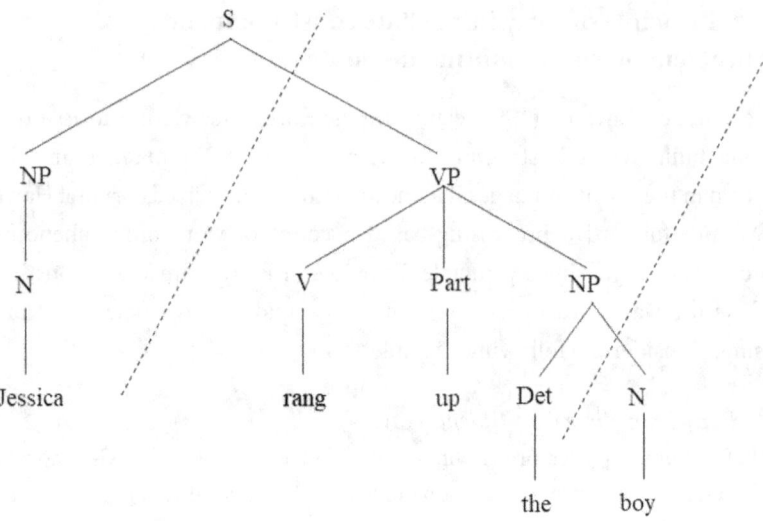

Figure 3.3 Structure for *Jessica rang up the boy*.

structural unit that is quintessential in getting the full picture of the linguistic structure. This makes good sense in verb-early order languages. Questions arise as to measuring the CRD, how to determine the predictability of the theory in verb-final languages, and whether the minimal distance pair will always be chosen as the most optimal option. Besides, measuring the CRD in verb-final languages with 'flexible' word orders will be more challenging as the size of CRD can vary to a great extent. I think it is sensible to assume that it is a sequence of particles which yield prediction on the CRD rather than verbs in these languages. Such questions are not easily resolvable without modifying fundamental assumptions on competence grammars.

In addition, Hawkins' way of word-counting faces some unavoidable problems. Simply counting words may not be able to accurately capture the domain's length. It is perfectly possible for a single word to be longer than a group of three (e.g. 'a red book' versus 'accommodation'), and these words can be spoken at highly variable articulation rates by different speakers in different conditions.

Sherr-Ziarko and Kiaer (2019) showed that prosodic variables would be more predictively useful than segment counting in explaining minimized domain in heavy NP shift. They showed that speakers are making an effort to 'squeeze' longer object NPs in order to shrink the domain of the phrasal verbs (Figure 3.4).

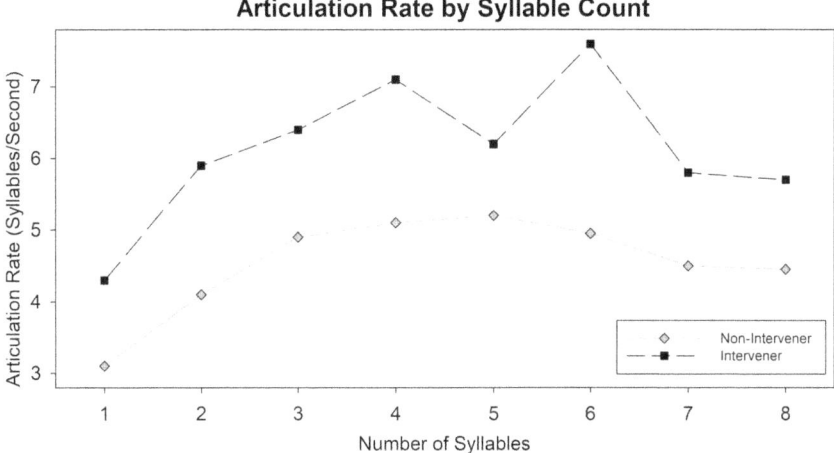

Figure 3.4 Articulation rate (s/second) by number of syllables for both interveners and non-interveners.

3.3.2. Problems of un-forced revision

Further works by Phillips and his colleagues also face problems in explaining verb-final languages. To explain incrementality within the Anglo- and Eurocentric frameworks, one has to start with many ad hoc assumptions about structure-building. Aoshima et al. (2004) have argued that in Japanese the sentence-initial *wh*-dative NP undergoes *un-forced revision* during the online structure building, to be interpreted within the 'most' embedded clause. Consider the following examples:

(19) [Japanese]
   a. Scrambled, declarative complementizer: Typing mismatch effect
Dono-seito-ni tannin-wa koocyoo-ga hon-o yonda-to tosyositu-de sisyo-ni iimasita-ka?
which-student-DAT teacher-TOP principal-NOM book-ACC read-DECL library-at librarian-DAT said-Q
'Which student did the class teacher tell the librarian at the library that the principal read a book for?'
   b. In-situ, declarative complementizer: Typing mismatch effect
tannin-wa koocyoo-ga dono-seito-ni hon-o yonda-to tosyositu-de sisyo-ni iimasita-ka?
teacher-TOP principal-NOM which-student-DAT book-ACC read-DECL library-at librarian-DAT said-Q

'Which student did the class teacher tell the librarian at the library that the principal read a book for?'

c. Scrambled, question particle: No typing mismatch effect

Dono-seito-ni tannin-wa koocyoo-ga hon-o yonda-ka tosyositu-de sisyo-ni iimasita
which-student-DAT teacher-TOP principal-NOM book-ACC read-Q library-at librarian-DAT said
'The class teacher told the librarian at the library which student the principal read a book for?'

d. In-situ, question particle: No typing mismatch effect

tannin-wa koocyoo-ga dono-seito-ni hon-o yonda-ka tosyositu-de sisyo-ni iimasita
teacher-TOP principal-NOM which-student-DAT book-ACC read-Q library-at librarian-DAT said
'The class teacher told the librarian at the library which student the principal read a book for?'

Aoshima et al. found that both when the *wh*-phrase was in situ as in (18b) or in (18d) or when they are scrambled long-distance as in (18a) or in (18c), Japanese speakers were surprised to encounter a declarative complementizer *-to* in the embedded clause instead of a question particle. Based on this result, they argued that Japanese speakers at first posit a gap in the matrix clause as in Figure 3.5 but revise it into the most embedded clause as shown in Figure 3.6.

According to Aoshima et al. (2004), the shift from Figure 3.5 to Figure 3.6 is 'unforced'. Nevertheless,[8] they still assumed that the motivation of such revision is feature-checking.[9] In other words, Aoshima and her colleagues have argued that the slowdown in the embedded clause with a declarative marker is caused because of the failure to check the *wh*-feature. Aoshima et al. (2005) argued that therefore referential NPs in a sentence-initial position do 'not' undergo un-forced revision. However, given that the strength of *wh*-feature in Japanese/Korean is very weak (Grewendorf 2001), it is hard to see why native speakers can and do make distinctions needed for the future structure building from the two types of NPs at such an early stage.

Aoshima et al. (2004) also argued that the parser prefers to satisfy requirements brought from the initial dative NP as soon as possible, hence, within the most embedded clause, since in Japanese and Korean the most embedded verb comes earliest and the matrix verb comes last. However, without getting the full picture of a structure, it is impossible to know how many embedded structures are used in the given sentence. Hence, we can't see from which source structure such revision should take place until the end of the processing of structure is reached.

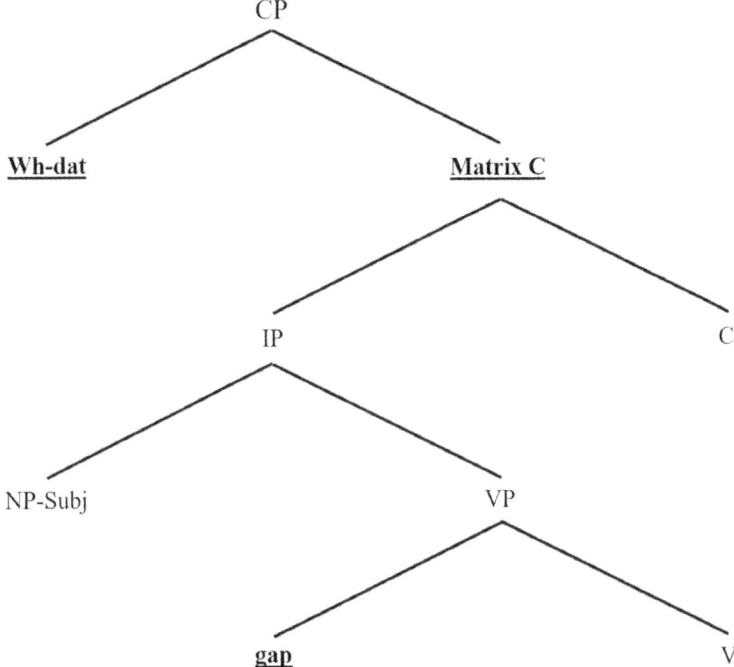

Figure 3.5 Gap in the matrix clause.

The problems in Aoshima et al.'s account regarding *un-forced revision* is naturally expected within the GB/MP framework, where structural uncertainty is not tolerated at any stage of structure-building. Hence, in the system, parsers are expected to make fundamental structure-building decisions as early as possible.

In terms of hierarchical distance assumed in GB/MP, the matrix clause will always be the first option for the initial NP, since it is the structure unfolded first from a strictly top-down view. Yet, in terms of processing the string, the matrix verb is the most non-local option for the hearer to choose in terms of string length, given that it will be the last constituent of all. Given this conflict, un-forced revision analysis might seem a possible solution.

As we've seen so far, threading incrementality into existing grammar formalisms is hard in the given configurational template (see Miyamoto 2002: 312, for a similar discussion). This is because incrementality inevitably involves the notion of underspecification or earlier structural uncertainty (i.e. underspecified head in Miyamoto's term) and time linearity in the course of derivation. Yet, using indeterministic, in other words, partial information to

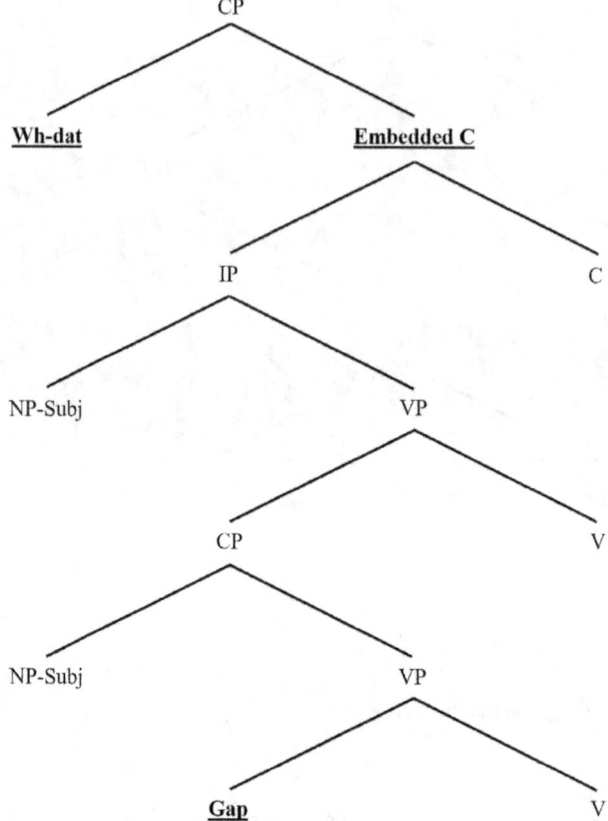

Figure 3.6 Gap in the embedded clause.

predict further structure was criticized in the GB/MP framework, given that it is at best tentative but lacks full determinism. These are the reasons why indeed much sentence processing evidence seeks an independently motivated parsing strategy.

3.4. Searching for the new framework

The status quo in the field has however been far from striking the right balance for an empirical foundation: either it has been very close to ignoring them all, taking the view that there is no way to prove anything empirically in a strict sense or, conversely, it has put a heavy emphasis on achieving new empirical findings, ignoring altogether what their implications are for the theory of syntax. In one sense, efforts to incorporate empirical challenges into the architecture of grammar have been made repeatedly since the outset of Chomskian linguistics. Nevertheless, I believe that their role has overall been often misrepresented. If they supported theoretic, grammar-internal claims, they were well received. However, in cases where the data did not support the claims made, generative linguists tended to invoke an independent parsing theory, instead of rethinking the properties of the grammar and its architecture. Yet without radical changes at the heart of the grammar, it is impossible to grasp the essential knowledge of human language.

Although the works of Hawkins and Phillips were hugely meaningful, in my view, these efforts did not bring about any fundamental change in syntactic architecture and basic assumptions which was necessary in explaining cross-linguistic evidence found in verb-final, flexible order languages. Instead, it seems that they have managed to settle or negotiate their findings within pre-minimalist version of generative syntax, yet without further justifying the choice of the particularly form of GB/MP architecture. With this choice of framework, it is inevitable to introduce an ad hoc assumption like *un-forced revision*. Without fundamentally rethinking and unthinking basic properties of GB/MP, it will remain always challenging to explain structural variations within verb-final Asian languages.

Pre-minimalist version of generative syntax is also popular in linguistic pedagogy of Asian languages for foreign learners. Teachers and researchers tend to pick and choose pre-minimalist versions of Chomskian schemata in explaining the grammar. And even in flexible order languages where case particles play crucial roles, they hardly seem to receive attention. Consider the following quote from Tsujimura (2005).

> *It should be cautioned, however, that syntax is full of controversy, partly because there are great many competing theories and also because syntactic issues tend to be more abstract than, say, phonological ones. For this reason, the current chapter faces a limitation . . . discussion of each topic will not employ the degree of depth that syntacticians might wish to see; nor do many of the analyses taken up here reflect the most current syntactic theory. The primary goal of this chapter, instead, is to observe and discuss a wide range of syntactic phenomenon and the theoretical issues related to them.* (Tsujimura 2005: 160; emphasis mine)

Tsujimura (2005), given the complexity, proposes to use a simpler syntactic framework. However, this framework is not necessarily suited to describe and explain Japanese in an intuitive way. Note that in Figure 1.1, particles are almost treated as non-existent. Most linguistics textbooks designed for Asian languages

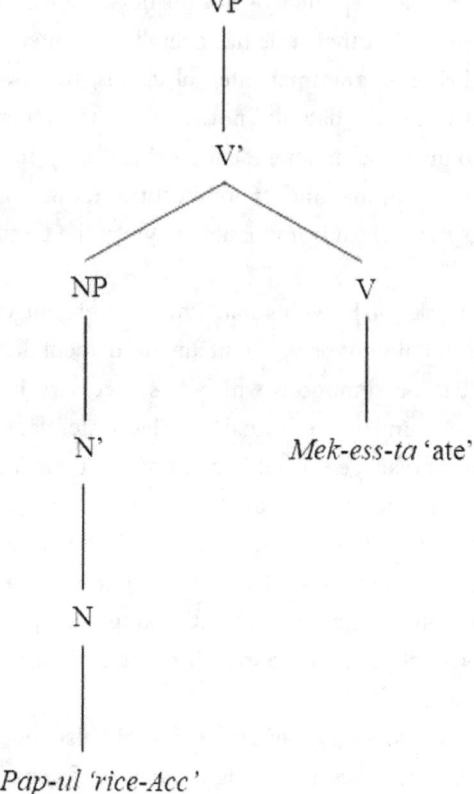

Figure 3.7 Syntactic structure of Korean sentence.

choose the pre-minimalist formal model as a simpler model yet without much justification other than logical simplicity compared to the recent MP work.[10]

Consider the following Japanese, Korean and Chinese examples from major linguistics textbooks, which demonstrate the lack of consistency in modelling particles and structures. As mentioned earlier, particles are treated as non-existent.

The situation is similar in Korean grammar too.

Lee et al. (2016: 111) adopt X-bar theory. Lee states: '*With the phrase in Figure above, we see the structure of a phrase, consisting of a head, a specifier and an adjunct confirming to X-bar theory.*' For Lee et al. (2016), the dative particle is marked as the head of the phrase, whereas the accusative particle is treated as non-existent. Hence, the treatment of case particles lacks logical consistency (Figures 3.7 and 3.8).

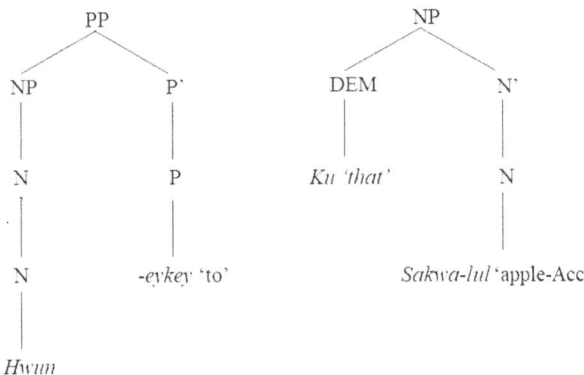

Figure 3.8 Syntactic structure for dative NP versus accusative NP.

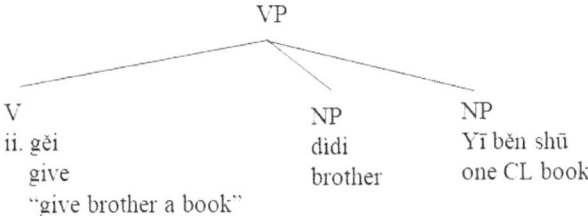

Figure 3.9 Syntactic structure for Chinese: Ternary structure.

On the other hand, in Chinese syntax, ternary structure is assumed as in Sun (2006: 162) (Figure 3.9).

Perhaps what is needed for learners may be nothing more than simple bracketing. One can say that this is 'pedagogical' material – written to be accessible to those who are unfamiliar with linguistic terminology. But there is no explanation that could justify the choice of formalism (Philips 2009: 13).

> I think that it would help a great deal if more linguists were to take more seriously the mentalistic commitments to which they profess. Most generative linguists would assent to the notion that their theories should be responsive to learnability consideration.

This touches one of the serious drawbacks of contemporary Asian linguistics, where it has lost its pedagogical implication altogether. If indeed the theory is explanatorily adequate, it is expected that it is also useful in learning. In my view, it is not fair for learners of the Asian language and linguistics to be prepared to understand some of the yet-to-prove logical mechanisms in contemporary linguistics to deepen their understanding of the languages they are learning.

That will explain why most Asian language courses provided by higher education institutions do not offer contemporary linguistics courses, with few exceptions.

There is no doubt that understanding structural properties of language is hugely important in language learning, yet not to the depth and degree which is often presented in the 'contemporary/modern' linguistics teaching materials. In learning syntax of flexible word-order languages with rich case particles, for instance, what is more adequately needed is the in-depth understanding of particles in syntactic architecture than the knowledge on word orders.

In explaining Asian languages in an explanatorily adequate manner, the ideal formal system needs to provide sensible accounts for the key features found in these languages, for example, flexible syntactic structure building via diverse combinatory force (e.g. particles, prosody, context and structural routines) and pragmatic principles of structural update, regardless of the location of a verb.

3.5. Summary

In this chapter, we have observed so far that natural language syntax is resource-sensitive – in particular, we showed that locality and incrementality matter in efficient structure building. I propose that the ordinary speaker's ways of building up the components of their sentences is done on the basis of maximizing the efficiency in communication. From a structure-building perspective, the essence of this efficiency is catalysed as 'locality'. Put simply, people build structures locally, check locally and then locally pack up their linguistic input – *as* they hear. Being free from written input, we can then easily realize that this way of structuring – *as* you hear – bit by bit, is a quintessential property of human language. This is found in almost every aspect of structure building, from recognizing the basic structural unit, assembling, assessing and then closing off the local structures.

Hawkins and Phillips are pioneering, yet, have a clear limit as their explanation is set somewhere in the generativist frameworks with a host of assumptions (i.e. verb-centredness, base-order assumption, intolerance for allowing structural building or assessment for not-yet-complete sequences). In order to provide an explanatorily adequate account on the key features related to syntactic fluidity and efficiency observed in Asian languages, we need a framework that could provide an explanatorily adequate account in a procedural manner – regardless of the location of a verb and flexible word orders.

4

Multidimensional meanings

Particles play an essential role in unfolding the structural skeleton of our target languages. On the other side of the coin lies a particle's roles in expressive, attitudinal and interpersonal meanings. As we shall explore in Chapter 9, particles contain a rich repertoire of emotional and attitudinal meanings such as encouragement, enthusiasm, endearment, friendliness, affection, (dis) agreement, surprise, (un)belief, doubt or certainty. Some particles can make the utterance sound feminine, whereas others make it sound masculine. Besides this, particles can strengthen or soften the utterance and make it casual, assertive or formal. These rich expressive and attitudinal meanings, however, have thus far received relatively little attention in formal linguistics. This is because the multifaceted nature of particles and their complex meanings are hard to capture and explain in traditional semantic terms. In this book, I introduce Potts' theory of expressive semantics and show that particles are expressive, projecting multidimensional, expressive and attitudinal meanings.

This chapter sets out some foundational issues and a background with key examples from a few languages. A wider range of cross-linguistic evidence will be explored in depth in later chapters. The linguistic competence of ordinary speakers in Asian languages is often measured by their ability to choose a set of particles appropriate to the socio-pragmatic context. The modulation process will be discussed in Chapter 5. In this chapter, I introduce Potts' theory of expressive semantics and show how particles project multidimensional, expressive and attitudinal meanings.

Particles do not seem to follow the typical agreement patterns set out in English and many European languages. However, until now it has been implicitly assumed and unquestioned that grammatical agreement plays the key role explaining Asian languages just as it does in English and many Western European languages (see Chapter 2). In fact, the repertoire of meaning reflected by particles in Asian languages is far richer and diverse than that conveyed by auxiliaries in English and other European languages. As we shall now explore, expressive semantics enables us to understand and formulate the rich array of meanings projected by particles in Asian languages.

4.1. Expressive meanings

4.1.1. Multidimensional meanings

In this book we assume that the meanings of what has been said are multidimensional. For the last three decades since Grice (1975), semanticists and pragmatists have mainly been concerned with propositional meaning. However, Potts (2005), following the earlier works of Kaplan (1989) and Kratzer (1999), shed fresh light upon non-propositional meaning. Potts argued for the necessity of considering the non-propositional, expressive dimensions of meaning and showed that there are two types of meaning, namely, (i) *at-issue* (inherently-lexical) meaning and (ii) *commitment* (inherently-pragmatic) meaning. As Potts points out throughout his book, in the tradition of contemporary semantic and pragmatic research, commitment meaning, which comprises an important part of conventional implicature, has been understudied or simply put aside as being unimportant. Potts (2005: 193) quotes Kaplan (1989: 555–6): 'I do not see that the existence of the pseudo de-re form of report poses any issue of theoretical interests to make it worth pursuing.' Potts, however, proves that these kinds of meanings, often assumed to be peripheral, marginal or additional, are at the very centre of linguistic meaning. He also argues that sometimes commitment meanings – particularly those of expressives – are so powerful that speakers cannot use these expressions at all without wholly committing themselves to the expressive content. Consider (1) from Potts (2005).

(1) That <u>bastard</u> Kresge is famous.
    a. Descriptive meaning: 'Kresge is famous.'
    b. Expressive meaning: 'Kresge is a {bastard/bad in the speaker's opinion.}'

The underlined expression *bastard* contributes to a dimension of meaning that is separate from the regular descriptive meaning. That is, no matter whether the propositional meaning of (1) is true or false, the expressive meaning projected by the word 'bastard', which reveals the speaker's attitude towards *Kresge*, is not affected at all. Consider more examples in (2) from Potts (2005). Similarly, the underlined words contribute to the expressive dimension, or the speaker's attitudinal/commitment meanings.

(2) a. *Ed refuses to look after Sheila's <u>damn</u> dog.*
    b. *Right after he agreed to help out, that <u>jerk</u> Chuck boarded a plane for Tahiti.*

One of the main proposals of Potts (2005) is to show that 'commitment' meanings are as crucial as lexical meanings. It is almost impossible for us to utter anything in a vacuumized situation, immune of how we as speakers view the event. In exploring the meaning of natural language (particularly spoken language), it is not only impossible but also incorrect to extract and study 'purely' lexical meaning alone, excluding the real-life dimensions of what constitutes meaning.

In an extension of Potts' view, I assume that both the meanings of known-to-be-problematic instances (as in those addressed earlier) and the meanings of linguistic expression in general need to be understood in tandem between the 'at-issue' meaning (that which is under discussion) and 'commitment' meaning (that which is being said about that which is under discussion). It depends on each situation. As addressed earlier, the particularities of such commitment meanings are in that they escape the typical truth values of the sentence and are independent of such judgement. Consider (3). No matter whether *a damn paper* is in a positive sentence or in a negative sentence, this doesn't change the speaker's judgement about the paper.

(3)
    a. *I had to write a <u>damn</u> paper on fruit flies.*
    b. *I didn't have to write a <u>damn</u> paper on fruit flies.*

Speaker-commitment meaning not only provides an independent meaning to the whole proposition but also surpasses other meanings. For instance, if I say '*Amazingly, John gave all his money to a charity*', the whole proposition sits under the scope of 'amazement'. If I say, '*I don't want to look after John's damn dog*', my attitude towards the dog which Potts collectively classifies using predicate BAD is true beyond the surface meaning of the sentence. Cross-linguistically, we can find the many emotive predicates that play a role as an expressive. Consider some English examples:

(4) Affectionate emotion
    a. *My <u>sweet little</u> girl didn't come home yet.*
    b. *<u>Dear old</u> Sarah came to my dad's eightieth birthday.*

(5) Dis-affectionate emotions
   a. This <u>bloody</u> car is bloody expensive.
   b. I won't look after John's <u>damn</u> dog.

Sometimes, the dis-affectionate predicate can be used as an affectionate predicate. When the English speaker says 'damn good', the speaker doesn't necessarily have a negative attitude towards the proposition.

4.1.2. Particles carry attitudinal meanings

Most of our target languages have particles with a complex and rich repertoire of emotional, attitudinal and interpersonal meanings, far beyond that which English and other auxiliaries can express, as we can see in Chapter 9.

For instance, particles that play the role of clause enders do not just wrap up and close off a structure but add the speaker's emotions or attitudes towards the hearer for the just-complete proposition. Consider the following Korean example. Let's say the speaker is talking to the hearer over the phone.

(5)
   a. 오-냐?
      o-nya
      COME-Q
      Lit. 'Are you coming?'
   b. 오-십니까?
      O-sipnikka
      Come-UPNI-Q
      Lit. 'Are you coming?'

It is worthwhile to note that the verbal stem *o-* (오-) does not have any attitudinal meaning, but the choice of ending particle specifies the nature of the interpersonal relation between speaker and hearer. *Nya* (-냐) signals that the speaker and the hearer have an intimate, close relation, that they are speaking in an informal situation and that the speaker is senior to the hearer. On the other hand, *sipnikka* (십니까) signals that the speaker and the hearer are speaking in a formal situation and that the speaker is junior to the hearer. These meanings are conveyed through the particle(s). These are not propositional meanings but a kind of expressive meaning that occurs through the use of particles.

Similarly, in Tagalog, the presence of the particle *po* or *ho* is used to indicate politeness in more formal settings, most notably when a younger person is speaking to an elder. (6a) and (6b) are the same except the presence of *po*.

(6) Tagalog
    a. *Umuulan sa labas.* [Standard]
       Raining LOC-outside.
       'It is raining outside.'
    b. *Umuulan po sa labas.* [Polite]
       Raining PO LOC-outside.
       'It is raining outside.'
       'The speaker is speaking politely and formally to possibly an elder.'

Consider the following Lao example, too.

(7)
    a. *Saam khon dtaay*   [Lao]
       Three person die
       'Three people died.'
    b. *Saam khon dtaay **bor***
       Three person die QPLR.
       'Is it the case that three people died?'
    c. *Saam khon dtaay **dti***
       Three person die QPLR.PRESM
       'Surely I am correct in thinking that three people died?'
    d. *Saam khon dtaay **waa***
       Three person die QPLR.INFER
       'Do I rightly infer that three people died?'

Based on the particle choice, the utterance can have additional meanings beyond question-hood.

Enfield (2007: 43) shows how the interrogative particle in Lao also reveals emotions and attitudes. Table 4.1 is a modification from Enfield (2007: 43).

4.1.3. Expressive meaning is register-sensitive

Expressive meanings are register-sensitive. For instance, in computer-mediated communication (CMC), emojis or various emoticons are used like particles to convey different emotions and attitudinal meanings. Very often, in CMC, if traditional particles are used without any emoticons or emojis, this is understood as a rather incomplete or unhappy mood.

Table 4.1 Interrogative particles in Lao grammar (Modified from Enfield 2007: 43)

Interrogative particle	Meanings
bor	polar question, unmarked
waa	polar question, proposition newly inferred
dti	polar question, proposition independently presumed
noa	polar question, seeks agreement
goa	content question, asks for information currently presupposed

In Korean, when a request is made and the answer is given with a full stop, the message sounds solemn, implying that the sender, though they may have approved the request, is not thrilled (Figure 4.1b). On the other hand, if a request is answered with a simple emoticon ^^, the message implies the sender's generous approval (Figure 4.1a). The same is the case in Chinese as in Figures 4.2a–4.2b.

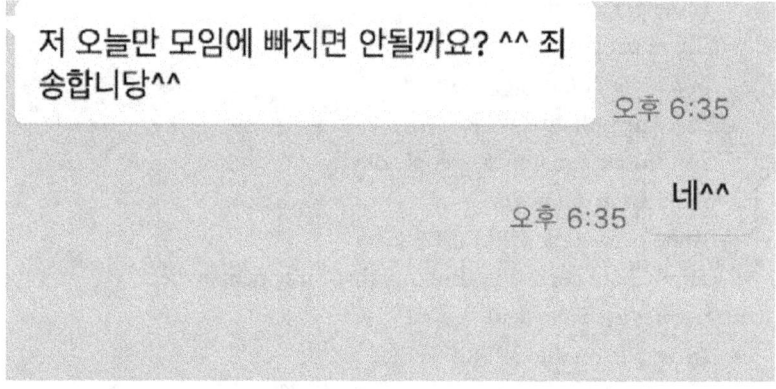

Figure 4.1a Approval with emoticon.

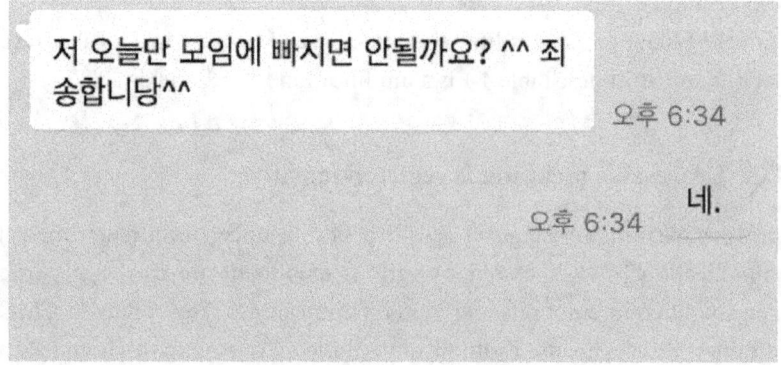

Figure 4.1b Approval without any emoticon.

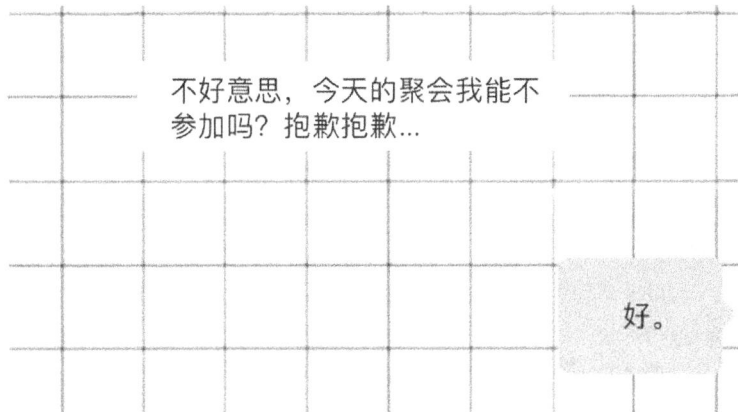

Figure 4.2a Approval without any emoticon.

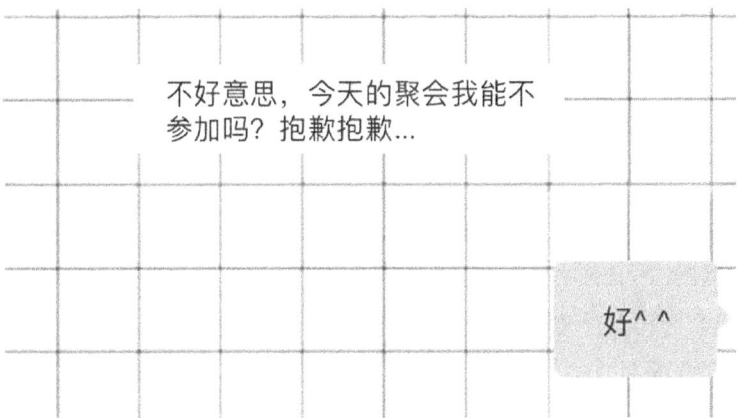

Figure 4.2b Approval with emoticon.

The meanings of Figures 4.1 and 4.2 are as follows:

'Excuse me, is it ok if I don't go to today's party? I'm so sorry about it.'
'OK.'

Though there are stylistic and individual differences, most ordinary speakers of Korean and Chinese will find the answer without the emoticon unkind and harsh; in contrast, the answer with emoticon sounds kind and generous. The uses of emoticons or emojis in instant messaging (IM) are gradually becoming a social convention. The use of a simple ^^ in Korean CMC, for instance, expressing one's benevolent attitude towards others, is crucial in ensuring the success of communication. It is important to make the communication *emphatic* by expressing benevolence to each other in order for the communication to flow naturally and smoothly. We shall return to this in Chapters 5 and 7.[1]

4.1.4. Interpersonal meanings can't be hidden

Attitude or interpersonal relations are crucial in language use. One cannot completely hide an attitude or emotion to a hearer, even in writing. At times, the speaker decides to leave it unspecified in order to avoid social awkwardness or any tension. Yet, in most cases, Asian language speakers express their attitudes towards the hearer. This process can become visible through the use of address terms, personal pronouns and, most importantly, different layers of particles. In speech, intonation matters, and in instant messaging and other online communication, different emojis, emoticons or stickers play the same role. Compared to languages like English where expressive powers lie mainly with auxiliaries, one can say that Asian languages project much more fine-grained interpersonal relations in everyday language use.

4.1.5. Particles are expressives

Potts (2005) claims the following properties to be expressive criteria. Particles meet all these criteria.

Expressive meaning criteria

1. Independence:
    - *Expressive content contributes a dimension of meaning that is separate from the regular descriptive content.*
2. Non-displaceability:
    - *Expressives predicate something of the utterance situation.*
3. Perspective dependence:
    - *Expressive content is evaluated from a particular perspective. In general, the perspective is the speaker's, but there can be deviations if conditions are right.*
4. Descriptive ineffability:
    - *Speakers are never fully satisfied when they paraphrase expressive content using descriptive, that is, non-expressive terms.*
5. Immediacy:
    - *Like performatives, expressives achieve their intended act simply by being uttered; they do not offer much other content.*

6. Repeatability:
   - *If a speaker repeatedly uses an expressive item, the effect is generally one of strengthening the emotive content, rather than one of redundancy.*

In the following section I shall further explain each criterion.

4.1.5.1. Non-displaceability

Expressives cannot (outside of direct quotation) be used to report on past events, attitudes or emotions, nor can they express mere possibilities, conjectures or suppositions. They always tell us something about the utterance situation itself. This is the *non-displaceability* property. Therefore, particles cannot be learned or taught imitatively, as they contain information encoded from the speakers' perspective. Consider the following example.

(8) Pragmatically inadequate dialogue because of simply particle copy by the hearer

Supervisor: *Mike-ya. Ne kongpwu-lul cincca yelsim-hi hayss-kwuna*. [Korean]
   (i) 'Mike, you have studied really heard.'
   (ii) 'I (=speaker) am expressing surprise to the junior person.'
Mike: *kamsahamnida*.
   'Thank you.'
(. . . .)
Mike: ??? *sensengnim-to scarf cengmal yeppu-kwuna*. [pragmatically inadequate]
   'You too teacher, your scarf is very nice.'

In this dialogue, Mike's (the student) comment about his teacher's scarf is pragmatically inappropriate. This is because he just copied the exclamatory ending that his teacher used in the previous sentence of the conversation. *-kwuna* cannot be simply copied/repeated and displaced (by the learner in this instance) because the meaning of this particle not only includes an exclamation but also reveals the interpersonal relations between speaker and hearer and the speaker-hearer dynamics occurring at that particular moment, with *-kwuna* imparting a social hierarchy where the speaker is senior to the junior.

Consider examples from Hindi in (9) and (10).

(9)
   tu (intimate) *a*   'you come'
   tum (informal) *ao*   'you come'
   ap (polite) *aiye*   'you come'

There are three pronoun levels in Hindi. Verbs in Hindi agree with the pronoun. The *tu* form of the verb is the verb stem. The *tum* form is verb stem + *o*. The *ap* form is the verb stem + *iye*. Even when the pronoun is not explicit in the sentence, the verb form will reflect the appropriate politeness level in the second person. The socio-pragmatic necessity of choosing the correct ending to correspond to the appropriate pronoun is significant in Hindi. If the verb ending is not chosen skilfully according to the interpersonal relationship between speaker and hearer, awkwardness or offence may arise as in the case of (10). The verbal endings and pronoun system are identical to other Hindustani languages such as Urdu (Jain, D and Cardona 2007: 61–2). I shall return to this in Chapter 5.

(10)
    ??? *tu* (intimate) *ao*   'you come'   [Hindi]
    ??? *tum* (informal) *aiye*   'you come'
    ???*ap* (polite) *a*   'you come'

4.1.5.2. Perspective dependence

The perspective encoded in the expressive aspects of an utterance is most likely to be that of the speaker's (Potts 2005; Potts and Kawahara 2004). For instance, in (11) the regret clearly comes not from the sentence subject *John* but from the speaker – who is commenting on John's behaviour.

(11) *John-i ka **peri-ess-e**.*   [Korean]
    John-NOM go <u>completely yet regretfully</u>-PAST-DECL
    (i) 'John left.'
    (ii) He's completely gone and this I (=the speaker, not John) found it regretful.

4.1.5.3. Descriptive ineffability

The meanings of most particles that we discuss in this book are challenging to describe because of the interpersonal meanings that particles project – hence, it is hard to describe their lexically independent meanings. This is why particles are particularly difficult to teach to second language learners. In second or foreign language acquisition, it is often observed that if the learner has a marker for a concept in their mother tongue, the acquisition of this concept in the target language is easier. However, if such a marker doesn't exist, acquisition may be cognitively difficult. When it comes to the use of particles, even ordinary native speakers of the target language need to pin down the necessary points of reference each time and negotiate. The multidimensional nature of particles is hard to be summed up as one descriptive property. Furthermore, even if there is a similar grammatical morpheme existing in English and Western European languages, the way in which the particles behave are different – for instance, plural particles in our target languages refer to vague plurality rather than propositional non-singularity (see Chapter 6).

4.1.5.4. Immediacy

The effect will arise immediately. Even if one reports an event that occurred in the past, the attitudinal meanings are present in the 'here and now' of the utterance time. In (12) for instance, the speaker's deferential attitude is expressed instantly during the utterance and it is also noticeable that the attitudinal meaning is applicable at the time of utterance, not the event time when the subject-hearer (i.e. hearer who also happens to be the subject) was ill.

(12) *ece apwu-si-ess-ta-ko-yo.* [Korean]
 Yesterday sick-HON-PAST-DECL-COMP-POL
 a. 'I heard that you were sick yesterday.'
 b. The speaker is showing respect to the hearer-subject 'at present' – at the time of utterance.

4.1.5.5. Repeatability

Repetition means that the emotional state is being emphasized. For expressives, the basic observation is that repetition leads to strengthening rather than redundancy. Harada (1976) argues that the use of honorifics in both embedded and matrix clauses as in (13) is somewhat 'too polite'. However, examples like (13) are not ungrammatical nor rare. They appear when the speaker wants to strengthen expressive meanings. This is observed in many languages.

(13) *Yamada sensei-wa [Karuizawa ni **o-ide** ni nar-u] **koto o-kime** ni nat-ta.*
 [Japanese]
 Y.Prof-WA Karuizawa HON-go DAT become-IMP COMP HON-decide DAT become
 'Professor Yamada decided to go to Karuizawa.' (matrix and embedded honorifics)

Similarly, in Thai, *ná* is often used in conjunction with other particles. This simply makes the statement increasingly respectful in (14).

(14)

Kɔ̀ɔp	*kun*	***ná ká*** [Thai]
Thank	you	[particle combination]

'Thank you [polite]'

In Tagalog as well, *O* is used in informal situations either after a polite request that includes *nga*, in which it increases the urgency of the request, or to direct the attention of the person(s) addressed, in which case it is equivalent to the English 'Look!', for example.

(15)

Tulungan	*mo*	***nga***	*ako,*	***o.***	[Tagalog]
help	you	please	me,	O	

'Come on, help me, please.'

4.2. Layers of expressive meanings

A sequence of particles projects layers of expressive meanings. If we regard a complex of meanings to look like an onion as in Figure 4.3, the propositional meaning in both example (16a) and (17a), 'it is good', would be like the outer-most part of the onion-like meaning complex.

(16) Single layer of expressive meaning
    a. *jot-**supnita**.* [Korean]
    b. *ii **desu.*** [Japanese]
       'It is good.'

(17) Multiple layers of expressive meanings
    a. *jot-**kess-tako-saynggak-i toy-pnida*** [Korean]
    b. *ii **kamoshirenai to omoimasu*** [Japanese]
       'I think . . . it might be . . . good.'

Both examples in (16) and (17) share this outer-most part: the same truth-conditional meaning. However, while the sentences in (16) reveal a single expressive layer of formality through *-supnita* (K) and *-desu* (J) endings, the examples in (17) reveal multiple expressive layers – a mixture of honorific, polite

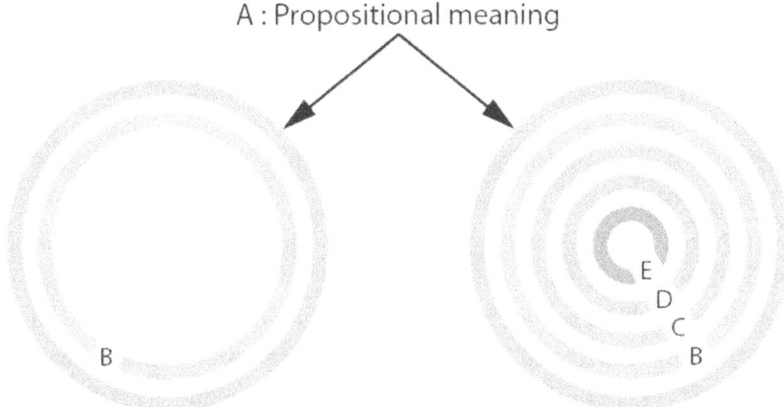

Figure 4.3 Layers of expressive meanings.

and humble meanings. As a result, though the propositional content is the same, examples in (16) sound less sophisticated and even a little abrupt compared to those in (17). Of course, adding layers is not necessarily always the best way to communicate. Finding the pragmatically appropriate layer and adding the right number of layers is indeed what comprise pragmatic competence in these languages.

4.3. Implicit and vague communications: Beyond face-threatening act (FTA)

Brown and Levinson (1978/87) undertook important and probably the most influential work in the study of politeness theory. Brown and Levinson argue that speakers choose to manifest politeness in order to minimize the risk of incurring a FTA. They introduce the notion of 'face' in order to illustrate 'politeness' in the broad sense. That is to say, all interlocutors have an interest in maintaining two types of 'face' during interaction: 'positive face' and 'negative face'.

Brown and Levinson define 'positive face' as the positive and consistent image people have of themselves, and their desire for approval, whereas, 'negative face' is 'the basic claim to territories, personal preserves, and rights to non-distraction' (p. 61). 'Positive politeness' is expressed by satisfying 'positive face' in either of the two ways: first, by indicating similarities among interlocutors or, second, by expressing an appreciation of the interlocutor's self-image. 'Negative politeness' can also be expressed in two ways: first, by saving the interlocutor's 'face' (either 'negative' or 'positive') by mitigating FTAs, such as advice-giving and disapproval; or, second, by satisfying 'negative face' by indicating respect for the addressee's right not to be imposed on.

In short, 'politeness' is expressed not only to minimize FTAs but also to satisfy the interactants' face regardless of whether an FTA occurs or not. Brown and Levinson proposed five politeness strategies as follows: (i) not to do FTA; (ii) to go off the record (i.e. giving only a hint); (iii) to use negative politeness (=showing deference); (iv) to use positive politeness (=appealing to intimacy, friendliness and/or camaraderie); and (v) to do an FTA (i.e. to say straightforwardly what one wants to accomplish).

Hasegawa (2014: 270) provides an example to show how those strategies are implemented in Japanese. The vague request as in (18a) is considered politest, and the straight request as in (18d) is regarded most impolite and rude. What we can see is the fine-grained nature of realizing politeness in Japanese. This is also found in most of our Asian target languages.[2]

(18) Politeness in Japanese
    a. Off-the-record strategy [intention: pay-raise request]
       Sumimasen- ga, watashi- wa koko 3-nen shoukyuu- ga Nain-desu -ga
       'I'm sorry, but I haven't received a pay raise in three years.'
    b. Utilize negative politeness
       Anoo konna koto- wo iu-no- wa totemo kokoro-gurushii no desu-ga, kyuuryoo-wo sukoshi age-te itadake-masen deshou-ka?
       'I'm awfully sorry to say this, but may I have a small pay raise?'
    c. Utilize positive politeness
       Nee shachou motto ganbaru kara, kyuuryoo chotto age-te yo.
       'Uh, Chief, I'll make more of an effort, so raise my salary, please.'
    d. Do an FTA without redressive action
       Oi, kyuuryoo age-ro yo.
       'Hey, raise my salary.'

The so-called off-the-record vagueness strategy is prevalent in Asian languages. In particular, I propose that 'intentional' vagueness can be a good tool for 'cooperation' (cf. Cook 1990), and is a way of revealing the speaker's benevolent attitude towards the hearers and ultimately making the conversation flow more harmoniously. I shall return to this in Chapter 5. I argue that the motivation for such linguistic behaviour can be directed by the speaker's individual desire to show their emotions and empathy, which is also broadly encoded in Asian languages and cultures.

Ide (1982, 1989) showed the limits and challenges in applying Brown and Levinson's work to Japanese. The essence of the argument is that the motivation of politeness is not just to minimize the impact of FTA. Ide argued that often politeness is selected as a socially obligatory choice in languages like Japanese. That said, honorifics and politeness can freely and frequently occur even when no FTA is involved. I think this is quite a normal behaviour found among Asian language communities. Ide introduces *volition-based politeness* and *discernment-based politeness* (i.e. *wakimae*). Discernment-based politeness affirms a culturally prescribed norm, which is independent of the speaker's rational intention (Ide 1989: 242) and is akin to a grammatical requirement, forming a socio-pragmatic concordance system.

Later, Eelen (2001) argued, unlike many researchers (like Ide) who assume that impoliteness is lack of politeness, that a dichotomy indeed cannot capture the extent to which polite and honorific expressions work in these languages. Furthermore, Eelen (2001) argues that the proper use of honorifics indicates one's *socio-pragmatic competence*. I agree with Eelen (2001) in that the use of honorifics and politeness strategies reveals socio-pragmatic competence rather than purely grammatical competence. The use of politeness and honorifics can make a conversation flow nicely but can also cause the hearer to feel distant and uneasy if used too much or in an inappropriate way. Thus, the ability to choose honorifics and politeness expressions suitably in a given situation is crucial.

The semantic and sociolinguistic aspects of honorifics or politeness are difficult to capture with the simple, binary criterion adopted by Brown and Levinson. The meanings of these expressions are much more complex than what is argued. In many languages, mixing positive and negative strategies is quite common and normal. Ultimately, Brown and Levinson view politeness as binary phenomena with one dimension, but with the progress in research since then, it has become obvious that politeness strategies are complex phenomena with multidimensional meanings. Hence, their original theory falls short when trying to explain the intricacies of the socioculturally negotiated interpersonal expressions exhibited by Asian languages.

4.3.1. Manifesting 'Asian-ness': Age, order and desire for unanimity

It is almost impossible to describe the essence of Asian-ness because Asia is too diverse and broad to be generalized. But from the evidence we have gathered in this book, we can find some commonality among Asian languages; they have a rich repertoire of interpersonal expressions which reflect the complex and dynamic nature of relationships formed in the community, where age-oriented social hierarchy and intimacy often carry significance in a manner not seen in Western Europe.

For example, the more senior individual in a relationship is expected to embrace the junior and act benevolently. The junior, on the other hand, downplays their position – either through humbling, making themselves invisible or expressing their good feeling towards the other through attentive communication. This is often manifested in repeated use of particles, prosody, gestures in offline communication, or through the use of emoticons in online communication. Though the general theme of benevolence is commonly observed in Asian languages and cultures, the surface-level linguistic realizations differ from one language to another.

Within this context, the desire to remain unspecific is strong across Asian languages. An implicit and vague communication, which can be viewed as a way of establishing a non-threatening, safe and comfortable relationship, is prevalent in these languages.

The vagueness effect involves different softening and humbling strategies and is common to many Asian languages. We can see some examples in Korean, Japanese and Chinese as follows.

(19) Vagueness strategy in Korean, Japanese and Chinese
    a. Using fillers like *chyotto* or *jom*.
       com *pikyecwullay*? [Korean]
       chotto *doitekurenai*? [Japanese]
       *rang***yixia** *haoma*? [Chinese]
       'Can you move (out of my way) "a bit"?'
       Instead of saying 'Can you move (out of my way)?'
    b. Using approximation expressions even though the speaker does not need to in order to form a clear statement – frequent use of expressions like *about* are underlined.
       nayil 3myeng **cengdo** *kukoss-uro kapnita.* [Korean]
       ashita 3nin **bakari** *sochirani ikimasu.* [Japanese]
       mingtian **dagai** *huiyou sangeren qunaer.* [Chinese]
       'Tomorrow about three people will get there.'

c. Using self-humbling expressions.
     na-kattun/ttawyi-saram. [Korean]
     wo zhezhong ren. [Chinese]
     'A person like me (lowering/humbling oneself)'
  d. Expressing a statement as a guess/supposition using various conjectural/suppositional endings at the end (see underlined expressions which means 'seems to').
     *ka-**nun-kess** **kass**sumpnida*. [Korean]
     *ta **hoaxing** zoule*. [Chinese]
     'He seems to be going.'

In this book, I propose that a speaker's motivation to choose unspecific, blurry expressions is rooted in the sociocultural characteristics of Asian languages and cultures. The essence of one's choice lies in the speaker's desire to be accepted as a 'good' member of a harmonious society – not only through avoiding trouble-making, but also through attempting not to stand out by making oneself visible. Indeed, one common way of expressing benevolence in Asian languages is by establishing a sort of conflict-free zone using hedges, softening and distant or vague expressions. Making personal pronouns invisible is another strategy which is employed to make communication vague and avoid any unnecessary directness. Whether to overtly articulate a personal pronoun or not depends on various socio-pragmatic factors. However, the desire not to stand out but to be a good citizen can be easily misunderstood in Western contexts. Often, Asian pupils are known to perform well, yet show a lack of engagement in class. Shyness or passiveness are typical attributes ascribed to Asian children. However, very often, this is not a consequence of disinterest, but an attempt to pay the proper respect to their teachers.

The negotiation process in showing both respect and intimacy is never easy, but rather requires careful thought in each situation. The social pressure to make a distant and formal relationship can conflict with a desire to establish a close, intimate relationship, similar to Ide's (1989) proposal. This again is far more complicated than what is found in Western European languages. The Confucian ideology of 長幼有序 *jangywuywuse*,[3] which states that there must be order between child and adult, or young and old, is still manifested in every aspect of language use in East Asia, where seniority, which refers to both age and length of service in an organization, is highly valued (Chen and Chung 2002). The crucial role played by age and order in language use is also seen in Southeast Asian[4] languages. Perhaps this is due to the influence of Buddhism – the Buddhist ethos of minimizing the suffering of self and other may manifest itself in the language strategies discussed earlier; vagueness and softening work to curtail any potential suffering on the part of the listener. Modesty is another Buddhist value that is reflected in the politeness techniques of Asian languages.

4.4. Summary

In this chapter we engaged in various discussions regarding how particles play crucial roles in realizing *expressive* and *interpersonal* meanings. We touched upon the point that native speakers' linguistic competence in these languages is often measured by their ability to choose pragmatically appropriate particles. Based on Potts' recent theory of expressive semantics, we argued that particles project multidimensional, expressive meanings. As Potts' works do not provide a taxonomy of expressives required for the actual analysis of different types of expressives, I proposed an attitudinal modality, in particular proposing this attitudinal modality as the way in which the speakers' attitudes are reflected in the meanings and functions of particles. In section 4.1 we took a new approach to the dynamic meaning complex of expressive meanings and saw how meanings are multidimensional. In section 4.2 we saw how, based on Potts' expressive criteria, particles function as expressives. We usefully paralleled the dynamic meanings of expressive particles in sentences to the 'layers of an onion' with predicate content as the outer layer and expressive meaning providing the (fresher) inner layers. Particle sharing and spreading across clauses was also visited in brief. In section 4.3 we discussed implicitly vague expressions in Asian language and the socio-pragmatic motivations to use them. We discussed the FTA theory and its limitations when being employed to explain Asian languages.

5

Socio-pragmatic meanings

This chapter discusses the socio-pragmatic characteristics of particles. Interpersonal relations, often reflected through particles, play a crucial role in language use. In Asia, age-oriented seniority and respect towards one's elders or bosses within a community or workplace play a crucial role in building interpersonal relations. This phenomenon is observed across Asian languages, in not only the premodern era but also the modern era, though it has been greatly simplified in contemporary society.

The umbrella terms 'honorifics' or 'politeness' do not adequately express the full range of possible interpersonal meanings. In contemporary linguistics, features such as [+HON], [+HBL/HUMBLE], [+RESPECT] or [+IN(FORMAL)] are occasionally introduced to explain different interpersonal relations. However, as we shall explore, these features require a much more fine-grained, formal framework to adequately capture the multidimensional, subjective and socio pragmatically sensitive meanings that are presented. In this book, therefore, I shall introduce a lexical matrix to fully capture the interpersonal dynamics manifested in particles (Chapter 6).

Particles used in the same utterance are not chosen randomly but rather are used to gradually form and maintain or reinforce socio-pragmatic meanings set between interlocutors. Particles are tuned and modulated throughout the utterance – in both verbal and non-verbal channels of communication. I shall show how both verbal and non-verbal interpersonal expressions within a single unit of utterance are modulated and incorporated to build interpersonal meanings. In order to explain this, I also propose the multimodal modulation hypothesis (MMH). In this chapter, I also show the meanings and distributions of second-person pronouns and address terms in our Asian target languages, which are far more complex than those found in Western European languages.

5.1. Interpersonal expressions

In this book, I propose a lexical matrix in order to capture and explain the dynamic and interpersonal characteristics of particles. I tentatively propose the following dimensions for the lexical matrix dedicated to socio-pragmatic meanings. For a fuller description, I will return to this issue in section 6.3. Every particle does not specify every dimension, and when a dimension remains unspecified, it does not automatically suggest that an opposite meaning is being conveyed. For instance, the lack of an explicitly polite or honorific dimension does not mean that the speaker is 'impolite' or expressing something impolitely. It only means that the speaker wishes to not 'explicitly express' his or her deference, politeness or benevolence to the hearer. The following points show the dimension of socio-pragmatic meanings I propose in this argument.

(i) *Social hierarchy*: a particle can reveal a speaker-hearer dynamic. That is, it can refer to a relationship where the speaker is senior to the hearer (S > H), equal (S = H) or junior to the hearer (S < H).
(ii) *Interpersonal relations* (e.g. intimacy, respect): a particle reveals a close/intimate and benevolent or respectful relationship between speaker and hearer.
(iii) *Mood and emotions*: a particle can express the speaker's attitudes, emotions and moods towards an utterance.
(iv) *Style:* a particle can reveal whether an utterance is used in monologue, dialogue or genre such as poetry or prose. It can also show whether it has a masculine or feminine voice.
(v) *Perspective and attitude*: a particle can express the speaker's attitude and perspective.

In this chapter, I shall focus on how different dimensions can be negotiated and expressed through particles. In particular, I show how interpersonal meanings are realized and how the dynamic negotiation between different functions yields socio-pragmatically (in)adequate results.

5.1.1. Interpersonal dynamics: Age, social status, intimacy and beyond

Asian languages reflect complex interpersonal dynamics. Social hierarchy is mainly established through age and rank within a community. Gender, class and religion also play some roles in this dynamic. Although in the modern day they are much more simplified compared to those before the twentieth century, these factors still influence daily language use.

In the essence of this dynamic relationship, hierarchy-based respect and intimacy are at the heart of negotiation. Language users struggle to find suitable expressions, that is, attitudinal particles or address terms, that show proper respect yet at the same time the right distance and intimacy.[1] Unlike in European languages, such negotiation is in flux in Asian languages. Many a time, language users must freshly negotiate their interpersonal relationships and find the right way to communicate with one another. This is because even when a relationship is securely established, many other sociocultural factors can still influence communication. For instance, register plays a crucial role in languages like Thai – it matters whether one speaks in 'street' register or 'formal' register. In the case of Burmese, particles to express respect towards male are different from those used for female. The presence of the third person or being in a public setting also influences the way interpersonal relations are established and expressed. In the following section I shall show Korean as a case study to demonstrate how interpersonal relationships are established in flux. While the precise negotiation process and factors may differ, similar dynamic and complex factors in the negotiation between respect and intimacy can be observed in most languages in Asia, as we shall explore later.

5.1.1.1. Korean case: Respect, intimacy and dynamic negotiation

The Korean language is sensitive to the relationship between the speaker and the addressee. Most expressions in Korean have a dimension depicting the hierarchical relation of the interlocutors and the speaker's attitude towards the addressee. Korean politeness dictates that certain formalities must be maintained when speaking to a person older than oneself, such as the dropping of personal pronouns.

Koreans rarely call each other by first names alone, always seeking to use a proper address term. Finding the appropriate address term is a dynamic process in which one must consider multiple factors, such as the age and social status of the person to whom one is speaking as well as the psychological distance one wishes to establish with the addressee.

Age is by far the most important factor in determining which speech style is appropriate for a given situation. To my knowledge, age plays a more critical role in Korean than in any other language I have investigated, except perhaps Thai.[2]

As in Korean, in Thai respect is primarily shown through the manner in which one addresses the other person (i.e. second-person pronouns) and usage of particles. Age, social status and closeness are important in determining how much respect to relay. For example, it is not uncommon for adults to ask each other their age and birthdate in order to determine who is พี่ (*pîi*) and who is น้อง (*nɔ́ɔng*). *Pîi* is the title and second-person pronoun reserved for people older than the speaker and *nɔ́ɔng* is used for those younger than the speaker. There are different registers and levels of respectfulness across different second-person pronouns as we shall return.

In addition to age, social status and hierarchy are also important factors. Especially in the workplace or hierarchy-based contexts like the military, rank matters more than age. Koreans often feel uneasy when speaking to a younger boss because of the juxtaposition of rank and age. If they come across each other outside the workplace, they tend to avoid speaking altogether because re-adjusting relationships could cause awkwardness. This is particularly visible in male-to-male interaction (Kiaer et al. 2019).

Even when the two parties calculate age and social status correctly, finding the correct address terms is still not simply a straightforward matter. In this calculation, one also must figure out whether they want to have a respect-oriented, polite relationship or an intimacy-oriented, informal relationship. Of course, relational dynamics change over time; hence, the two speakers need to make the right turn at the right time, making necessary adjustments or negotiations in order to make the conversation flow nicely.

Balancing intimacy and respect in interpersonal relations is not easy – not only for learners of Korean but also for ordinary Korean speakers. For instance, Kiaer et al. (2019) report that the incorrect use of address terms or speech styles can even cause serious violence.

It is noticeable that in Korean one must find the right address term right from the beginning, even when conversing with a stranger. This is why Koreans tend to ask each other's ages only a few minutes after meeting. Sometimes, the questions can go on and may cover things like whether the other person is married or has children. These are questions that foreign speakers can find quite overwhelming, but they are necessary to find the right address terms and make the conversation flow smoothly. Additionally, one also needs to consider the environment – whether it is a private or public space. One has to further decide how one is postulating his/her relationship with the addressee, and whether to put more emphasis on respect or intimacy.

In Korean, as in many other Asian languages, it is impossible to hide one's attitude towards his/her addressee. That is, the choice of address terms directly reflects one's attitude towards the person whom he/she is talking to or about.

For instance, the use of an honorific suffix or particle such as -*nim* (님) or – *kkeyse* (께서) reflects the speaker's respectful attitude towards the addressee. A teacher can be addressed in the following ways when used as a subject of the sentence as in (1). The degree of respect shown in (1) increases from (a) to (c). (1b) shows more respect than (1a), and (1c) expresses more respect than (1b), though the propositional meanings are all the same.

(1) Degree of respect: a<<b<<c
    a. *Kim sensayng-i hay-**yo**.*   [Korean]
       Kim teacher-NOM do-POL
       'Teacher Kim, can you please do that?' (casual – perhaps between colleagues)
    b. *Kim sensayng-**nim**-i hay-**yo**.*
       Kim teacher-HON-NOM do-POL
       'Dear teacher Kim, can you please do that?' (respectful)
    c. *Kim sensayng-**nim-kkeyse** ha-sey-**yo**.*
       Kim teacher-HON-HON$_{NOM}$ do-HON-POL
       'Dear teacher Kim, can you please do that?' (more respectful)

Similarly, Matsumoto (1988) shows the obligatory choice of honorific or plain forms of copulas in Japanese. All examples have the same propositional meanings but show speaker's different attitudes towards the hearers.

(2) Degree of respect: a<<b<<c
    a. *Kyoo wa doyoobi da.*   [Japanese]
       Today TOP Saturday COP
    b. *Kyoo wa doyoobi desu.*
       Today TOP Saturday HON-COP
    c. *Kyoo wa doyoobi de-gozaimasu.*
       Today TOP Saturday Super HON-COP
       'Today is Saturday.'

5.1.2. Navigating interpersonal dynamics through non-verbal expressions

Though particles project interpersonal meanings such as politeness and respect, in real communication, they are always accompanied by non-verbal expressions such as prosody and gestures to make these attitudinal meanings full and real. In fact, the most crucial parts of socio-pragmatic meanings, and in particular interpersonal meanings, are communicated through non-verbal channels. Concepts such as respect and politeness attitudes, which carry huge importance in Asian languages, are always learned together with culturally embodied gestural primitives. Hua et al. (2019) showed how the translingual and transcultural notions of respect and politeness were learned through karate practice. It is simply impossible to fully grasp the notion of respect and the manners with which to negotiate respect and intimacy through the use of verbal expressions alone. Meanings such as respect are therefore composed and expressed not only with verbal particles but also with less abrupt prosody and diverse gestural primitives – for example, posture, eye contact/gaze, nodding and bowing.

Gesture is indeed an important part of non-verbal communication. While it has frequently been argued whether gesture can be considered linguistic, an argument which hinges on their manifest deliberate expressiveness, such discussions tend to disregard aspects of gesture more specific to an Asian context (Kendon 2004; Wharton 2009). This is because many Asian gestures are related to politeness, not in the traditional sense of strategic politeness described by Levinson and Brown (1987). Areas of non-verbal communication may vary across different cultures. Some important cultural factors are individualism versus collectivism, and high power-distance versus low power-distance (Moore, Hickson, Stacks 2014: 22–3). However, many high-profile discussions of non-verbal behaviour fail to recognize cultural differences in intentional, culturally motivated gestures. Knapp and Hall (2005: 448–56) describe non-verbal communication in terms of communicating intimacy and dominance, assuming that showing dominance rather than subordination in social situations is always desirable. While this may be true in a Western context, Asian cultures often require interlocutors to take a position of deference, distinct from either dominance or subordination. For interlocutors in an Asian context, communicating deference non-verbally is often an important 'face-saving act' (Brown and Levinson 1987).

Just as the pragmatic aspects of language related to deference are often glossed over in the Euro-centric perspective of standard linguistics, when explaining the gestures common to Asian languages, pragmatically deferential gestures also do not seem to fit in the categories defined by previous discussions.

Deferential gestures in and Asian context, such as bowing, nodding, gaze or the positioning of the hands are prevalent and prominent. However, as they are rare in a European context; they have hardly been studied in the field thus far. For instance, in the case of Korean, bowing or repeated nodding is important in completing one's deferential attitude towards the addressee. Bowing and posture are related to a certain extent. Compared to the senior, the junior in the relationship tends to have a less straight, slightly bent posture.[3]

Similarly, hand shaking in East Asia is very hierarchical. The senior in the relationship initiates the handshake, and the junior must use two hands. Depending on the degree of formality and the distance in hierarchy, the two hands may be clasped around the other person's hand, or they may gently clasp the other's forearm. This method of shaking hands is found in Japan and Korea, as well as in very formal situations in China. Handshaking in this manner sends a specific message regarding who has seniority in the relationship. The length and lingering nature of the handshake also send a message about closeness, but this may be harder to categorize as intentional or having specific linguistic motivation. Handshakes are almost always accompanied with a bow.

Eye contact or gaze has also been shown to differ depending on cultural background (Moore, Hickson, Stacks 2014: 386). In many Western contexts, and particularly in the United States, a steady gaze signals confidence and trustworthiness, while in an Asian context broadly it may come across as threatening and signal a desire to intimidate the other. In an Asian context, particularly in East Asia, interlocutors are strategic about how they make eye contact with their superiors and inferiors, depending on power and intimacy, and often show deference by avoiding maintaining eye contact.

Patting is another interesting way to express intimacy from a senior to a junior.[4] If the patting happens in another direction, from a junior to a senior, it may create intimacy, but it will also portray rudeness. Hence, this may make communication socio-pragmatically awkward. In successful communication, the whole message – the verbal message of respect and the non-verbal message of patting – are realized in a well-tuned, synchronized manner. What heritage speakers often find most challenging is the ability to bring about the non-verbal expressions and synchronize them with verbal messages sensitive to the social register.[5] Touch can generally be the expression of affection and intimacy. Yet, in India, touching feet by a junior to a senior/elderly is viewed as an expression of respect.

Another interesting aspect of non-verbal communication is avoidance. In many Western contexts, this may happen vocally, through back-channelling or stutter-starts in speech (Moore, Hickson, Stacks 2014: 427). In an Asian context, explicit verbal requests may be considered particularly rude or even insolent when made to social superiors and seniors. As a result of this, people will often use non-verbal cues, such as raising a hand to the mouth or scratching the head, or even discreetly clearing the throat. Interestingly, clearing the throat in such

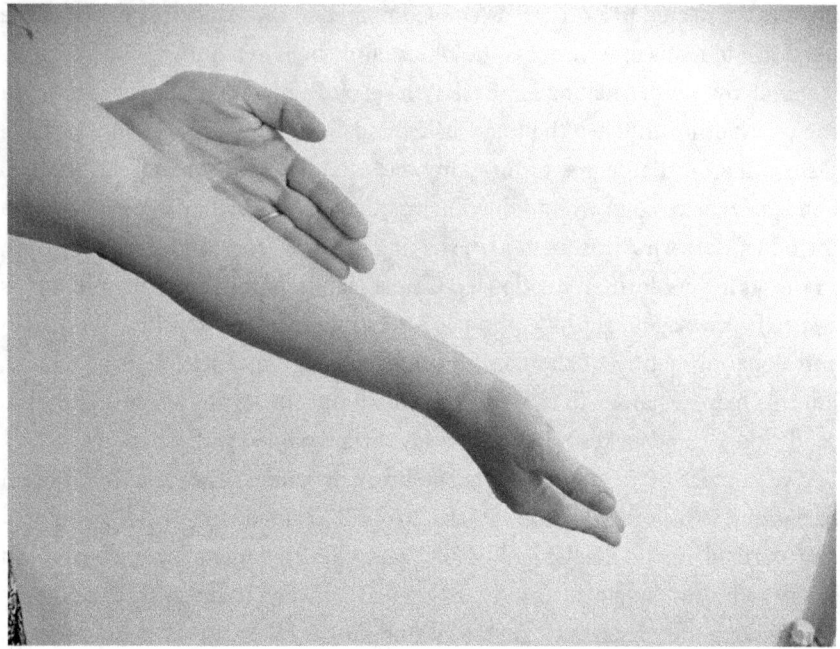

Figure 5.1 Hand gesture.

a situation is seen as very impolite in many Western contexts (Moore, Hickson, Stacks 2014: 261).

Hand gestures are frequently used in Korean to solidify the relationship between juniors and seniors in everyday movements. The hand gesture in Figure 5.1 is used by juniors when presenting an item to their seniors. Since it humbles the speaker in comparison to their interlocutor, this action can naturally never be used the other way around (i.e. by a senior presenting something to a junior). Though these gestures are certainly not defined nor standardized, they virtually always accompany honorifics or any other form of deferential interaction, to the extent that their absence may undermine the honorific function of verbal honorifics in actual communication.

In computer-mediated communication (CMC), emojis play an important role in creating intimacy and further benevolent utterance environment (see Figure 5.2).

This emoji is very interesting in that it can be used as a prayer, or thank you, or please. The same semiotic primitive can have various meanings depending on the cultural context or the text-sender's intention and the utterance environment. In India the emoji in Figure 5.2 is very common and can create a benevolent

Figure 5.2 Prayer or thank you.

environment, normally to convey the gratitude. This may not be the case in English-speaking world or other part of Asia. Different cultures have a different emoji that plays the same empathy-creating role in CMC.

5.1.3. Case study: Learning culturally embodied concepts through drama; The case of Korean

Learners of Korean have increased sharply in recent years as a result of the Korean wave, with K-pop and K-drama providing the main motivation for these learners. Through the watching of dramas, learners with a basic or zero knowledge of the Korean language are able to pick up on and learn socio-pragmatic meanings. The following interview extracts from Kiaer (2017b) show how learners pick up different attitudes from prosody and other non-verbal expressions.

5.1.3.1. Prosody in Korean

Often, girls say 'aiiiiiing'. That sounds quite annoying but also cute.
   Many times Korean girls use this kind of nagging tone.
   I learned how to be sarcastic. Joa means good in Korean, but johtha! means that it is not at all good. There are many tones in Korean that show irony like this.

5.1.3.2. Nodding

'Koreans are always nodding or bowing. Miso, in *Working Mum and Babysitting Daddy*, is saying sorry to her daughter's teacher. But, interestingly, she is constantly bowing down to someone who is not even visible – who is on the phone.'

5.1.3.3. Eye contact

'Koreans do not normally have eye contact when they talk. Once I saw a clip where Seoyoung is rebuked for having eye contact with her mother in law.'

5.1.3.4. Hand movement

'In watching *Working Mum and Babysitting Daddy*, I saw that Koreans use both hands when they pour out alcohol to their boss.'

5.2. Multimodal modulation hypothesis (MMH)

Socio-pragmatic meanings are achieved and modulated simultaneously via different channels of communication in a holistic manner. This is hard to capture and explain by observing a single written sentence as the linguistic interaction. Social interaction in language use occurs in a fully multimodal manner. Consider Enfield (2007) for a similar insight.

> Moreover, these linguistic structures occur in fully multimodal contexts, where people simultaneously employ rich semiotic resources which are meaningfully related to their talk (e.g. gesture, eye gaze, bodily comportment). Again, I am painfully aware of these important components of what it takes to speak Lao, and of the consequences of bracketing them out of the present work. (Preface)

In this book, I propose the necessity of looking at different dimensions of meaning to capture the fine-grained socio-pragmatic meanings projected by particles in Asian languages and also propose the principle of modulation, operating between different dimensions of meanings. In many languages across the world, in particular Asian languages, socio-pragmatically appropriate language use is critical. Often, the incorrect use of address terms or endings or the inappropriate use of non-verbal expressions can cause a serious problem in communication. However, in the generativists' tradition, a socio-pragmatic mismatch, sometimes referred to as a politeness mismatch, between second-person pronominal and the verb endings has often been ignored, as Ferguson (1991: 183) describes.

Agreement phenomena, by which one grammatical element matches another in terms of some categorial feature, present a challenge to contemporary theories of grammar. <u>Agreement in features of politeness has, however, received very little attention, often not being noted in lists of possible agreement features.</u> (Emphasis mine)

As Ferguson notes in the case of Hindi, the broad, pragmatic modulation process has been largely ignored in Asian linguistics. This is quite natural in the setting of modern linguistics, whose basic concepts are built upon English and European languages, where pragmatic modulation is less obvious than in Asian languages. In English, the second-person pronoun *you* can be used for all addressees in principle, and the verbal ending does not reflect based on one's attitude towards the addressee.

However, in Asian languages, socio-pragmatic modulation is crucial at every stage of communication. From beginning to the end, what is attuned, or orchestrated, harmoniously[6] is not only verbal input but also non-verbal input. Information from all dimensions are integrated in a way that builds a rich yet socio-pragmatically consistent and enhanced utterance. Within this background, I propose an MMH as follows:

(3) **MMH**

The core linguistic ability found in human communication is to be able to modulate or attune/orchestrate different levels/modes of information in a harmonious way, sensitive to the socio-pragmatic needs of each situation. If conflicting or inconsistent meanings are communicated, the communication will become socio-pragmatically inappropriate, insincere or unreliable.

For instance, if one begins with an honorific attitude which postulates S < H relation, the speaker needs to maintain this attitude throughout. Otherwise, the utterance appears unnatural or even sarcastic due to semantic and pragmatic inconsistency. Hence, if the utterance-initial vocative particle shows S < H and a respectful attitude, the following expressions also need to maintain this, although the degree can be expressed stronger. If a conflicting expression occurs, the utterance becomes inconsistent, unnatural, insincere or sarcastic. If the verbal expressions show S < H and a respectful attitude, the prosody and gesture should have S < H properties.

According to MMH, non-verbal expressions should be used with verbal expressions in a harmonious way to maintain, strengthen and specify the meanings of the utterances in a consistent manner. For instance, in India, touching feet is a gesture followed by Hindus largely to show respect to one's elders within a family or community. This deferential gesture can be used to strengthen the deferential meaning expressed verbally. In actual communication, the message sent non-verbally could be even more powerful and effective than verbal messages. If non-verbal expressions such as gestures are used inappropriately, however, they could jeopardize interpersonal relations set out by verbal interaction. In the following section, I shall show the application of MMH from diverse Asian languages.

5.2.1. MMH: Cross-linguistic evidence

Cross-linguistically, some expressions show S > H attributes, whereas other expressions show S < H attributes. Some will also express intimacy and informality, whereas the other expressions will reflect formality and respect. If the examples with conflicting attributes are used together in one utterance, this will violate MMH and cause socio-pragmatic unnaturalness.

5.2.1.1. Korean

In the following section, I shall discuss how meanings of social hierarchy, respect and intimacy are modulated in an utterance in a stepwise incremental manner. Consider the following example (4). Examples (4a) and (4d) are socio-pragmatically unnatural compared to (4b) and (4c) because of the mismatch between the vocative particle and ending particle.

(4)   ??? a. *Mina-**ya**, kongpwuha-**seyo***. [Korean]
       M-VOC study-POL+DECL.
       'Mina, please study.'
       b. *Mina-**nim**, kongpwuha-**seyo.***
       M-VOC study-POL+DECL.
       'Mina, please study.'
       c. *Mina-**ya**, kongpwu **hay***.
       M-VOC study-POL+DECL.
       ???d. *Mina-**nim**, kongpwu **hay***.
       M-VOC study-POL+DECL.
       'Mina, please study.'

For the same reason, compared to previous examples given in (4), (5) is socio-pragmatically awkward because of the mismatch between the vocative particle and the ending particle.

(5)   ??? *Kim sensayng-**a** ha-se-**yo**.*
       Kim teacher-VOC do-HON-POL
       'Dear teacher Kim, can you please do that?'[7]

In cases (4a) and (5), awkwardness occurs because the vocative particle -*a*/-*ya* creates a prediction of a close, informal relationship between the speaker and the hearer where the speaker is senior to the hearer. This prediction is jeopardized by the use of -*seyyo* which indicates a relationship where speaker wants to establish a polite yet distant relationship. In the case of (4d), the particle -*nim* creates the relationship where speaker wants to have some polite, hence distant relationship, and the hearer is set to be senior to the speaker. Such anticipation, however, is jeopardized by -*hay* particle at the end, which is often used to create a close, informal relationship between the speaker and the hearer where the speaker is senior to the hearer.

When mismatch occurs, the speaker's attitude becomes insincere, and therefore socio-pragmatically inconsistent. The awkwardness can be seen as sarcastic at times – but generally it is received as inappropriate and awkward. If we simply gloss each particle -*a* and -*yo* as VOC (for vocative) and POL (for polite), respectively, we cannot explain the inappropriateness observed in (4a and d) and (5). Socio-pragmatic meaning for each particle therefore needs to be illustrated in a more fine-grained way (as in (6)) than simple glossing to show how MMH is violated in the examples given earlier.

(6)
   a. Interpersonal matrix for the particle -*a*/-*ya*: [+ s > h], [+intimacy]
   b. Interpersonal matrix for the particle -*hay*: [+ s > h], [+intimacy]
   c. Interpersonal matrix for the particle -*seyyo*: [+ s < h], [+ polite]
   d. Interpersonal matrix for the particle -*nim*: [+ s < h], [+ polite]

In a single utterance, speakers must use expressions which indicate the same interpersonal dynamics. One can of course choose different dynamics in another utterance. Yet, within the unit or domain of a single utterance, it is necessary for a speaker to keep the utterance within the tenet of MMH. For instance, in Korean, the expressions within one utterance need to be from the same group – either from (i) or from (ii). If they are from different groups, they will violate MMH and cause socio-pragmatic unnaturalness.

(i) S > H, benevolent intimacy-oriented expressions[8]
   a) Utterance-initial particles:

—interjections: *ung* 'yes', some interjections can sound like swearing words, for example, *aissi, eissi*[9]
—vocative particle *-a/ya* shows intimacy
b) First- and second-person pronouns:
—first-person pronoun: *na*
—second-person pronoun: varies according to the fine-grained interpersonal dynamics between the speaker and the hearer.
c) Utterance-final particles:
—half-talk style[10] particles are preferred.
—non-verbal expressions (exclusively allowed in S > H) relation: patting, pointing

(ii) S < H, respect-oriented expressions
a) Utterance-initial particles:
—interjections: *yey* 'yes'
—suffix particle *-nim* attached after the address term: shows respect
b) First- and second-person pronouns:
—first-person pronoun: *ce/je*
—second-person pronoun: generally avoided
c) Utterance-final particles:
—polite, honorific, formal ending particles are used.
—non-verbal expressions: nodding, bowing
—less abrupt prosodic tones will be used
—softening tendency is much more preferred. If the S << H is set (i.e. when the hearer is much more senior to the speaker) the honorific or polite particles, prosody and gestures are more frequently used, spreading out the utterance.

As described earlier, the modulation does not happen at the verbal level alone but also in multimodal channels including non-verbal level of representation.

5.2.1.2. *Thai and Lao*

Consider Lao example in (7).

(7)
<u>**Kho**</u> *hai mii sukhaphaap khaenghaeng* <u>**der**</u>   [Lao]
<u>**Request**</u> cause have health strong [polite particle]
'We wish you good health'

In these examples, *kho* introduces a somewhat polite discourse and this expectation is met through the use of *der* which strengthens the polite tone. However, Thai examples (8) and (9) show the expectation at the beginning of an utterance is not met at the end.

(8)
??? **muŋ** yàak hây chăn tham àray phûa **khun** [Thai]

You (extremely informal) want cause I do what for you (formal)

(9)
??? **gɛ̀ɛ** yàak hâi chăn tam à rai **kráp** [Thai]

You (informal) want cause I do what [respectful particle]

In (8), the second-person pronoun is extremely informal, yet the ending shows speaker being serious and formal towards the second person. On the other hand, in (9) the second-person pronoun shows the speaker's casual/informal attitude towards the second-person addressee yet, the ending shows one's respect. Hence, in both cases MMH is violated and as a result, socio-pragmatic unnaturalness arises.

In the Lao example, the word '*dooy*' is very important in expressing respect. It is used to politely acknowledge a question asked by an elder (i.e. parent, teacher, government official, etc.) before an answer is given, with another polite particle following at the end. The use of these paired particles enhances socio-pragmatic naturalness.

(10)
Jao gin khao laew br [Lao]
You eat rice already or
Have you eaten yet?

Dooy *gin laew*
Yes ate already
Yes, I've already eaten [polite][11]

5.2.1.3. Persian

Consider a Persian example.

(11) shoma   **farmud-i**   emruz   tu   xune   nist-I   [Persian]
     you   told-2PL   today   at   house   aren't-2SG

'You told me you are not at home today.'

?to	**farmud-i**	emruz	tu	xune	nist-i
you	told-2SG	today	at	house	aren't-2SG

'You told me you are not at home today.'

Fermudan is a verb that shows respect to the second-person addressee. Hence, *shoma* is expected as it shows respect, whereas the singular pronoun *to* lacks respect. When 'to' is used, it is a little bit unnatural. Yet, the degree of unnaturalness is weaker in the case of Persian, compared to Korean or Urdu/Bengali, for instance. Note that from language to language socio-pragmatic appropriateness can be realized differently in terms of dimensions and degrees.

The awkwardness as shown in the Persian example is difficult to grasp with the generativists' tool box and will either be ignored or be understood as an exception. The conventional glossing of a single dimension cannot demonstrate where and why the mismatch of prediction occurs. In order to capture what's happening, the fine-grained, multidimensional information needs to be shown.

5.2.1.4. Chinese

In the same vein, in Chinese, *nǐ* (你, 'you') is used for equals and all people, and *nín* (您, 'you') is used to show respect to the hearer. For example, *nǐ* may be used between friends, colleagues or strangers, but *nín* is usually used when speaking to a teacher, or by an employee to a customer.

(12)
    a. *nǐ xìng shénme*
       you surname what
       'What is your surname?' [casual]
    b. *nín guìxìng*
       you noble surname
       'What is your surname?' [polite]

Chinese speakers may find the examples (12c) and (12d) socio-pragmatically awkward because of the inappropriate use of *nǐ* and *nín*.

    c.
       ???***Lǎoshī**, nǐ* xiànzài yǒu kòng ma?
       Teacher, you now have a minute?
       Lit. 'Teacher, do you have a minute now?'
    d.
       ???***Jessie**, nín* xiànzài yǒu kòng ma?
       Jessie, you now have a minute?
       Lit. 'Jessie, do you have a minute now?'

In the Beijing dialect of Mandarin Chinese, to express strong feelings (especially negative ones) to someone, a neutral tone suffix *-ei* may be attached to certain address words. It is most commonly applied to the word 孙子 (*sūnzi*, 'grandson'), to form *sūnzei*, meaning approximately 'Hey you nasty one!' Another example is 小子 (*xiǎozi*, lit. 'kid; young one'), resulting in *xiǎozei* 'Hey kiddo!' This suffix again may cause socio-pragmatic awkwardness if they are attached to address terms such as *Lǎoshī* 'teacher'.

5.2.1.5. Urdu

In Urdu, *tū* is used only when addressing a small child in one's own family. It can also be used as an insult, or as a reproof to a servant or subordinate. Yet, it can occur commonly in poetry where the poet addresses his/her beloved as in (13). In our lexical matrix, there is a style dimension. *Tū* will have [+poetry] as a style attribute in (13).

(13)
tū kyā khā rahā hai?
What are you eating?

The term '*tum*' is used when addressing one or more persons of lower status, children or close family members younger than oneself. Persons of equal status may address each other as *tum* in informal social situations.

(14)
tum itnī rāt gaē kahām̐ jā rahī hō?
Where are you going so late at night?

The term '*āp*' is used when addressing one or more persons of higher status, persons to whom respect is due or family members older than oneself. It is also used by young persons to elderly persons (even if the elder is a servant), to skilled persons (of all socio-economic ranks) and by parents to children, to teach them good manners. Finally, persons of equal status generally address each other as *āp* in formal social situations, such as an office or a formal event.

(15)
āp baithiē
You please sit down (to an elder).

(16)
āp sē darxāst hai ke hamēm̐ apnē fann sē navāzēm̐
He (an honoured poet) is requested to favour us with his art.

In Urdu, requests conform to the levels of *tū, tum* and *āp* (Schmidt 1999: 104).

Table 5.1 Urdu expressions sensitive to social hierarchy between speaker and hearer

Examples:	S > H forms and usage	S < H forms and usage
Second-person pronouns	*Tū* (very intimate) *Tum* (familiar)	*Āp*
Requests	Verb root alone for *tū* khānā khā bētē Eat your food, son Suffix ō khānā khā lō Eat your food.	Verb root plus *iē* caliē Please walk

(17)
    a. The *tū* form is the verb root alone.
       khānā khā bētē
       Eat your food, son

    b. The *tum* form has the suffix *-ō*
       khānā khā lō
       Eat your food.

    c. The *āp* form has the verb root and suffix *-iē*
       caliē
       Please walk

If the wrong request particle is used for the corresponding second-person pronoun, it causes socio-pragmatic awkwardness. The observation made in Urdu can be presented as in Table 5.1.

5.2.1.6. Hindi[12]

In Hindi, the second-person *tuu* form is the most impolite and must be used with care. The most honorific form is *aap*. If the relationship becomes close, speakers may change to *tum*. *Tum* is only suitable for equals and inferiors. Additionally, in Hindi, as for the third-person pronoun, *vah* is used when the subject is lower than the speaker and *ve* is used when the subject of the utterance is higher than the speaker.

(18)
    a. **tum** kal zaruur aanaa yaar
       'You must come tomorrow, dear friend.'
    b. kyaa **aap** kal dilii jaa rahe hāī
       'Are you going to Delhi tomorrow?'

Table 5.2 Hindi expressions sensitive to social hierarchy between speaker and hearer

Examples:	S > H forms and usage	S < H forms and usage
Second-person pronouns	*Tuu*	Aap
	Tum	

As discussed in Chapter 4, the verbal ending also differs based on the choice of second-person pronoun. Hence, (19) is socio-pragmatically inadequate.

(19)
 ??? *tu* (intimate) *ao* 'you come' [Hindi]
 ??? *tum* (informal) *aiye* 'you come'
 ???*ap* (polite) *a* 'you come'

This can be summed up as in Table 5.2.

5.2.1.7. Bengali

There are three levels of politeness in Bengali second-person pronouns: familiar, polite and intimate. There are two levels of politeness for third-person pronouns: ordinary and honorific. As shown in Table 5.3, the third-person honorific is used to speak about people in a respectful way, regardless of the speaker's relationship with them. It is usual for a wife to refer to her husband with the honorific pronoun when speaking to anyone outside the immediate family.

As in the case of Urdu, verb conjugations distinguish person, formality (honorific- and non-honorific distinctions) and tense but not number and gender (Thomson 2012: 48). Each personal pronoun requires different verbal endings as shown in Table 5.4.

Table 5.3 Bengali expressions sensitive to social hierarchy between speaker and hearer

Examples:	S > H forms and usage	S < H forms and usage
Second-person pronouns	*tumi, tui*	*āpni*
Third-person pronouns	*e*	*Ini*

(i) First-person *ami*
(2) Second-person familiar *tumi*
(2I) Second-person intimate *tui*
(3) Third-ordinary *se*
(H) Second-person polite and third-person honorific *apni, tini*

Table 5.4 Bengali verbal conjugations based on person pronouns

	First person	Second-person familiar	Second-person intimate	Third ordinary	Second-person polite and third-person honorific
Present simple	-i	-ô	-is	-e	-en
Present continuous	-chi	-chô	-chis	-che	-chen

If the wrong verbal particle is used, the utterance will also cause socio-pragmatic awkwardness.

5.2.1.8. Japanese

Japanese makes extensive use of honorific titles for the purpose of addressing individuals. Before any sort of relationship is established, <last name + san> is often used, and after becoming close, <first name + san> becomes more common. *Chan* and *kun* are both considered intimate. The first name alone may be used in very close relationships. Junior students do not refer to their seniors without a suffix or title but may be much more casual with friends of the same or lower position. The plain form is used when the speaker is of a higher social standing than the listener. The *desu/masu* form is always used in formal situations, or when a speaker is socially lower than the hearer.

Such speakers may also use honorific verb forms when the listener or a socially higher third person is the subject of the sentence. The misuse of these may cause socio-pragmatic tension between the speaker and the hearer (see Table 5.5).

5.3. Realization of second-person pronoun: Asian evidence

In literature on the subjecthood, it is often assumed without further explanation that second-person pronouns are arbitrarily dropped in some Asian languages. But as we shall explore, the realization of second-person pronouns is far from

Table 5.5 Japanese expressions sensitive to social hierarchy

Examples:	S > H forms and usage	S < H forms and usage
Speech styles	Plain form	*Masu* form
Honorific forms	Standard form	Honorific form
Titles	-kun, -chan	-san, -sama, -sensei

arbitrary. On the contrary, such linguistic decisions are very sensitive to age, social hierarchy and systems of respect and intimacy in Asian languages. The use of second-person pronouns is socio-pragmatically sensitive and complex and they are systematically replaced with address terms, kinship terms or sometimes non-verbal expressions to avoid socio-pragmatic awkwardness.

The social convention of referring to elders in the community as kin or family members in order to show both intimacy and respect is extremely common in Asian languages and cultures. Simultaneously, some occupational titles such as teacher are frequently used as a respectful address term. This socio-pragmatically sensitive approach to argument realization, however, is not found in English or any other Western European languages.

While English does not have the same complex politeness system, most of the Western European languages have binary distinctions, as in *tu* versus *vous* in French. Hence, there is also a level of socio-pragmatic complexity which calls for the proper understanding of interpersonal relations. For instance, in French, 'you' can be separated into two different levels of politeness; *tu* and *vous*. *Tu* is the casual 'you' and can be used with everyone with whom one is intimate, from one's friends and close colleagues to one's parents, husband or wife.

On the other hand, *vous* is used with people one does not know, such as older people with a substantial age gap and people in positions demanding respect, such as a teacher or superior at work.[13] Moreover, since *vous* is the plural form of *tu*, *vous* is always used when talking to a group of people. It is thus safer to use *vous* rather than *tu* in circumstances of which one is unaware, although *vous* may potentially create an undesirable distance when used to a close friend or family.

Nevertheless, the complexity and dynamic nature of negotiation in Asian languages is far more complex than what we observe in European languages. According to WALS, among Western European languages, Romanian, Hungarian and Lithuanian exhibit multiple politeness distinctions. Yet, the nature of the politeness distinction is incomparably simpler than what we observe in Asian languages. In the case of Romanian, the additional second-person singular form *domina voastră* is a highly polite form yet is rarely used and considered obsolete (Braun 1984). In the case of Hungarian, the additional second-person singular pronoun *magá* is known to be used by less educated people and etymologically is a third-person reflexive pronoun (Keresztes 1992). Among the three, Lithuanian shows the most diverse singular/plural second-person pronouns, yet the age and seniority-sensitive linguistic considerations that we observe in Asian languages are not manifested so clearly, even in Lithuanian.

Table 5.6 Bengali: Pronominal (Thomson 2012: 70)

Singular	Nominative
2nd ps fam	*Tumi* 'you'
2nd ps int	*Tui* 'you'
2nd ps pol	*Apni* 'you'
3rd ps ord, U	*Se* 'he/she'
3rd ps ord, N	*e* 'he/she'
3rd ps ord, F	*O* 'he/she'
3rd ps hon, U	*tini* 'he/she'
3rd ps hon, N	*Ini* 'he/she'
3rd ps hon, F	*Uni* 'he/she'

The inventory of second-person pronouns in Asian languages is much more fine-grained than in Western European languages and is highly sensitive to interpersonal relations. For instance, personal pronouns in Bengali also have levels such as familiar (fam), intimate(int), polite(pol), ordinary(ord), honorific, near and far as shown in Table 5.6. In the following sections, I shall give examples from different Asian languages in order to show how second-person pronouns are encoded.

5.3.1. Bengali

Bengali shows a rather complex nature of second-person realization. As shown in Table 5.6, Bengali distinguishes people on the basis of their status. Honorific pronouns and verbs are used for respected people – for professionals like doctors, teachers, lawyers and politicians, or for parents, grandparents and other relatives (Thomson 2012: 61). The way second- and third-person pronouns are used also reflects the complex aspects of sociocultural and interpersonal relations in Bangla. That said, according to Thomson (2012: 68), second-person pronouns distinguish three degrees of politeness: 'intimate, familiar and polite'. Third-person pronouns distinguish two degrees of status: ordinary and honorific. The second-person polite *apni* is the usual form of address between strangers, acquaintances and work colleagues, but also for particularly respected members of the family.[14]

Though the inventory of second-person pronouns is far richer in Asian languages, as in the case of Bengali, than it is in Western European languages, second-person pronouns are further avoided in many Asian languages in spoken communication. WALS shows that second-person pronouns are avoided if necessary in the following seven languages, which are all Asian: Burmese,

Japanese, Indonesian, Khmer, Korean, Thai and Vietnamese. In these languages, very often, the second-person pronouns are replaced with appropriate address or kinship terms or sometimes with non-verbal gestures. Each of these languages has a complex set of rules surrounding the use of second-person pronouns. In the following, I shall show how the second-person and address terms are realized in the these languages.

5.3.2. Thai

There are at least five registers which are used in different contexts, including a street register and a formal register, along with registers for use in public speaking, with royalty and with religious figures. Honorific language is not restricted to a certain register but can be used even in the street register. Its use is based on age, social status and intimacy and is used by adding special particles to the end of utterances. A significant part of the honorific system in Thai is also found in the use of the first-person pronoun. This is used differently based on the gender of the speaker and the social status or intimacy of the interlocutors. Given names are seldom used and are replaced with nicknames instead.

5.3.2.1. Street register

There are a few terms for 'you' in the street register including the following:

/mʉng/ Extremely impolite when used outside of close relationships equal in social status.
/təə/ Used in close relationships. Usually refers to females.
/gɛɛ/ Used in close relationships. Refers to both male and female.
/nŭu/ Refers to children and young women.

Often times, familial terms are used as second-person pronouns in the street register. Note that these pronouns can be used outside of immediate family. For example, a child could refer to an elderly woman who is not her own grandmother as *yaai*.[15]

Younger sibling: /nɔ́ɔng/
Older sibling: /pîi/
Mother: /mɛ̂ɛ/
Father: /pɔ̂ɔ/
Elder uncle: /lung/

Younger aunt: /náa/
Older aunt: /bpâa/
Grandmother: /yaai/
Grandfather: /dtaa/

Titles can also be used as second-person pronouns. More formal titles such as professor may slip into the formal register.

Medical doctor: /mɔ̌ɔ/
Teacher: /kruu/
Professor: /aa jaan/
Village chief: /pûu yài bâan/
Boss: /naai/

5.3.2.2. Formal register

/kun/ means 'you' but can also be used for titles including Ms, Mrs and Mr. This can be combined with other titles including doctor or teacher to increase formality. /tân/ is more formal than *kun* and is often used in public speaking and meetings.

5.3.2.3. Religious register

/yoom/ This pronoun is used particularly in addressing monks.

5.3.2.4. Royal register

/prá ong/ This pronoun is used particularly in addressing a king or god.

5.3.3. Khmer

Khmer is very similar to Thai. Second-person pronouns are often unsaid to avoid any socio-pragmatically awkward situations. Names are often replaced with nicknames or titles. There is a complex set of social registers, which, similar to Thai, differ depending on the social status of the speaker, the listener and the referent. Verbs change to reflect honorific action, and pronouns can be changed to honour or to humble. Social registers include language for commoners, royalty and religious figures. Within the commoner class, there are intimate and respectful ways of speaking. The royal and religious types of speech are not used frequently by commoners, who may feel uncomfortable using them.

5.3.4. Burmese

The Burmese language is indeed very age-oriented. The choice of address terms reflects relative age, seniority and respect. The use of address terms in Burmese is also gender sensitive.

The use of honorifics before personal names is the norm, and it is considered rude to call a person just by their name without an honorific, unless one has known them since childhood or youth or in the case of a younger underling. Young males are addressed as *Maung* or *Ko* (lit. brother), and older or senior men as *U* (lit. uncle). Likewise, young females are addressed as *Ma* (lit. sister), and older or senior women as *Daw* (lit. aunt), regardless of their marital status. First- and second-person pronouns are age-dependent and vary depending on whom one is speaking to. Elders are spoken to in a more respectful manner and a special vocabulary exists for speaking to Buddhist monks. We can see in the next example how the use of second-person pronouns is much more fine-grained and complex in actual usage:

/nìN/ informal, equal/inferior
/mín/ informal, equal/inferior
nyì, informal, equal/inferior
/ɲí/ informal, by females to equal/inferior females
/tɔ̀/ informal, by females
/meiʔhswei/ 'friend'
/kʰəmjá/ formal, by males
/ʃìN/ formal, by females
/(ə)θìN/ formal, by either
/hyiñ/ formal, by females, 'master'
/hkiñbyà/ by males, 'master'

Second-person pronouns are avoided not only in imperative forms but also in conversation.

* *U* – Adult males (from younger to their seniors)
* *Daw* – Adult females (from younger to their seniors)
* *Ko* – Younger males (most commonly used)
* *Ma* – Younger females (most commonly used)

When talking with or about monks, part of the basic vocabulary is replaced by special honorific forms. Examples are *ɕauʔ* 'tell (a monk)' for colloquial *pyɔ́*, *tɕwá* 'go' for colloquial *θwà*, and *pín* 'invite' for colloquial *pheiʔ*, among many others.

A layperson addressing a monk uses the pronoun *dəbé.dɔ* (male speaker) or *dəbé.dɔ.má* (female speaker) to refer to themselves, literally 'disciple'. The appropriate term to address a monk is *ʔəɕin-phəyà* 'holy lord', while a nun is addressed by *shəya.lè* 'little teacher'. Examples of possible utterances in a conversation with a monk are the following (Jenny and Hnin Tun 2017: 488).

(20)
    *mə-θí-bù **phəyà**.*
    NEG-know-NEG holy
    'I don't know.'
    *shùn.phòun-pè-pì-bi là **phəyà**.*
    eat-give-finished-NSIT PQ holy
    'Have you eaten?'

A monk speaking to laypeople has a wider range of terms, including *ʔùzìn* (also sometimes used as a term to address a monk), *tɕouʔ, ŋa, phòun.dʑì*, according to the relationship between the monk and the layperson. The politeness markers *khəmya* (male speaker) and *ɕin* (female speaker) are replaced by *phəyà* 'holy (object, person) Buddha' when speaking to a monk. The following are some special second-person address terms that are used within a Buddhist context:

    hsăyah̲kălei either, speaking to nuns
    ăhyiñhpăyà either, speaking to monks
    bhun informal between monks
    pasang informal between monks
    a. hrang bhu.ra formal between monks
    chara dau formal between monks

5.3.5. Japanese and Korean

In Japanese and Korean, it is common to simply omit the pronoun entirely, unless giving emphasis or introducing the second person as the new sentential subject. In Japanese, after the appropriate relationship is established, it is typical to refer to the second person as name plus title (see Table 5.7).

In Japanese, the most important variable is intimacy. This is related to in/out-groupness, where one shows politeness to the people in one's out-group. Rank within an in-group is also important in finding the right address term. However, age is not as important as in-groupness and social position compared to Korean.

Table 5.7 Second-person pronouns and address terms in Japanese

Address terms	Usage	Examples
-san	used between equals of any age, or a socially lower speaker to a socially higher addressee	*Takayama-san* 'Mr. Takayama'
-sama	used to address guests, customers, divine gods, or show a greater level of respect than *-san*	*okyaku-sama* 'Customer' *kami-sama* 'God'
-kun	used to address younger males than the speaker in informal situations	*Takeshi-kun* 'Takeshi'
-chan	used to address young girls in informal situations	*Rie-chan* 'Rie'
-sensei	used to address teachers or doctors	*Yamato-sensei* 'Teacher/Doctor Yamato'
anata/anta	used in informal situations, mainly between partners, or when the name of the addressee is not known, only used to equal or lower addressees	*anata wa dare?* 'Who are you?'
kimi	used by male speakers to a male addressee in a close relationship	*kimi wa nani wo suru?* 'What are you doing?'
kisama	used as an insult	*kisama!* 'You bitch!'
omae	used by a socially higher male speaker to mainly male addressees, or between males in a close relationship	*omae wa dou omou?* 'What do you think?'

There are numerous address terms replacing the second-person pronouns in Korean. Table 5.8 shows some examples.

However, choosing the right term can often be tricky. In such cases, Korean speakers use other attention seeking interjections or non-verbal expressions such as hand gestures, the same hand gesture used when giving something to the senior (see Figures 5.1 and 5.2).

5.3.6. Indonesian

In Indonesian, kinship terms such as *bapak*, *ibu*, *saudara* and *saudari* are used when addressing other people politely. *Bapak* and *ibu* stand for father and mother, and they can be used as respectful forms to older people or any adult of marriageable age. They can also be used as self-address terms when older people are talking to younger people. *Saudara* is used to address male siblings and

Table 5.8 Second-person pronouns and address terms in Korean

Address terms	Usage
Ne	From a senior to junior in an informal setting where the two are very close, possibly between family members or school friends.
Tangsin	This can be used as a swearing word if used between strangers. Husband and wife can call each other with this to show affection (e.g. honey, darling) or it can be used as an honorific pronoun if used in religious context.
Sensengnim	This means teacher. Koreans use this term however to show respect regardless of their actual job.
Samonnim	This means teacher's wife, originally. Koreans use this term however to show respect to the older woman particularly in sales setting.
Imonim	This means aunt. Koreans use this term however to show family-like intimacy to the older woman, for example, to refer to a serving lady in the restaurant.

saudari for female siblings, but they can also be used as second-person polite address terms for people of the speaker's generation or younger. There are also *engkau, kau, kamu* and *kalian,* which can be used to address children or used between equals who have a close relationship with one another; they cannot be used as a polite second-person pronoun in other situations. The third-person bound pronoun *-nya* can sometimes be used as a polite form for second-person address. The other politeness strategy is to avoid person pronoun usage at all. It is easy to see that both age and intimacy play an important role in the politeness strategy in Indonesian. There are strict restrictions on the address terms usage according to the speakers and hearers' age and their relationship, which is like Korean where age has been considered as one of the most important factors that influence language politeness.

5.3.7. Vietnamese

In Vietnamese, job titles, status terms and kinship terms are used as alternatives for polite personal pronouns. For example, job titles such as *bác-sĩ* (doctor), *giáo-sư* (teacher, professor), *thây giáo* (teaching master) and *thây thuoc* (medicine master) are used to address other people politely. There are also specific terms for addressing high ranking officials such as *ngài/ ngườì*. Kinship terms hold a large portion of the expression for person pronouns, and the kinship terms are also used selectively according to the speaker and hearer's age and their relationship. For example, *anh* stands for elder brother and *chi* stands for elder sister, and they can also be used to address people of lower class or servants and labourers. However, an elder labourer is normally addressed politely as *ong* (grandfather) or *bà* (grandmother). *Ong* and *bà* can also be used to address other older people politely, while *chi* and *anh* cannot be used in the same way. There are also *em* (younger brother), which can be used to address younger children politely, and *mày*, which can only be used as an abrupt form that expresses deep familiarity. Therefore, it is not hard to see that age and social status are the two most important factors that influence politeness strategies in Vietnamese. There are specific terms for people of lower class, but people with different ages are addressed differently – older people are usually addressed in a politer form.

In many Asian languages, not only those mentioned earlier, second-person pronouns are simply avoided when their use may potentially cause social awkwardness. In spoken communication, they are replaced by address or kinship terms as discussed, or with appropriate non-verbal expressions such as hand gestures. In many Asian languages, pointing or hand gestures accompanied with other verbal and non-verbal expressions, such as eye contact and/or bowing, are used to refer to the second person. It is worthwhile to note that no Western European languages share this property. Similar tension may arise in languages like French or German, yet not to the degree and extent which we have observed in Asian languages. For instance, even in some awkward situations, second-person pronouns will not disappear altogether from an utterance.

5.4. Summary

In this chapter, we have discussed socio-pragmatic particles in Asian languages. In Asia, age-oriented seniority and/or respect towards one's elders or bosses within a community or workplace play a crucial role in building interpersonal relations. The typical terms 'honorifics' or 'politeness' do not adequately express the full range of possible interpersonal meanings. These features require a much more fine-grained, formal framework. This book introduces a lexical matrix to fully capture the interpersonal dynamics manifested in particles.

Particles used in the same utterance are not chosen randomly but rather are used to gradually form and reinforce socio-pragmatic meanings set between interlocutors. Particles are tuned and modulated throughout the utterance – in both verbal and non-verbal channels of communication. In order to explain this, I proposed the MMH in this chapter.

6

Particles as a meaning complex

6.1. The limit of current particle researches in Asian languages

In this book, I suggest that the meanings of particles are multidimensional, proposing a lexical matrix to include multidimensional information. As discussed in Chapter 1, the multifaceted nature of particles that reflect constructive and/ or socio-pragmatically complex, expressive and attitudinal meanings have often been overlooked in contemporary linguistics. In this section, I shall show some of the limits of particle research in Asian languages within contemporary linguistics.

6.1.1. Subjectivity of particle use: The limit of glossing particles

Very often, the complex and expressive nature of meaning is pinned down as one single glossing that matches the categories found in most European languages. However, the number of semantic primitives and the degree to which meanings are represented through particles in Asian languages differs greatly from Western European languages.

The function and behaviour of particles are not necessarily similar just because the glossing patterns are the same. For instance, plurality is often defined purely based on the number of items. The typical definition is as follows: *A plural number is a number that expresses reference to a quantity greater than that expressed by the largest specific number category in a language, such as 'more than one' in English, and 'more than two' in some other languages.*[1]

According to Dryer (2013a), most of the world languages under investigation had morphosyntactic devices to code nominal plurality.[2] Only 9 per cent of the languages (98 languages among 1,066 languages) do not have any plural marking. However, the ways in which plurality is understood and expressed differs from language to language. Many of our Asian target languages do not mark plurality in the way that English does. Plurality is not marked automatically as in English or in other Western European languages. Plurality is encoded differently from how it is encoded in English and other Western European agreement-based languages. In most cases, a plural particle is used not to express the mathematical number of entities but rather when the speaker aims to express or emphasize the severalness or multitude nature of the entities. Animacy or humanness also plays an important role. Consider some of examples from Asian languages as follows.

6.1.1.1. Persian

In Persian, a plural verb (for inanimates) is sometimes preferred when the subject is seen as individuals rather than a mass of things or when the subject needs emphasis or is personified in some way (Yousef 2018: 178).

6.1.1.2. Bengali

In Bengali, the plural marker -(e)ra can be used with animate nouns, but only to emphasize their plural-ness.

(1)
amader konna
'Our daughter'
amader konnara
'Our daughters'

6.1.1.3. Lao

In Lao there is no plural. The word 'many' may be used, or a specific number can be stated. A word can also be reduplicated.

6.1.1.4. Khmer

Khmer has no plural. Like Lao, the word 'many' (/craən/) may be used, or a specific number can be stated. A word can also be reduplicated.

6.1.1.5. Thai

In Thai, there is no plural. Like Lao and Khmer, the word 'many' may be used, or a number and classifier word can be used. A word can also be reduplicated.

(2)   *năngsɯ̌ɯ săam lêm*
       'book three classifier'

6.1.1.6. Kazakh

The plural is marked by the suffix *-lar* as follows.

(3)
>*uyɣïr* 'Uyghur'
>*uyɣïr-lar* 'Uyghurs'

This plural particle is only used on unmarked nouns.

6.1.1.7. Turkish

The third-person plural suffix *-lar* is used when it is attached to a non-case-marked subject complement.

(4)
>*Tutsáklar*
>prisoner-lar
>'They are prisoners.'

In Turkish, cases have plural forms so the marker is not always necessary.

6.1.1.8. Tagalog

In Tagalog, '*mga*' is a plural marker. It occurs before the word it pluralizes and is only used for emphasis or if plurality is not obvious.

(5)
>*libro*
>'book'
>*mga libro*
>'books'

6.1.1.9. Tibetan

The plural marker *tshō/tso* appears with demonstratives and personal pronouns, or acts as a definite article for plurals on human nouns.

(6)
>*āma-tso*
>'the mothers'
>*lōptrawa-tso*
>'the students'

In the case of unambiguous plural readings of animals or inanimate nouns, demonstratives are used: *cōktse thetso* 'those tables'.

6.1.1.10. Japanese

The suffix *-tachi* can be loosely translated as 'and company'. It can be attached to any noun or pronoun to make a quasi-plural representing a group of people.

(7)
> *kodomo-tachi*
> 'The children'
> *Yuki-tachi*
> 'Yuki and company'

6.1.1.11. Korean

The suffix *-tul* is used, but is also used when the speaker aims to represent severalness (see Kiaer 2010).

6.1.1.12. Chinese

The plural marker *men* (们; 們) has limited usage. It is used with personal pronouns, as in *wǒmen* (我们; 我們, 'we' or 'us'), derived from *wǒ* (我, 'I, me'). It can be used with nouns representing humans, most commonly those with two syllables, such as *péngyoumén* (朋友们; 朋友們, 'friends'), from *péngyou* (朋友, 'friend'). Its use in such cases is optional.

6.1.1.13. Burmese

It is possible to change a word in its plural form by adding *myar*. In such a case, it designates the noun more specifically as a group or collective body of things.

(8)
> *thit pin*
> 'Tree'
> *thit pin myar*
> 'Trees'

As shown here, plural particles in most of our target Asian languages are used only in marked situations to emphasize plurality or severalness. This is very different from the way plurality is marked and agreed in European languages. The use of particles is found to be context-bound and subjective, which is again different from European languages, where plural marking is chosen automatically based on the absolute number of entities under discussion.

Furthermore, as discussed in Chapter 5, interpersonal meanings often show interactional dynamics and again cannot simply be glossed as honorific (HON) or polite (POL). There is a much wider range and degree of attitudinal particles in Asian languages which reflect interpersonal relations that are sensitive to multiple socio-pragmatic factors, such as social hierarchy, gender or styles. Hence, simple glossing is insufficient for describing the complex meanings projected by particles.

Another set of particles that has received much attention in contemporary linguistics includes the so-called topic and focus particles. There are some problems, however, in the research on these particles, as we shall now discuss. The way these particles function is expressive in nature and hard to narrow down to one discourse function as might be possible in most European languages. Let's take an example using Korean (K) and Japanese (J) topic particles which have been frequently discussed in theoretical linguistics.

6.1.2. Case study: -*un/nun* (K) and -*wa* (J) as difficult-to-define topic markers

In the literature, -*un/nun* (K) and -*wa* (J) have most often been understood as 'topic' particles and glossed as TOP. On the other hand, -*i/ka* (K) and -*ga* (J) have been often understood as 'focus' particles and glossed as FOC or nominative particles as NOM. However, glossing the -*un/nun* (K) and -*wa* (J) as *topic particles* has a clear limit in terms of describing and explaining the overall behaviours related to the pairs of particles.

6.1.3. Limit of previous studies: Prevalent uses of non-typical -*wa* (J) and -*un/nun* (K)

Many Western European learners of Japanese and Korean do not have topic markers in their first language, therefore making the acquisition of markers in Korean and Japanese very challenging for them. The difficulties are based on the fact that the topic marker is in competition with the subject particle, which generally occupies the same place in the sentence. The explanations given in textbooks are not sufficient for learners or for teachers, because they start with a concept which is not clear for most learners.

For many years in Korean and Japanese linguistics, -*un/nun* (K) and -*wa* (J) have been discussed in relation to -*i/ka* (K) and -*ga* (J). In these languages -*wa* (J) and -*un/nun* (K) were regarded as a morphological topic marker (see Kuno 1973). Though having been studied over a long period, the continued definition of topic and topic marker/particle in Korean and Japanese is not so straightforward, and indeed a general consensus on the definition of 'topic' is yet to be achieved in linguistics.

Among the different criteria put forth, it has at a minimum been assumed that -*wa* (J) and -*un/nun* (K) mark expressions referring to 'old information' that is 'given' already in a text or discourse, whereas -*ga* (J) and -*i/ka* (K) marked expressions refer to new information that is not yet *given* in the text or discourse (see Shimojo 2005 and Vermuelen 2007). However, often this sort of definition of these pairs is applicable to 'short-nominal, referential NPs' only. Although Shibatani (1990),[3] among many others, argues that genuine topic marking is related to short-nominal, referential NPs, the actual data, such as that of spontaneous speech corpora, shows that -*wa* (J) ~ -*un/nun* (K) can freely and frequently occur beyond short, nominal and referential NPs. The NPs in these cases are difficult to analyse with old/given versus new information criterion. It is important to notice that both -*un/nun* (K) ~ -*wa* (J) and -*i/ka* (K) ~ -*ga* (J) can be used in these NPs. Consider example (9).

(9) Non-typical NPs with -*un/nun* (K) and -*wa* (J): referring to neither *given* nor *old information*

    a. *wh*-indefinite expression plus -*un/nun* (K) and -*wa* (J) or *i/ka* (K) or *ga* (J)

    b. (long) fact clause plus *un/nun* (K) and -*wa* (J)

    c. Adverbial expression plus -*un/nun* (K) and -*wa* (J) or *i/ka* (K) or *ga* (J)
For example, *onul{un/i} sarah nal-i-ya.* [Korean]
kyou-{wa/ga} Sarah-no hi-na-no. [Japanese]
'Today is Sarah's day.'

    d. Repetition of -*un/nun* (K) and -*wa* (J) – this is not for a double contrast.
uri oppa-nun kyesan-un hwaksil-hay-yo. [Korean]
?? *watashi no onii-san-wa keisan wa tokui desu.* [Japanese]
'My brother is good at calculation.'

These uses of -*wa* (J) and *un/nun* (K) are neither exceptional nor rare. Fitt (2017) shows that more than half of the collected examples with -*wa* (J) in fact include examples with non-typical NPs, in that they are not short, nominal referential NPs. What these show is that the term 'topic' is limited as an overarching term that could capture the semantics and pragmatics of *-wa* (J) ~ *-un/nun* (K) marking.

6.1.4. Interchangeability of particles

In fact, frequently, the two particles *-un/nun* (K) ~ *-wa* (J) and *-i/ka* (K) ~ *-ga* (J) are easily interchangeable.

(10) a. *khokkiri-ka kho-ka kil-ta.*   [Korean]
       zou ga hana ga nagai   [Japanese]⁴
       elephant-KA/GA nose-KA/GA big-DECL
   b. *khokkiri-nun kho-ka kil-ta.*   [Korean]
       zou wa hana ga nagai   [Japanese]
       elephant-NUN/WA nose-KA/GA big-DECL
       'Elephants have a long nose.'

These are just two of the main problems which show that the meanings of the so-called topic and focus particles in these languages are hard to narrow down as one single semantic feature. Topicality is associated with the old information and focality is associated with new information to an extent, but this is only a part of the meanings presented by these particles. Indeed, in many languages, topic and focus particles reflect a combination of different meanings. Often, these particles are used to convey exhaustive and/or contrastive meanings, yet this depends greatly on the context. Due to the complex nature of meanings, it is better to gloss these particles in their transliterated forms. Consider examples drawn from different Asian languages that are often known as topic and focus particles.

6.1.5. Beyond Korean and Japanese: Evidence from other Asian languages

In the following I present diverse particles, known as topic and focus particles. As in the case of Korean and Japanese, the meanings of these particles are complex and hard to narrow down as one single feature.

6.1.5.1. *Hindi/Urdu*

The particle *hii* is a focus particle, adding the meaning of exhaustiveness and emphasis.

(11)

> *Rita* *hii*   *ayi*
> Rita   only   came
> 'Only Rita came.'

Hindi/Urdu also has a thematic or topic particle *to* which expresses contrastive meaning. The particle *to* here builds the item as contrasting with the other items/books.

(12)

> *ye   lo!   hindī kī   kitāb to   tumhen kal   dūngī*
> these take Hindi of   book   TO   2.DAT   tomorrow give.FUT.1SG
> 'Take these! The Hindi book, I will give it to you tomorrow.'

The following sentence can be used to contrast, if someone else said something like 'I can see two of them.' Here, *to* acts as contrast to the speaker before him (as for me . . .)

(13)

> *mujhe   to   tīn   nazar   ā   rahī   hain*
> 1SG.DAT TO   three look   come   PROG   PRES
> 'As for me I (but if you ask me) I can see three of them.'

6.1.5.2. Burmese

Burmese has an exhaustive particle *hma*. *Hma* is a constituent focus particle which adjoins to a focus-containing constituent. It acts like Japanese *ga* and Korean *i/ka* in the exhaustive listing meaning.

(14)

> *Aung-ga   ye-ko-hma   tahuq-keh-deh*
> Aung-NOM   water-ACC-HMA   drink-PAST-NONFUT
> 'It's WATER that Aung drank.'

This particle has another use as a focus particle:

(15)

> *Aung-ga   ye-ko-hma   ma-thauq-keh-dar*
> Aung-NOM   water-ACC-HMA   NEG-drink-PAST-dar
> 'Aung didn't even drink WATER.'

Burmese also has an IMPORT (importance) particle, INTENS (intensifier) particle and EMPH (emphatic) particle. All of these can be better grouped together as perspective and attitude particles, as we shall return soon.

6.1.5.3. Vietnamese

Vietnamese also has a focus particle *nam*. It appears prepositionally with the focus constituent.

(16)

Mỗi	*[Nam]F*	*mua*	*cuốn*	*sách*
only	NAM	bought	CL	book

'Only [Nam]F bought the book.'

Vietnamese also has focus-sensitive particles like thậm chí/đến 'even', cả 'also' and chỉ/mỗi 'only' that indicate semantic focus. Each of these focus-sensitive particles is associated to another particle introducing information that is already part of the common ground. In the case of *thậm chí, đến* 'even' and *cả* 'also', the *cũng* particle is mandatory, as shown in the next example. The use of double emphasis/focus markers increases the emphatic attitude.[5]

(17)

<u>cả</u> Hàn Quốc *<u>cũng</u>* ăn thịt chó
FOC_EVEN Korean BG_EVEN/ALSO eat meat dog
'Even Koreans eat dog meat.'

6.1.5.4. Lao

Lao has a focus particle ka^0, appearing immediately before the main verb phrase (including its left aspect-modality marking), and immediately after the sentential subject. It is a sentence-level marker, and cannot appear inside clauses which are tightly subordinated, such as relative clauses or controlled complement clauses.

(18)

Dtae khoi ga* bor jer kak bandai
'But then I can't remember very clearly.'

6.1.5.5. Mongolian

Mongolian has a focus particle *ch* that is postpositional.

(19)
emee ch / megden sandarch
'As for Granny, / [she] got anxious.'

Consider (20), *chiny* is a possessive topic marker which refers the highlighted topic to the previous context and are used mainly for contrastive topics, when the speaker opposes one item with another.

(20)
Bi chiny / yamaa baiturai, hüühed ch erhlüülzh üzeegüi hün
'As for me, / [I] am the [kind of] person who has never indulged even children, not to speak of goats.'

As shown earlier, in many Asian languages, it is hard to tell the difference between contrastive topic and focus markers. The main meaning which both sets of particles present is aboutness, emphasis and contractiveness.

6.1.5.6. Chinese

Classical Chinese had 者 zhě.
Chénshèng zhě yángchéng rén yě.
'Chen Sheng is a Yangcheng person.'

Some scholars argue for the following particles as topic particles in contemporary Chinese: *a (ya), ne, me, ba*.

(21)

Hua	(a),	Zhangsan	hen	xihuan	meiguihua.
flowers	TOP	Zhangsan	very	like	roses

'As for flowers, Zhangsan likes roses very much.'

There are also two focus particles *jiu* 'only' and *dou* 'even'.

What we observe is that the diverse meanings which these particles project from various languages are hard to confine by the topicality or focality that are often assumed to be easily definable as single semantic features in contemporary linguistics. In order to provide a better description and analysis for these particles and other attitudinal particles in Asian languages, I propose *perspective and attitudinal particles* as an overarching term responsible for the speaker's perspective and attitudes towards the proposition he/she is making or to the addressee. The meanings and functions of the particles presented above, often glossed as topic or focus particles, are better understood as perspective particles which can have multiple dimensions of meanings. In the next section we see the kinds of particles that could come under perspective and attitudinal particles. These particles are much more fine-grained in languages such as Thai, Lao and Burmese than in other Asian languages. These are also the languages where personal pronouns are extensively developed based on interpersonal dynamics and socio-pragmatic factors. Buddhism may have played an important role in this, but that is a topic for another book.

6.1.6. Perspective particles

Attribute/dimension	meaning
SUBJECTIVE	particles which show subjective perspective
OBJECTIVE	particles which show objective perspective
EMPHASIS/FOCUS/IMPORT	particles which show emphasis, focus or importance
FORG	particles that are used for foregrounding
TOP	particles that mark referent as topical, in the centre of interest

6.1.7. Attitudinal particles

Attribute/dimension	meaning
SOFTENING	particles that are used to soften the utterance
HEDGE	particles are used to signal caution or probability versus full certainty
HES	particles that show hesitation
DOUBT	particles that show doubt
(UN)BELIEF	particles that show (un)belief
CERTAINTY	particles that show certainty

For instance, as perspective particles *un/nun* (K) ~ *-wa* (J) and *-i/ka* (K) ~ *-ga* (J) can have dimensions of meanings such as subjective and objectiveness as well as topicality, contractiveness and emphasis.

6.1.8. Subjective versus objective particles

So-called topic and focus particles in Korean and Japanese can also reveal the speaker's subjective or objective attitude. In the case of *-ga* (J) and *-i/ka* (K), particles reveal the speaker's 'objective' attitude, whereas the choice of *-wa* (J) and *-un/nun* (K) reveals the speaker's 'subjective' attitude towards what he/she is talking about. Often, in science-related statements such as weather forecasts, *-ga* (J) and *-i/ka* (K) are preferred to *-wa* (J) and *-un/nun* (K) as in (22), yet in subjective statements such as personal opinion, *-wa* (J) and *-un/nun* (K) are preferred to *-ga* (J) and *i/ka* (K) as in (23).

(22) Weather forecast (GA/KA is strongly preferred)
   a. *oxford-e nwun {no particle, i, nun } mani narikyesssupnita.* [Korean]
   b. *oxford-ni ooyuki{no particle, ga, wa} furi-masu.* [Japanese]
   'Heavy snow will fall in Oxford.'

(23) Personal opinion (-WA/NUN is strongly preferred)
   a. *cho seongjin {no particle, i, nun } nwuka mwelayto chopinuy taykarako poa.* [Korean]
   b. *cho seongjin {no particle, ga, wa} dare-ga nan-to it-te-mo chopin-no tatsujin da-to omou.* [Japanese]
   'No matter what anyone else says, I think Seongjin Cho is the master of Chopin.'

'Subjectiveness' and 'objectiveness' are not mutually exclusive terms; being subjective and objective is a gradient phenomenon. As we can see in Figure 6.1, there is in fact a large portion of grey area, where the speaker's perspective can be a mixture of subjectiveness and objectiveness. The two perspectives can be swapped very easily, yet crucially without changing propositional meanings. In this sense, we argue that the meaning contribution that these particles make is *expressive* and *modal* in nature.

In principle, particles are chosen based on what perspectives and attitudes one has and hence there are many factors which influence their realization. In the following section, I shall discuss the pragmatic realization of particles (see Figure 6.1).

6.2. Particle realization: A complex matter

Particles contribute to the speaker/writer's perspective or attitude towards what is under discussion. Hence, as a rule, they are only obligatory when the speaker wishes to express his/her view. The meanings, functions and distribution of particles in our target languages are complex and multidimensional, and therefore difficult to capture in a one-dimensional view. In this section, I showcase Korean and Japanese examples to reveal the complexity of particle behaviour.

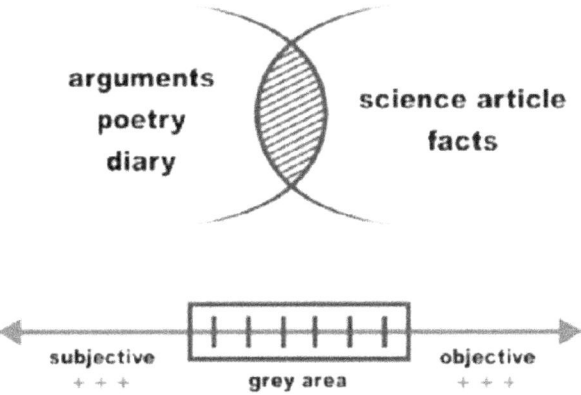

Figure 6.1 Subjectiveness and objectiveness scale.

As we have discussed in Chapter 1, particles do not have to appear obligatorily. In particular, the accusative particles tend to be less present when the structural relations of the host expression become obvious. For instance, in Bengali, direct object case particles are used when it is necessary. Mostly, they are used to add expressive meanings: (i) to indicate a treatment of inanimate things as animates or (ii) to show an author's personal engagement. Consider (24) from Thomson (2012: 264).

(24) ækj_n cikits_k hisabe khub kach theke jībônke dækhar [Bengali]
      one doctor as very close from life. OBJ see
      suyog gh_t_e.
      opportunity occur
      'As a doctor he has the opportunity to see life from close up.'

This phenomenon is found across our target languages and has been referred to as the *particle omission* phenomenon.

6.2.1. Object particle realization: The case of Korean

Kiaer and Shin (2012) showed the role of prosody in the distribution of object particles -*LUL* in Korean. They argue that the distribution of -*LUL* cannot be explained purely by semantic constraints. It is often argued that the object particle is the focus marker, and if the object particle is absent, it is then used as a contrastive topic marker. However, this is not always the case as shown in (25b). Examples like (25) are common in Korean.

(25) a. *ne sakwa mek-ullay? Banana mek-ul-lay* ? [Korean]
    you apple eat-will/intend banana eat-will/intend
    'Will you eat an apple or a banana?'
  b. *banana mek-ul-lay.*
    Banana eat-will/intend
    'I am going to eat a banana.'

Lee H (2003, 2006) showed that if expressions have features such as [+Human], [+Contrastive Focus] and [+Definiteness], then object particles are most likely to be realized (i.e. overt marking) than to be elliptical. However, Kiaer and Shin (2012) showed that realization of object particles depends much more on contextual factors than the semantic characteristics mentioned earlier.

Consider (26). According to Lee H's (2006) claim, the object particle should be realized in (26). But, (26b) without the object particle is more natural than (26c) with the overt object particle. Using an object particle in (26c) sounds very much redundant and unnatural.

(26) A: *Ne Jina mannasse? Mina mannasse?*
    You Jina met Mina met
    'Did you meet Jina or Mina?'
  B: *Ung, Mina mannasse.*
    Yes Mina met
    'Yes, I met Mina.'
  C: ??*Ung, Mina-lul mannasse.*
    Yes Mina-LUL$_{ACC}$ met
    'Yes, I met Mina.'

Lee S (2006), on the other hand, argued that the omission of the object particle adds habitual, repetitive and more or less generic meanings. Yet, as we can see in (27b), this is not always the case. Example (27b) does not have any meaning addressed earlier.

(27) a. *Mwe hay?*
    What do$_{Informal}$
    'What are you doing?'
  b. *pap meke.*
    Meal eat$_{Informal}$
    'I am having a meal/eating.'

Particle realization is sensitive to the registers. It becomes much more visible in speech or in informal registers than formal registers. It is also sensitive to the prosody. Lee S (2006) argues that (28) is unnatural because the particle is omitted.

(28) ?? *Hama-nun mwul coahanta.*
   Hippopotamus-NUN[6] water likes
   'Hippopotamus likes water.'

However, if (28) is spoken in a natural, informal situation with a rising tone as in (29), (28) is restored as a perfectly natural utterance.

(29) *Hama-nun mwul coahanta* (H%)
   Hippopotamus-NUN water likes
   'Hippopotamus likes water.'

Alternatively, when the speech style changes into an informal style, the sentence becomes very natural.

(30) *Hama-nun mwul coahay.*
   Hippopotamus-NUN water likes
   'Hippopotamus likes water.'

Particles contribute the speaker/writer's perspective or attitude towards what is under discussion. Hence, as a rule, they are only obligatory when the speaker wishes to express his/her view. In English, functional words or grammatical morphemes, such as plural suffixes and tense suffixes, must be present explicitly. However, this is not the case in most Asian languages, including Korean. Instead, they are realized when they make a meaningful contribution or are useful in building a structure.

6.2.2. Particles and perspective

Lee D (2002) takes the position that explicitly unmarked NPs involve the 'zero particle' rather than 'particle omission'. In Lee's view, the zero particle has two key functions within an utterance: (i) absolute specification and (ii) compensatory reinforcement. The zero particle is typically used in spoken Japanese, where interlocutionary attitudes are developed between two or more speakers. Consider the following examples from Lee D (2002):

(31)
   a. *Watashi Ø bikkkuri shichatta.*
      I was.surprised
      'I was surprised.'

    b. *Watashi Ø Sushi Ø daisuki!*
       I Sushi like.a.lot
       'I love Sushi!'

According to Lee, the use of the zero particle heightens the speaker's feelings/emotions, leading to stronger interactional attitude between the speaker and the listener. Lee's view is close to my proposal on perspective particles. Very often, particles can remain implicit rather than being expressed explicitly, depending on the situation and the speaker's viewpoint.

Consider the following Korean examples (32) and (33). With the use of *-ka*, it seems that the speaker is putting emphasis on the situation. For instance, in (32), the presence of particles is more natural than when there are no particles as in (33), because pragmatically it is a little 'surprising' to have rain in April.

(32) With particle *-ka*
    sawel-in-tey pakk-ey pi-ka o-ney. [Korean]
    'It is April but, it is raining outside.' (I (=speaker) am emphasizing the surprising aspect of this event.)

(33) Without particle *-ka*
    a. *sawel-in-tey pakk-ey pi o-ney.* [Korean]
       'It is April but, it is raining outside.'

Particle realizations are also very sensitive to registers. So, in formal registers, particles are likely to occur, whereas in informal registers they are replaced by prosody or non-verbal expressions. I propose in this book ternary instead of binary distinctions in realizing the speaker's perspectives. Having no particle implies that the speaker does not intend to express his/her perspective in a specific mood or remain solemn.[7] On the other hand, in choosing a particle the speaker wishes to express his/her perspective specifically and wants to do so by making the target of talk prominent.

6.3. Particles as meaning complex

As we have discussed, it is of primary importance to understand that the meaning complex each particle projects is multidimensional. This understanding will benefit not only theoretical linguists but also educators and learners. That said, what is usually being taught in classrooms is only the constructive or lexical meanings of particles, rather than the socio-pragmatic dynamic meanings. As a result, though proficiency may be quite high, many learners fail to learn the uses of particles and often face social embarrassment and even disputes. As discussed in Chapter 1, even the CEFR surprisingly does not include any discussion about particle acquisition in our target languages. Consider the following proposed dimensions for a lexical matrix projected by particles.

(A) **Constructive dimension**
Particles can be used in the building up and unfolding of a clause or the closing off of a clause. Or, they can be used in linking the currently built structure to a higher level of structure (i.e. subordination) or other equal structures (i.e. coordination).

(B) **Socio-pragmatic dimension**
   a. *Social hierarchy*: a particle can reveal the social hierarchy between the interlocutors. That is, it can refer to a relationship where the speaker is senior to the hearer (S > H), equal (S = H) or junior to the hearer (S < H).
   b. *Interpersonal relations*: a particle reveals speaker-hearer's close/intimate and benevolent or respectful relationship.
   c. *Mood and emotions*: a particle can express the speaker's attitudes, emotions and moods of the utterance.
   d. *Style*: a particle can reveal whether it is used in monologue, dialogue or genre such as poetry or prose. It can also show whether it has masculine or feminine voice.
   e. *Perspective and attitude*: a particle can express the speaker's attitude and perspective.

The degree to which the various dimensions are prominent differs between particles. For instance, constructive roles may be more significant in some particles, whereas interpersonal roles may be more significant in other particles. Among the particles where interpersonal roles play crucial parts, some particles may be sensitive to register and styles, but some others may not be.

6.3.1. Lexical matrix for Korean utterance-final particles

These criteria can apply to many Asian languages, but in the following we specifically showcase examples in Korean. The idea of these matrices is a hand-me-down from lexical theoretic formalisms (e.g. LFS and HPSG). In the following, we begin by examining Korean particles, but the matrices can be easily applicable in other languages as well.

If one expresses the proposition 'Jina is very pretty,' in Korean, one needs to consider whether he/she wishes to present the proposition in an informal speech context or in a formal writing context; and that question becomes easy when the interpersonal meanings of particles *-yo* (요) and *-upnita* (-습니다) are considered. The matrix reveals the complexity of meanings projected by the particle that is underlined. We can naturally expect the semantic concordance between meaning complexes projected in one proposition expressed as a single unit of utterance.

The inventory of attributes and the values for each attribute need to be refined in future studies. Yet, what we demonstrate here is the necessity of using fine-grained approaches to analyse the meanings of particles. The dimension of social hierarchy and interpersonal relations are merged into interpersonal dimensions in the matrix. Consider the following examples.

(34)
    -yo (-요) [Korean] (falling tone ↘)
    For example, *Jina cham yeppe-yo*.
    'Jina is very pretty.'

$$\left\{\begin{array}{l} \text{Constructive Dimension}\left[+\text{CLOSE OFF}\right] \\ \text{Mood and Emotion Dimension}\left[+\text{DECL}\right] \\ \text{Interpersonal Dimension}\left[+\text{INTIMACY}\right],\left[+\text{POLITE}\right],\left[+\text{S<H}\right] \\ \text{Style Dimension}\left[+\text{INFORMAL}\right]\left[+\text{SPEECH}\right] \end{array}\right\}$$

What (34) shows is that *-yo* closes off the utterance together with the falling tone; it reflects declarative mood; it implies intimacy, politeness and hierarchy where the speaker is deferent to the hearer; and it is informal in register and used in speech.

(35)
    -upnita (-습니다) [Korean] (falling tone ↘)
    For example, *jina cham yepp-upnita*.
    'Jina is very pretty.'

$$\left\{\begin{array}{l}\text{Constructive Dimension}\left[\text{+CLOSE OFF}\right]\\ \text{Mood and Emotion Dimension}\left[\text{+DECL}\right]\\ \text{Interpersonal Dimension}\left[\text{+POLITE}\right],\left[\text{+S<H}\right]\\ \text{Style Dimension}\left[\text{+FORMAL}\right]\end{array}\right\}$$

Hence, if one is speaking in a formal context, using *-upnita* will be more suitable than using *-yo* as an ending particle. Yet, if the intimacy is the real value that the speaker is seeking, the *-yo* ending will be more suitable to use than the *-upnita* ending. Evaluating the suitability of these endings is dynamic and depends very much on contexts and speakers' perspectives and attitudes. Consider (36), which we discussed in Chapter 4.

(36) Pragmatically inadequate dialogue due to simple particle copy
Supervisor: *mike-ya. ne kongpwu-lul cincca yelsim-hi hayss-kwuna.* [Korean]
        'Mike, you have studied really heard.'
    Mike: *kamsahapnida.* [Korean]
        'Thank you.'
        (.)
Mike:??? *sensayngnim-to scarf cengmal yeppu-kwuna.* [Korean]
        'Teacher, your scarf is very nice.'

In Chapter 4, we showed that the reason in example (36) is pragmatically inappropriate is because Mike simply copied the exclamatory ending that his teacher used in the previous (sentence of a) conversation. *-kwuna* cannot be simply copied because the meaning of this particle not only includes exclamation (mood dimension) but also includes interpersonal meaning that indicates the speaker is senior to the hearer. This is why (36) becomes pragmatically inadequate.

We can show this process using lexical matrix for particles. From an incremental perspective, we can see that at first, lexical matrix is projected by the vocative particle *-ya* which projects the following meaning complex:

$$\left\{\begin{array}{l}\text{Constructive Dimension}\left[\text{+CLOSE OFF}\right]\\ \text{Mood and Emotion Dimension}\left[\text{+VOC}\right]\\ \text{Interpersonal Dimension}\left[\text{+INTIMACY}\right],\left[\text{+S>H}\right]\\ \text{Style Dimension}\left[\text{+INFORMAL}\right]\left[\text{+SPEECH}\right]\end{array}\right\}$$

Then, at the end, the exclamative particle *-kwuna* projects the following meaning complex:

$$\begin{Bmatrix} \text{Lexical matrix projected by } \textit{-kwuna} \\ \text{Constructive Dimension [+CLOSE OFF]} \\ \text{Mood and Emotion Dimension } [++\text{EXCL}] \\ \textbf{Interpersonal Dimension}\, [+\text{INTIMACY}], [+\text{S} > \text{H}] \\ \text{Style Dimension}\, [+\text{INFORMAL}]\,[+\text{SPEECH}] \end{Bmatrix}$$

The two matrices which the two particles project are compatible. However, when *-nim* is used instead of *-ya* in (36), it becomes incompatible due to clash at the interpersonal dimension. The use of *-nim* and *-kwuna* together violates MMH.

$$\begin{Bmatrix} \text{Lexical matrix projected by } \textit{-nim} \\ \text{Constructive Dimension}\, [+\text{CLOSE OFF}] \\ \text{Mood and Emotion Dimension}\, [+\text{VOC}] \\ \textbf{Interpersonal Dimension}\, [+\text{POLITE}], [+\text{S} < \text{H}] \\ \text{Style Dimension}\, [+\text{SPEECH}] \end{Bmatrix}$$

What is worthwhile remembering is that the semantic mismatch and the detection of unnaturalness occur at the point of facing the expressions rather than at the final stage of understanding. In this section, we provided lexical matrices for Korean particles only, but the method of adopting such lexical matrices can be easily extended into other Asian languages.

6.4. Summary

In Chapter 6 we have shown the limit of particle research and showed the complex nature of particle realization. In order to show that particles act as multidimensional meaning complexes rather than one-dimensional markers, I proposed a lexical matrix with four dimensions: constructive, mood and emotion, interpersonal and style. In this chapter I mainly showcased Korean, but more discussions from other languages will follow in later chapters.

7

Pragmatic syntax

7.1. Modelling particles in the grammar formalism

Particle behaviours are neither arbitrary nor peripheral, but they are systematic and consistently motivated by the speaker's pragmatic needs. As we have already seen and will explore in depth in later chapters, particles are realized in order to meet the syntactic, semantic and pragmatic needs. When the default word order is used or the grammatical roles are contextually inferable, particles are less likely to be used as a constructive primitive. This is often the case in an informal register where the utterance-exchange is short and fully context-bound, with rich non-verbal information such as prosody and gestures. In such cases, particle realization has more to do with the speaker or the interlocutor's desire to add his/her subjective perspective, emotions and attitudes. Of course, the absence of a particle doesn't mean the absence of an attitude. The absence of a particle can add neutral, formal and at times abrupt attitudes. Dialectal variations are often observed in particles. In that sense, the empathy or sense of belonging in the community can be drawn through the use of particles as we shall return to in section 7.2.

In order to explain the meanings, functions and distribution of particles, we need a framework which can incorporate sources other than word order in syntactic architecture. We also need a toolkit which enables resource-sensitive, procedural structure building – regardless of the location of a verb. In any case, we need a formal model which shows how pragmatic knowledge plays a role in syntactic structure building. However, as we already discussed in Chapter 2, this is not an easy task given the existing theoretical frameworks. Consider again how we classify our target languages in Chapter 1.

7.1.1. A group

This group consists of flexible word orders with rich case particles and pragmatic realization of expressions (i.e. pro-drop). In general, particle-rich languages are Arabic, Korean, Japanese, Tamil, Hindi, Urdu, Bengali, Tibetan, Tagalog, Turkish, Persian, Mongolian and Sanskrit (all these languages except Standard Arabic show strong verb-finality).[1]

7.1.2. B group

This group consists of flexible word orders yet with no case particles and pragmatic realization of expression (i.e. pro-drop). In general, particle-rich languages, mostly SVO order is preferred such as Mandarin Chinese, Thai, Indonesian, Vietnamese, Lao, Khmer and Burmese (SOV preferred).

The ideal framework would be able to describe and explain the syntactically, semantically and pragmatically interwoven behaviours of particles. For this purpose, I have adopted a dynamic syntax (DS, Cann et al. 2005) framework. In addition to the original framework, I propose a *pragmatic syntax* hypothesis, developed from Kiaer (2014), and argue that there are three major driving forces within structure building and particle realization: *efficiency*, *expressivity* and *empathy*. In explaining the logical foundation, I will show how the puzzling cases we saw earlier in section 2.1 (namely, (i) the surprising pre-verbal, constituent formation and (ii) left-right asymmetry) can be explained using the updated DS framework. Furthermore, I show how prosody and structural routines can be encoded within grammar.

7.2. DS: Left-to-right[2] growth of a structure as the basis of syntactic carpentry[3]

7.2.1. Overview

In this book I adopt DS (Kempson et al. 2001 and Cann et al. 2005) to model the role of particles in syntactic architecture and the composition of socio-pragmatic meaning in our target languages.

Based on DS, I will argue that reflecting the time linearity of the growth of interpretation is an essential part of grammar formalism, with intonation providing important clues to analysis. In DS, sensitivity to linear order forms an integral aspect of structure-building, replacing a strictly top-down configurational hierarchy. Hence, a structure is built incrementally along the left-to-right linear order. The core notion of DS is early underspecification of structure and its subsequent update at a later stage.

In this way, DS can capture fluidity in syntactic configuration – not only in English-like languages but also in languages with rich case morphology[4] and flexible syntax such as Korean, Japanese, Persian, Turkish, Mongolian and many Indian languages. In addition, it can explain those languages whose structural relations are in principle largely underspecified and rely on pragmatic resolution. Languages such as Lao, Thai and Mandarin Chinese belong to this group, where there seems to be no visible constructive cues, yet speakers hardly experience any problems in communication.

Instead of positing various movements or lexical triggers for word-order variation, DS assumes that in languages with flexible word orders, (i) constructive use of case particles, (ii) processes of structural abduction and (iii) pragmatic routines unfold argument structure, far ahead of the actual verb or grammatical head. For the cases of languages even without constructive particles, it is solely pragmatic knowledge that projects the structural skeleton. One may expect some confusing and chaotic situations when there are no morphosyntactic markers that signal grammatical relations, yet ordinary speakers do not have any problem in establishing interpretation. Within DS, it can be explained as a pragmatic update from the context. Flexible structure buildings in both A- and B-group languages can be therefore understood under the same structure-building mechanisms. I shall return shortly with examples.

Case systems in A-group languages contribute to the structural development of what is in other frameworks an S-node (i.e. sentence-node), whose relation to the containing overall structure is radically underspecified, since whether or not the case-marked NP is the argument of an embedded clause, a relative clause or a matrix clause can only be known at the end of parsing.[5] This view is contrary to the Rizzian view in which NPs are projected as part of a very high-level, fine-grained structure, regardless of their actual syntactic position (Rizzi 1997).

The use of structural underspecification and its subsequent update is essential in capturing incremental, time-linear structure building. However, the notions of underspecification and time linearity have been largely ignored by theoretical linguists, and though it has been adopted in a restricted way, it has been assumed that such notions are for a parser system that refers to an independent grammar.

In its original set-up, following the relevance theoretic claim made in Sperber and Wilson (1995), DS assumes that the initial and overall goal of structure-building is to form a proposition by progressively presenting and combining partial fragmentary information. In this stepwise structure building, detailed structure-building guidelines are only accessible after a certain step in the parsing. DS assumes that various structural requirements are to be met at various stages of incremental processing, rather than all at once at the very end. In DS, unlike the modelling of word-order flexibility with variation from a canonical order and no relation to the incrementality of language processing (as in minimalism, CCG, LFG, HPSG), a structure is built strictly in an incremental way from left to right. Let us take an example from English.

(1) Underspecified host structure:
    a. *To whom* . . .
    b. *To whom did Will say* that Jen was crying?
    c. *To whom* did Will think that Jen *was giving a present*?
    d. *To whom* did Will think that Jen was thinking of *giving a present*?

When the front expression like *to whom* in (1a) is read, initially it is not clear at which level of a structure it is to be interpreted. In other words, it is not clear whether *to whom* is interpreted within the matrix clause as in (1b) or within other embedded clauses as in (1c and 1d). However, speakers of English can at least expect a ditransitive, three-place predicate, even though the upcoming host structure is still unseen. The relevant host structure is decided on as the structure grows.

The same intuition can apply to language universally. Some information for the upcoming structure is given as one gathers the information, yet other information is available only at a later stage. What human parsers are able to do is to build a partial structure incrementally as the information is given. In verb-final languages, a draft structure is often unfolded by case particles, a minimal set of structure-building routines and other pragmatic strategies. There is no fundamental difference in the logic of structure building based on the location of a verb. Although the mechanism that is to be chosen differs from language to language, I argue that the paired notion of underspecification and subsequent update forms the basis of structural growth across languages.

Originally, DS assumes that the parser's initial and overall goal is to form a proposition by combining partial information. Furthering from original set-up in DS, Kiaer (2014) adopts the revised goal for structure building following the pragmatic syntax hypothesis. Kiaer (2014) argued that the goal of linguistic structure building is not just to obtain a proposition but to do so in the most optimal way as in (2). Later in this chapter, I will show how this optimization process is encoded in grammar through the process of routinization.

(2) Goal of linguistic structure building:
For efficient communication, ordinary language users aim to *optimize* their syntactic structure building (both production and comprehension) by achieving the meaningful, communicative proposition as quickly as possible with minimal structure-building effort.

Word-order variation emerges as a possibility via the assumption of early structural underspecification. The subsequent update of some constructed underspecified relation can be made by (routinized) lexical actions, for instance, case specifications. Since DS assumes that structure-building processes are triggered by the lexical expressions in order, left-right incrementality and structure-building are, by definition, coordinated.

In addition to case particles as the source of a combinatory force, Kiaer (2007) modelled the role of prosody[6] in incremental structure building within DS, using Korean as a case study. Based on DS, Kiaer (2007) showed the importance of capturing procedural aspects of interpretation within the grammar formalism, and the way prosody can be defined as interacting with word order to determine such interpretation. By definition, DS allows all information, including lexical information, structural information and context to be available at all stages, unlike other syntax-driven parsing approaches.

7.2.2. Left-to-right architecture for not-yet seen structure

DS[7] assumes left-to-right directional derivation. Such an assumption makes it possible to thread left-to-right incremental growth of a structure into the heart of the grammar. As mentioned earlier, both dependency grammar and LFG were also initially designed to allow incremental left-to-right processing without excessive derivational complexity, as summarized by Bresnan (2001). Yet, both of these grammars failed to preserve this insight in their most up-to-date architecture. As discussed in Chapter 2, in principle, most grammars and linguistic theories do not tolerate any structural indeterminism when they provide structural representations.

Within the Chomskian tradition, structural properties of language were assumed to be characterized entirely independently of the dynamics of language processing. Yet DS assumes that there is no gulf between grammar and parser. The first challenge DS faces is being able to state the interaction between the order of words and the interpretation within a sentence/utterance. This, as part of the problem of compositionality, has been the concern of theoretical linguists for a long time. The second challenge is to explain how the interpretation of words may be related to the previous context. This problem of context-dependency has so far been the concern within semantics and pragmatics. DS shows that these two problems, namely compositionality and context-dependency, are not independent. Instead, according to DS assumptions, the syntactic and semantic aspects of compositionality, together with the problem of context-dependency, must be addressed together (Cann et al. 2005: 3).

First of all, the compositionality problem for natural languages is the problem of how it is that humans are able to systematically build up complex sentences indefinitely (Cann et al. 2005: 3). Particularly puzzling cases are related to long-distance dependency, a problem which has long been recognized as not being reducible to purely semantic considerations. DS unfolds syntactic structure following the growth of left-to-right semantic representation, and constructions such as long-distance dependency can be naturally explained in terms of earlier structural underspecification and the subsequent update of semantic representation without adding any ad hoc constraints (Kempson and Kiaer 2010).

Consider example (3) and Figure 7.1 from Baldridge (2002: 149). Baldridge tried to provide a combinatory categorical account that could be applicable for both short- and long-distance scrambling in a unified way in languages like Tagalog and Toba Batak. In (3), *Kitabi* and *Fatma* are both simple NPs. However, though *Kitabi*'s type is only NP_a, *Fatma* is far-complex and type-raised as we can see in the circled expression from Figure 7.1. In CCG, for instance, type-raising for the expression *Fatma* needs to be decided at the time when the expression is parsed, yet it is impossible to do so because the whole structure is not yet visible at this early stage.

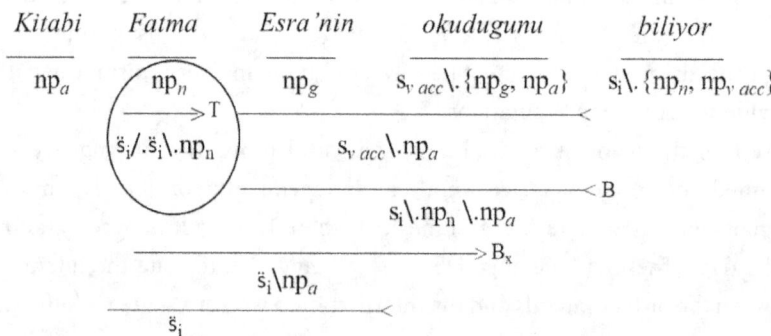

Figure 7.1 Pre-determined type-raising.

(3) *Kitabi Fatma Esranin okudugunu biliyor* [Turkish]
　　book-ACC Fatma-NOM Esraniin-GEN read know-PROG
　　'As for the book, Fatma knows that Esra read it.'

There is no mainstream syntactic theory designed specifically to be applicable to 'not-yet-seen' structures. Put simply, any analysis for an incomplete linguistic sequence is taken to be, in principle, illegitimate. This is one of the crucial reasons that left-to-right motivation has not been widely adopted in linguistic theories. It has been implicitly believed that the issues surrounding the incremental or partial growth of an incomplete sequence is what a grammar-independent parsing theory should seek to explain, rather than a competence-based linguistic theory. Within the DS architecture, on the contrary, the essence of syntactic knowledge lies in the ordinary speakers' ability to build a partial, provisional structure – an underspecified, not-yet-complete structure that is soon to be updated – in a bit-by-bit manner from left to right.

Phillips' (1996) approach is the closest to this idea of incrementality in terms of considering the direction of structure-building. However, his build-and-revise (= *build-and-destroy*, in his terms) approach has limits in capturing monotonic incrementality (see Chapter 3).

The problem of context-dependency did not bother syntacticians much thus far, as their remit of research has been only that involving one isolated sentence at a time in the Chomskian tradition. Yet, it is impossible to understand the meaning of a sentence without considering its context, particularly in Asian languages, where argument realization is decided by pragmatic and contextual needs. In many of Asian languages, a verb alone can compose a perfectly grammatical sentence. This is possible only because interlocutors can retrieve both subject and object from the context.

These two problems of compositionality and context-dependency, together with the intrinsic properties of syntactic structure, can be explained by considering time linearity, expressed by linear order and the growth of representation alongside it. The consequence of ignoring linear order in natural language syntax and assuming some canonical order as the point of departure is to yield numerous movements particularly in verb-final or relatively flexible word-order languages.

7.2.3. The unfolding of a structural template: Basic logic in DS

Following Sperber and Wilson (1995), DS takes establishing some propositional formula as interpretation to be the goal at the starting point in any parsing effort,

Table 7.1 Types in dynamic syntax

Type	Description	Example expression
Ty(e)	Individual term	*Fo*(*Mary*')
Ty(t)	Proposition	*Fo*(*sing*'(*John*'))
Ty(e→t)	(1-place) Predicate	*Fo*(*run*')
Ty(e→(e→t))	(2-place) Predicate	*Fo*(*like*')
Ty(e→(e→(e→t)))	(3-place) Predicate	*Fo*(*give*')

with this overall goal possibly leading to other sub-goals as more information comes in. In DS, there are three drivers of structure-building: (i) computational actions, (ii) lexical actions, or (iii) pragmatic actions. What is being built in DS is a representation of semantic content. A tree gives no indication of order, as this is a representation of content, inhabited by concepts, not by words of the string. In the following, we will discuss the basic types, relations and logic used in the DS.

7.2.3.1. Basic types

The basic types are defined as in Table 7.1, which is a simplified version of types taken from Cann et al. (2005: 36). This follows the general practice of formal semantics. *Ty* is a 'type' predicate/functor which takes a semantic type such as e for an individual term, and produces *Ty*(e), a type-logical combination used in DS. *Fo* is a 'formula' predicate/functor which takes a semantic content such as *Mary*' and produces *Fo*(*Mary*'), or abbreviated as *Mary*' as its value.

7.2.3.2. Basic relations

It seems that humans understand the flow of information based on anticipating what is coming ahead – in an incremental manner. I suggest this sequential mode of understanding to be the essence of cognition. On this basis, DS assumes that the basic linguistic relation is the repeated anticipation and then application of functor argument, as set out in a tree structure configuration. The basic observation is that each lexical item proceeds with such combinatory information and one expression plays the role of a 'functor' in terms of building a bigger expression, whereas the other expression plays the role of 'argument'.

Verbal predicates normally act as functors, but as we observe in many Asian languages and beyond, particles also play the role of functor in that they project structural requirements. As a convention, following Kempson et al. (2001),

Pragmatic Syntax

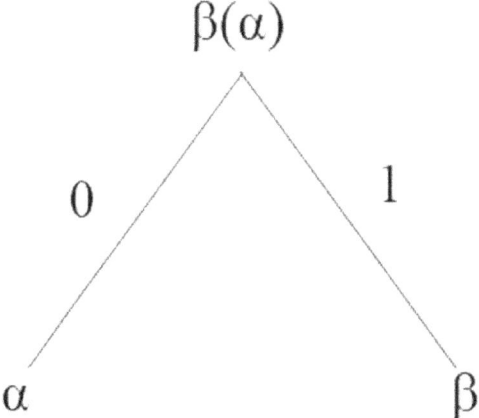

Figure 7.2 Binary, functor-argument relation.

throughout the book, I will assign '0' to the argument relation and '1' to the functor relation. In Figure 7.2, α is an argument and β is a functor. The basic functional application will yield a proposition β(α).

7.2.4. Verbal projection of a structure: The case of Korean

In the following, using DS logic, I shall show how a simple structure is built in Korean, one of the A-group languages, and Lao, one of the B-group languages.

(4) Bomi: *Hemi-ka Mina-lul ikiesse?* [Korean]
     Hemi-NOM Mina-ACC beat
     'Did Hemi beat Mina?'

   Kiho: *ung **iki-esse**.*
     Yes, beat-(PAST+INFORMAL)
     'Yes, Hemi beat Mina.'

Figure 7.3 shows the partial structure projected by the underlined verb *ikiesse* 'beat'.

Fragmental answers as in (4) are prevalent in Korean and our other target languages. The stem of the verb *iki-* 'beat' will project a draft structure as in Figure 7.3 with two arguments decorated with place-holding meta-variables *U* and *V* that need to be filled in from the context.

Because DS is committed to building representations of content rather than structure inhabited by words, it is able to characterize the flexible word order and pro-drop nature of head-final languages by assuming that the verb projects

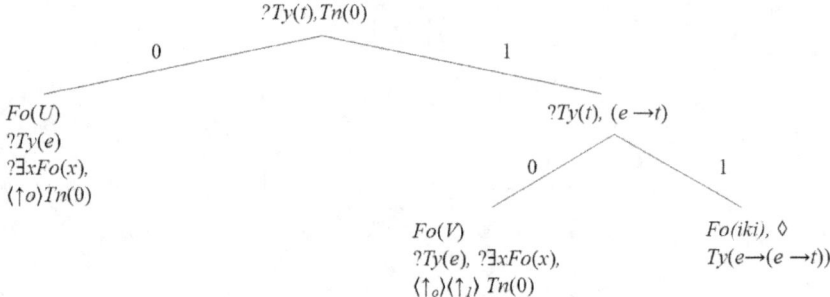

Figure 7.3 Partial structure projected by the verb *iki* 'beat'.

a full propositional structure, whose arguments are semantically underspecified (as though projected from anaphoric expressions). Such actions are part of the specification of each verb. For instance, *iki-* 'beat' projects the partial tree in Figure 7.3, with two argument nodes decorated with place-holding meta-variables *U* and *V*. As discussed in section 1.5, in most of our target languages, expressions are pragmatically realized. Hence, they appear when they are needed. Hence, if they are retrievable from the context, they tend to remain unsaid. The place holder in DS represents those expressions which are unsaid yet are to be updated by the context.

In the following, I will show the basis of logic of finite tree (LOFT; Blackburn and Meyer-Viol 1994), which forms the core architectural properties of DS using the tree given in Figure 7.3. At first, let's see the top node, labelled as $?Ty(t), Tn(0)$. $?Ty(t)$ is associated with the label of type $(=Ty)$, which deals with the combinatorial property of lexical items. What $?Ty(t)$ indicates is that a proposition is required. This is the overall goal of structure-building applicable in all languages and it is computationally driven (i.e. this goal will be set before any word is read). In our term, it can be rephrased as an overall goal to establish a meaningful, communicative proposition. In Kiaer (2014), I proposed that this goal needs to be met as soon as possible with minimizing structure-building effort. This can be understood as part of pragmatic strategy and real drive for structure building, as we shall turn to in section 7.3.

$Tn(0)$ is associated with the label of tree node $(=Tn)$, which has the information on the address of each node in the overall structure. What $Tn(0)$ informs us is that this node is the top node.

Now, let's move from the top node to the next node along with an argument (0) relation. The node under 0 relation in LOFT is the argument node and the node under 1 relation in LOFT is the functor node. The argument node of

$?Ty(t), Tn(0)$ is labelled as $\{Fo(U), ?Ty(e), ?\exists xFo(x), \langle\uparrow_0\rangle ?Tn(0)\}$. This node is to be a subject node. $Fo(U)$ and $?\exists xFo(x)$ are associated with the label of formula(=Fo), which has all content information. U is a place-holding meta-variable. Its content is to be updated by the context. $?\exists xFo(x)$ is the requirement for a formula/content value for the current node and is forcing its update at some point in its parse process. $\langle\uparrow_0\rangle Tn(0)$ refers to the modal relation, which states that from the current node, if the parser goes up (↑) along with 0 (=argument) relation, there is a top node (=$Tn(0)$).

The other daughter node under $?Ty(t), Tn(0)$ is the predicate node. This node is the functor argument. $?Ty(e \rightarrow t)$ is the type label, which indicates that a predicate is required. This node can be addressed as $\langle\uparrow_1\rangle Tn(0)$. From this node, two sub-nodes are further developed. First, let's move to the node along with the argument (0) relation from $?Ty(e \rightarrow t)$ node. This node is to be an object node. This node is labelled as $\{Fo(V), ?Ty(e), ?\exists xFo(x), \langle\uparrow_0\rangle \langle\uparrow_1\rangle Tn(0)\}$. $Fo(V)$ is another place-holding meta-variable, projected by the verb, whose value also needs to be identified in the context. $?Ty(e)$ is a type label, which denotes that $Ty(e)$ is required at the current node. $?\exists xFo(x)$ is also the requirement for a formula/content value for the current node. $\langle\uparrow_0\rangle \langle\uparrow_1\rangle Tn(0)$ is the tree-node address, which states that if the parser goes up along the argument (=0) node relation and then the functor node (=1) relation, there is a top node. Another argument node branched from $?Ty(e \rightarrow t)$ is the verb node. ◊ shows the current state of parsing. This node can be addressed as $\langle\uparrow_1\rangle \langle\uparrow_1\rangle Tn(0)$. The two arguments of the verb *iki*- 'beat' are local to each other based on the functor/argument spine. They will be updated as *Hemi'* for $Fo(U)$ and *Mina'* for $Fo(V)$, respectively, from the context in the process of structure building.

Unfolding a structure via verbs alone without an overt subject is common in languages such as Altaic languages, comprised of mainly Mongolic, Tungusic and Turkic languages. It is also a feature of some Indo-Iranian languages like Persian. In Persian, subject is not normally present because verbal particles carry the grammatical information of the subject.

(5) *Shenid-i?* [Persian]
    'Did you [2SG] hear?'

In understanding example (5), we can see that the verbal particle updates the meta-variable U as the second-person pronoun. The lexical action of the particle can be given as in the following section.

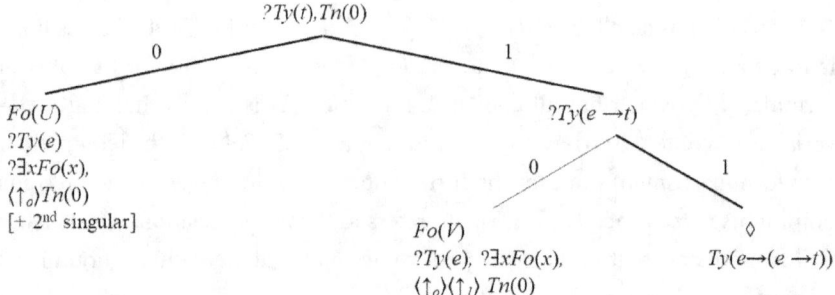

Figure 7.4 Persian verb ending updates the subject.

7.2.5. Verbal Projection of a structure: Lao

Modelling flexible word order does not cause any ad hoc device in DS. Consider the following example from Kazakh. All the examples have the same propositional meaning, and the partial structure built before reaching the main verb *äkel-di* will be the same[8] (see Figure 7.4).

(6)

Bolat	*üj-ge*	*mïsïq-tï*	*äkel-di.*	[Kazakh]
Bolat.NOM	home-DAT	cat-ACC	bring-PST	
Üj-ge	*Bolat*	*mïsïq-tï*	*äkel-di.*	
home-DAT	Bolat.NOM	cat-ACC	bring-PST	
Mïsïq-tï	*üj-ge*	*Bolat*	*äkel-di.*	
cat-ACC	home-DAT	Bolat.NOM	bring-PST	
Üj-ge	*mïsïq-tï*	*Bolat*	*äkel-di.*	
home-DAT	cat-ACC	Bolat.NOM	bring-PST	

'Bolat brought the cat home.'

Regardless of the word-order variation, the following information is collected before the verb. The dative particle *-ge* and accusative particle *-tï*: create an anticipation for the ditransitive verb, accumulating the partial requirements from each expression. Note that in Kazakh too, the nominative NP is not obligatory. In Chapter 8, I shall introduce the lexical macro which (a sequence of) particles project.

Consider the following example from Lao, which is a language belonging to the B group. In explaining Riau Indonesian, Gil considers how structural relationships in this language are largely underspecified and it is only context which updates it in the specified relation.[9] In Lao, argument and particle realization is very flexible. Adjectives, verbs or other nominal expressions can unfold a structural skeleton. The detailed expectation, for instance, the value for the meta-variable U and V, is only inferred from the context.

(7)
    a. *nyaaw* [Lao]
       long
       '(It was) long.'
    b. *leum*
       forget
       '(I have) forgotten (it).'
    c. *hen*
       see
       '(I) saw (it).'

It is assumed that the structure-building goal is universal across languages. Yet, the actual expectation of unfolding sub-structures varies between languages. As for pro-drop languages as in our target languages, it is possible that verb and verbal endings unfold a complete proposition with underspecified arguments. At the same time, in those languages, when verb or verbal endings are not yet available, NP clusters can build a partial structure through use of the particles we shall now turn to. In this way, a structure is built without any waiting or delay. Genre and style also produce a different projection. For instance, in poetry or in other literary genre, the normal syntactic projection will depend on the poetic or literary tools and these will also influence particle realization. It may be considered grammatical but unnatural, or even absurd, for subjects and objects to be all expressed explicitly in poetry – even in languages like English (see Figure 7.5).

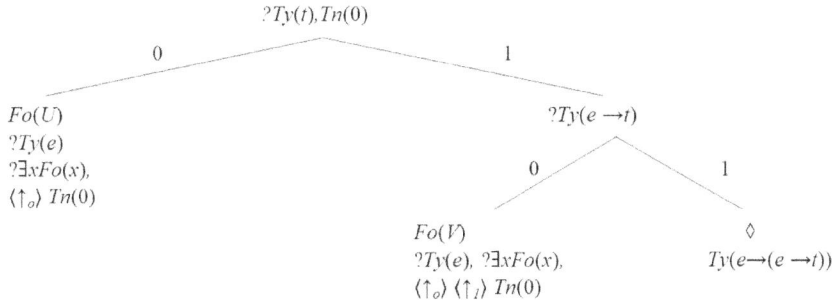

Figure 7.5 Lao verbs: Fo(U) and Fo(V) will be updated from the context.

7.2.6. Ways of structure-building: Locally versus non-locally

In DS, there are three methods of structure building: (i) local/immediate update (via an operation of local *Adjunction); (ii) non-local/non-immediate update (via an operation of *adjunction); (iii) a general update (via an operation of generalized adjunction). Here the Kleene asterisk (*) is used to characterize an underspecified tree relation. The essence of this relation is identical to the functional uncertainty adopted in LFG (Kaplan and Zaenen 1989).

In the original design, Kempson et al. (2001) and Cann et al. (2005) assumed that all the three structure-building options are in principle available at any point of structure building as long as their input condition is met. Put simply, DS assumes that, in principle, any argument can be resolved within its ongoing local predicate-argument structure, in some non-local, non-immediate propositional domain, or in a proposition that is not related to the local proposition through a predicate-argument relation. The availability of these three options can explain flexible structure building. Generalized adjunction rule are available but the structural relationship it projects is so weak in natural language it is therefore less useful in terms of making syntax predictable. In this chapter, we focus on local and non-local adjunction rules only.

Modality $<\uparrow_*>Tn(a)$ is an underspecified tree relation, ranging over any sequence of argument (0) or functor (1) relations. As it stands, $<\uparrow_*>Tn(a)$ shows a very weak relation in that the only thing it requires is for this node to be dominated by $Tn(a)$. The rule that builds such an underspecified relation is called *adjunction and a localized variant requiring resolution within a single predicate-argument structure is called local *adjunction (see Cann et al. 2005 for a detailed formalism).

7.2.6.1. Formal descriptions of *adjunction and local *adjunction

*Adjunction creates an unfixed structural relation that may be resolved either locally or non-locally.

*Adjunction $Tn(0), \ldots ?Ty(t)$

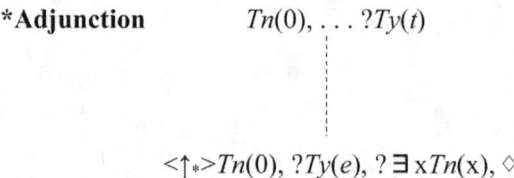

$?\exists xTn(x)$ is a requirement that the tree-node predicate Tn should have a value (i.e. the tree-node address should be fixed). $<\uparrow_*>Tn(0)$ is quite general, hence the host expression can be fixed in 'any' structure – local or non-local – matrix or any level of subordinate clause. There is a localized version of this rule called local *adjunction. Simply speaking, this rule specifies that the unfixed structural relation should be satisfied in the local domain.

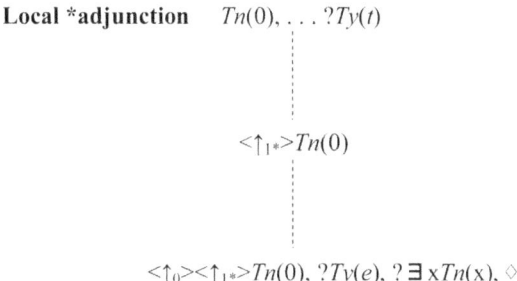

Local *adjunction $Tn(0), \ldots ?Ty(t)$

$\langle\uparrow_{1*}\rangle Tn(0)$

$\langle\uparrow_0\rangle\langle\uparrow_{1*}\rangle Tn(0), ?Ty(e), ?\exists x Tn(x), \diamond$

The modality [10] $\langle\uparrow*\rangle$ is an underspecified modal relation, which can be extended into any functor (1) or argument (0) relation. Some structural relations may be fixed later during the course of structure-building, even across clause boundaries. This is the basis of long-distance dependency. Non-local update can be formalized by the same modality $(=\langle\uparrow*\rangle)$ as the local update, but without any locality restriction.

7.2.7. Constructive case particle and local update

In many of our target languages, particularly those in A group, case morphology can induce the local update of argument nodes decorated by NPs from such an unfixed relation to a fixed relation before the structural array is unfolded by a predicate. It is cross-linguistically the case that a sequence of consecutive expressions, unless intervened by other factors such as prosodic break, tend to be interpreted in the same local domain. This local domain may turn out later as a simple matrix clause or this domain may be the part of a larger clause that is to be linked later through coordination or subordination. Such a decision will take place at the later stage, but what seems to be obvious is that the given case particles can project the structural array possibly in the same local structure in a default situation.

Consider the Korean example in (8). In (8), all three NPs underlined will be built in the same local structure. Yet, (8a) ends up as a simple clause, whereas (8b) is wrapped up as an argument of the larger, forthcoming clause. The later destiny is only known at the later stage, yet still Korean parsers can build a structure with the three consecutive NPs – all in one local domain.

(8)
   a. <u>Bill-hanthey Jina-ka cake-lul</u> cwu-esse [Korean]
      Bill-DAT J-NOM cake-ACC give-(PAST+INFORMAL+INTIMACY)
   b. <u>Bill-hanthey Jina-ka cake-lul</u> cwu-esseta-ko . . .
      Bill-DAT J-NOM cake-ACC give-(PAST)-COMP

In DS, case particles are defined as filters on the output. For instance, a nominative case particle is defined as a filter which fixes its argument in the local structure as the subject $(\langle\uparrow_0\rangle Tn(a), ?\langle\uparrow_0\rangle Ty(t)$ for some node $Tn(a))$, while an accusative marker is defined as a filter which guarantees that the argument is fixed at some point as the object $(\langle\uparrow_0\rangle\langle\uparrow_1\rangle Tn(a), ?\langle\uparrow_0\rangle Ty(e \to t)$. Consider example (9). In this Korean example, we don't see the verb yet but a sequence of two case-marked NPs:

(9)   Jina-ka Mina-lul . . . [Korean]
      J-NOM M-ACC

In the following, I shall show how the partial structure is built by each case particle. At the first stage (a), the lexical action shows the application of local *adjunction, as the general computational actions for introducing argument nodes. Then as in (b) when *Jina* meets the requirement of *?Ty(e)*, it fills the content value for the node. Then, as in (c) the case particle *-ka* fixes the node as the nominative argument of the local structure. A sample tree update induced by nominative case filter *-ka* in parsing a nominative NP *Jina-ka* is given in Figure 7.6.

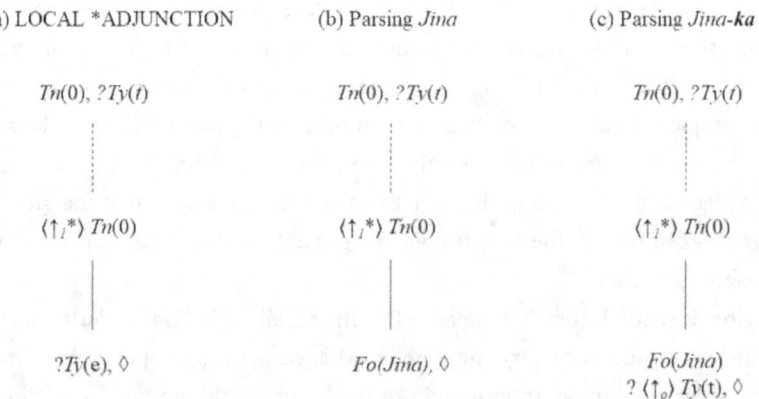

Figure 7.6 Local structure building via case particle *-ka*.

(5) Routinised Update

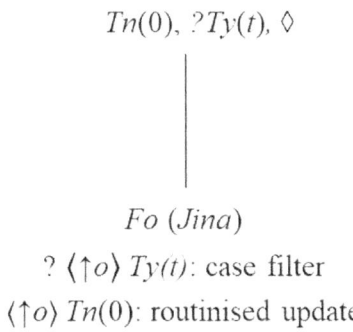

Figure 7.7 Routinized update via the accusative particle -lul.

Stage (c) in Figure 7.6 is triggered by a case particle which plays a role as a filter. Such an update is very common in A-group languages, hence often this process is automated and routinized within grammar. What I mean by this is simply that the parser does not search all the possible routes of structure building when they face nominative case-marked NP like *Jina-ka*. Instead, they will store the local structure-building option as a default routine unless otherwise stated and intervening prosody appears between expressions. Hence, a sample tree update induced by the accusative case filter *-lul* in parsing an accusative NP *Mina-lul* can be simplified as shown in Figure 7.7.

The application of local *adjunction is, however, not unrestricted. Without resolving the underspecified tree-node address, the parser cannot use the same adjunction rule again. This is the same with the application of *adjunction.[11] In parsing *Jina-ka* and *Mina-lul*, the unfixed tree node relation is immediately resolved after parsing *Jina-ka*. Hence, there is no clash of nodes. Stepwise enrichment as driven by the case filter in structure-building is analogous to anaphora resolution. In Chapter 8, I shall show how the routinization process induces a lexical macro and also will explore constructive particles in our target languages.

7.2.8. Locality as routine: Local update as routinized update

Because of constructive case particles, structural association can be made early far ahead of a verb. In principle, as mentioned earlier, the case particles only present structural requirement and do not specify the address of the host structure. That said, the node can be introduced in three ways: (i) local *adjunction (i.e. immediate growth), (ii) *adjunction (non-immediate growth), and (iii) generalized adjunction (i.e. arbitrary growth). Though in principle all three operations maybe available, Kiaer (2007, 2014) argued that localized options are stored as the default structure-building option. Kiaer (2007) proposes that in a default situation the underspecified node addressed in this way will be updated as $<\uparrow_0><\uparrow_1><\uparrow_1>$Tn(0) through local *adjunction.

This process of localization is prevalent not only in Korean but also in other languages. Cann et al. (2005) coined the term 'routinization' within DS formalism in order to explain the automated lexical actions. The evidence of routinization is found in typological variation as well as in language change. Neither diachronic nor synchronic variation displays all the logically possible alternatives, but mostly a certain very limited set of variations (Hawkins 2004, 2014). Kiaer (2007, 2014) further proposed for the localized structure building as a default structural routine in example (11).

(10) Preference routinized/encoded in the grammar
    a. Local *adjunction (i.e. immediate growth) > *adjunction (non-immediate growth) > generalized adjunction (i.e. arbitrary growth)

Following the principle of efficiency, I propose that human parsers will build a structure as locally as possible unless otherwise (i.e. intervened by non-local mechanisms such as prosodic break). This can capture a simple mechanism to build all nodes in the same domain if possible and update or specify its semantic and socio-pragmatic content as the communication grows. This is at the heart of efficient syntactic architecture across languages, which needs exploration and explanation. The locality proposal as shown in example (10) is in line with Hawkins' (2004) performance-grammar correspondence hypothesis as shown in (11).

(11) Performance-grammar correspondence hypothesis
    Grammars have conventionalized syntactic structures in proportion to their degree of preference in performance, as evidenced by frequency of use and ease of processing.

Although the role of case particles is crucial in unfolding a sentence, if the structural anticipation for the upcoming form is clear and predictable, then particles tend to remain unsaid (Kiaer and Shin 2012). This is particularly frequent in spoken data. It seems that the richer the context the utterance has, the richer the structural routines available. Sociolinguistic factors also play a crucial role in supplying register-specific cues which enable human parsers to build a structure in an incremental, predictable manner. The routinization patterns as these and diverse sources of incrementality in Korean and other languages need further attention in future study.

Sometimes, language-specific routines are set as a result of frequent uses over time. Hence, even when there is no morphological marker, as in B-group languages, routines will project a provisional structure where the interpretation can be built seamlessly. In (12), the Thai example shows a list of verbs without any subject, direct or indirect object. However, Thai speakers can establish the coordinated structures between two sets of verbs and reach the interpretation given in (12). This example is from Smyth (2002).

(12)
dtɔ̂ɔng rîip bpai sɯ́ɯ hâi [Thai]
must hurry go buy give
'(I) must rush off and buy some for her.'

This can be only explained by the structural routines that Thai speakers have already in their mental grammar.

7.2.9. Non-local structure building: Surprising constituent and intervening prosody

Local structure building supported by structural routinizations, however, is overridden when there is an intervening prosody. There is ample cross-linguistic evidence (see Kiaer 2007). In the case of Korean, intonational phrase (IP) boundary plays the role of triggering non-local structure building (Kiaer 2007). Similar function of IP boundary is found in Kazakh too (Christopher 2018). According to Jun (1993, 2000), in Korean an IP contains one or more APs and is marked by a boundary tone realized at the end of the phrase (e.g. L\%, H\%, LH\%, HL\%, LHL\%, HLH\%, LHLH\%). Consider (13). Kiaer (2007) reports that the final syllable of dative particle *-they* in *-hanthey* is significantly longer when the expression is interpreted non-locally than when it is interpreted locally.

(13)
    a. Direct-object and indirect-object NP cannot form a cluster due to the IP boundary

{Ku-teddy-lul}%	{Mina-hanthey}	emma-nun appa-ka	Christmas-senmwul-lo
The teddy-ACC	Mina-DAT	mum-TOP dad-NOM	Christmas-present-INST

Sarah-hanthey	cwusiessta-ko	malhaysseyo.
Sarah-DAT	gave-COMP	said

'Mother said to Sarah that dad gave a teddy to Mina as a Christmas present.'

b. Direct-object and indirect-object NP forms a cluster due to the IP boundary

???{Ku-teddy-lul	Mina-hanthey}%	emma-nun appa-ka	Christmas-senmwul-lo
The teddy-ACC	Mina-DAT	mum-TOP dad-NOM	Christmas-present-INST
<u>Sarah-hanthey</u>	cwusiessta-ko	malhaysseyo.	
Sarah-DAT	gave-COMP	said	

'Mum said to Mina that Dad gave a teddy to Sarah as a Christmas present.'

Kiaer (2007) reports through online cross-modal self-paced reading comprehension that (13b) shows significant delay when the second dative NP *Sarah-hanthey* 'to Sarah' (underlined) is read. This is before reaching any verb at the end. The delay occurs because the first dative NP *Mina-hanthey* is built in the same local structure together with the preceding accusative NP *ku-teddy-lul* 'the teddy' in (13b) unlike in (13a), where such a clustering is intervened through an IP boundary.

When the underlined cluster is formed as in (13b), it is obvious that it is to be interpreted within the embedded clause. Hence, when another dative *NP Sarah-hanthey* 'to Sarah' is read, the human parser cannot but be surprised as the slot is already filled by the dative NP *Mina-hanthey* 'to Mina'. As a result, the processing is delayed. This is a clear-cut evidence of pre-verbal, incremental structure building in Korean. Also it shows how prosody plays a role in whether to build the adjacent expressions together or not. The IP final syllable is lengthened significantly and is optionally followed by a pause. An AP contains one or more words (but often one word) and is defined by phrasal tones, either LHLH or HHLH. The AP initial tone can be high or low depending on the AP initial segment. Based on Kiaer (2007, 2014) I propose the constructive role of IP boundary in Korean as follows.

(14) Constructive meaning of IP boundary tones
    a. Absence of IP boundary tones: 'continue' the structure building. Structure building is not yet complete.
    b. Presence of IP boundary tones: either 'de-localize (or disconnect)' structure building and initiate a new structure or 'finish-off' structure building.

Pragmatic Syntax   153

Kiaer (2007, 2014) shows how the interaction between particles and prosody can explain the process of surprising constituent formation from real-time understanding perspective. Consider (15).

(15) <u>Password-lul</u>   Kim-kemsa-nun   Park-kica-ka   karuciecwuessta-ko
    <u>spy-hanthey%</u>
    Password-ACC   Kim-prosecutor-   Park-journalist-   told-COMP
    spy-DAT   TOP   NOM
    malhayssta.
    said
    'Prosecutor Kim said that it is journalist Park who told the spy the password.'

In understanding (14), when the sequence of two NPs *Password-lul spy-hanthey* 'Password to the spy' is parsed as underlined, the accusative particle *-lul* and dative particle *-hanthey* may build a partial sequence as circled. This structure is built locally in the same structure following structural routinization, which puts local structure building as a default option. This early cluster then will wait until the possible slot from the main structure becomes available. This process of de-localization is triggered by the IP boundary following the sequence (see Figure 7.8).

Figure 7.8 is from Kiaer (2007: 277) and it shows the step just before structure building for (15) is to be finished. What this step shows is that the structural anticipation built by a sequence of particles is finally met and confirmed by the verb. Crucially, the initial partial structure is built by the help of constructive particles, structural routines and prosody far ahead of reaching a verb, which only confirms the early structure building.

My hunch is that, cross-linguistically, it is the prosody at least in spoken communication that perhaps together with other non-verbal behaviours signals

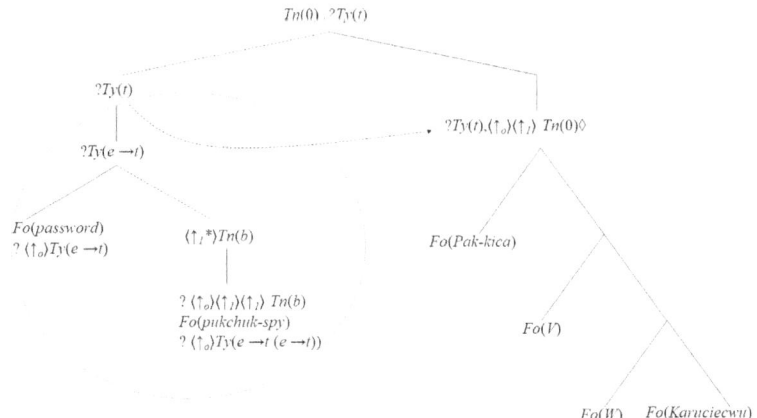

Figure 7.8 Pre-verbal constructions.

the end of a local clause. As we have seen in Chapter 2, it is not uncommon for expressions to occur even after the verb in SOV order languages or even after the particles that are known as morphological indicators for wrapping up a clause. However, in contemporary syntactic architecture, which focuses on written register only, the role of prosody in syntactic architecture is inevitably considered peripheral or even non-existent, disregarding its ever-crucial position in the syntactic architecture across world languages.

7.2.10. Explaining left-to-right asymmetry: The case of Korean

Localization of structure building is also expressed through left-to-right asymmetric structural interpretation and preference asymmetry as we discussed in Chapters 2 and 3. In short, leftward expressions are more flexible in terms of interpretation, although clear preference is given to the localized structure. On the other hand, rightward expressions do not have much freedom but are to be interpreted in the closest local structure only. These all show how localization is encoded in the grammar of Korean.

Consider examples (17) to (19) as discussed in Chapter 2. The dative NP in (16) can, in principle, be interpreted within three different structures:

(16)
Saca-hanthey   *holangi-nun*   *penguini-ka massissnun*   *cookie-lul*
lion-DAT   tiger-TOP   penguin-NOM delicious   cookie-ACC
mantwule-cwukessta-ko   *yaksokhayssta-ko*   *malhayss-eyo.*
make-will.give-COMP   promised-COMP   said-DECL

a. 'A tiger <u>said to a lion</u> that a penguin promised that he will make and give him a delicious cookie.'
b. 'A tiger said to somebody that a penguin <u>promised to a lion</u> that he will make and give him a delicious cookie.'
c. 'A tiger said to somebody that a penguin promised that he will make and <u>give a lion</u> a delicious cookie.'

DS can explain flexibility yet preference of interpretation sensitive to the linear order of the expressions as in (16a) and (16c). In principle, in (16) *Saca-hanthey* 'to a lion' can be built in the upcoming structure locally, non-locally, or in principle in any structure within DS as discussed previously. This captures how the three readings are possible when the dative NP appears at the left-peripheral position.

However, as discussed in Chapter 2, the initial NP is generally preferred to be interpreted within the local structure, in this case the matrix clause signalled by the following -*un* marked NP, rather than in any arbitrary structure. A structure-building choice such as this can be explained in DS as it is assumed that local structure building, considered to be the most cost-saving and efficient across languages, is routinized and chosen as a default option unless prosodic break intervenes. Consider (17) and (18).

7.2.11. Restriction at the right

(17) Dative NP can be interpreted only within matrix structures
Holangi-nun   penguini-ka   massissnun cookie-lul   mantwule-cwukessta-ko
tiger-TOP   penguin-NOM   delicious   cookie-ACC make-will.give-COMP
yaksokhayssta-ko   saca-hanthey   malhayss-eyo.
promised-COMP   lion-DAT   said-DECL
   a. 'A tiger said to a lion that a penguin promised that he will make and give him a delicious cookie.'
   b. 'A tiger said to somebody that a penguin promised to a lion that he will make and give him a delicious cookie.' (This reading is very hard to get.)
   c. 'A tiger said to somebody that a penguin promised that he will make and give a lion a delicious cookie.' (This reading is very hard to get.)

(18) Dative NP can be interpreted only within matrix structures
Holangi-nun   penguini-ka   massissnun   cookie-lul   mantwule-cwukessta-ko
tiger-TOP   penguin-NOM   delicious   cookie-ACC make-will.give-COMP
yaksokhayssta-ko   malhayss-eyo   saca-hanthey
promised-COMP   said-DECL   lion-DAT
   a. 'A tiger said to a lion that a penguin promised that he will make and give him a delicious cookie.'
   b. 'A tiger said to somebody that a penguin promised to a lion that he will make and give him a delicious cookie.' (This reading is very hard to get.)
   c. 'A tiger said to somebody that a penguin promised that he will make and give a lion a delicious cookie.' (This reading is very hard to get.)

The dative NP in (16) can be interpreted flexibly. On the other hand, the same NP is restricted in interpretation in (17) and (18). DS can explain the limited interpretation of (17) and (18) as the structure-building mechanism being sensitive to linear order. In the case of (17), the embedded clause structure building thus far is completed and wrapped up by the use of the complementizer -*ko*. No expressions can undo the already closed-off structure, particularly if the structure is an embedded clause. Once the complementizer seals off a structure building, nothing can be added. Hence, the only place for the dative NP to be interpreted is the matrix clause.

However, as in (18), if this happens at the end of the main clause, final prosody plays the role of closing off the local structure building. When the prosody doesn't clearly close off the structure-building or when the parser realizes the necessity of adding afterthought-like expressions, expressions can be added to the preceding structure and interpreted within the previous one. It is, however, noticeable that there is a clear limitation on the prosodic length of the post-verbal expressions as we have discussed in Chapter 2 (see Kempson and Kiaer 2010 for a detailed formal analysis). Examples in (16) to (18) show how interpretational freedom is sensitive to linear order. Without understanding the linear growth of a structure, the interpretational asymmetry observed earlier is hard to capture and explain.

7.2.12. Enriching meanings across structures: Expressing multimodal, multidimensional meanings

DS also allows the building of paired trees to ensure anaphoric and structural enrichment across a simple sentence via LINK relation. The concept of linking tree structures involves the projection of two tree structures in tandem and a flow of information from one tree to another (Kempson et al. 2001: 104). Initially, the link relation is used in characterizing relative clauses, topic and coordination structures (Cann et al. 2005; Kempson et al. 2001).

The notion of link is useful in explaining context-dependency in anaphora resolution, in that one partial tree is built to provide the context in which some other structure is then built. Tree growth/completion in both trees thus takes place in tandem. The process of completing the first tree takes place in the context of having constructed the intermediate tree first. Relative clause construal provides a core example. Consider English examples.

(19) Added information about *John* through LINK relation
    a. *John returned home.*
    b. *John, who left, returned home.*
    c. *John, who left, whom my mum didn't like, returned home.*
    d. *John, who left, whom my mum didn't like, real idiot, returned home.*

In (19b to d), for example, the added clauses form an independent proposition of $Ty(t)$ and the purpose of adding this clause is to enrich the formula *John* as a basis for interpreting the adjunct string. The relative pronoun *who* must therefore be understood as *John*. With this observation, DS formulates a link relation,

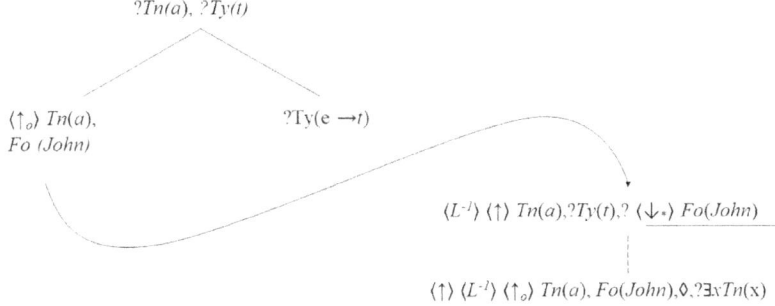

Figure 7.9 Parsing who in (19c).

which yields an independent proposition of $Ty(t)$ which has a copy of $Fo\ (John)$ in the proposed tree structure. The structural relation of the copied formula upon parsing *who* remains underspecified, since it can be either a subject or an object as in (19b) or (19c). Let's consider the building of LINK relation from the node decorated by $Fo\ (John)$. $L\char`^{-1}$ denotes backward link relation (Figure 7.9).

As shown in Figure 7.9, the node built in a LINK structure is structurally underspecified $(?\langle\uparrow_*\rangle L^{-1}\langle\uparrow\rangle Tn(a)$. Hence, it can be interpreted as a subject (19b) or an object (19c). Yet, crucially they share the term '$Fo\ (John)$': the extended structure and information is about *John*.

As in (19d), sometimes the pronoun is absent but rising intonation is used as an indicator that the two structures are linked.

The LINK operation provides an excellent way for us to formulate multidimensional, multimodal meanings that are incrementally built together with the propositional meaning. Most of all, I propose that particles project a LINKed structure which contains information stored in a lexical matrix as we proposed in Chapter 6. We shall explore the application of LINKed structures in other Asian languages in Chapters 8 and 9.

Consider the Korean example given in (20). Notice that *Jina-nun* is not a mere subject. Its grammatical role in the following appendix structure is completely underspecified. What is shared between the underlined structures is that it is the description about *Jina*. For the simplicity of discussion, I skip the detailed glossing for (20).

(20) *-nun* [Korean]
    a. *Jina-nun [cham yeppe.]*
       'Jina is very pretty.'
    b. *Jina-nun [Mina-ka cham joahay.]*
       'Jina, Mina really likes her (=Jina).'

c. *Jina-nun* [*Mina-lul ikiesse.*]
   'Jina, she beat Mina.'
d. *Jina-nun* [*Mina-ka key-lul jwun-saram-ul a-nun saram-iya.*]
   'Jina, she is the person who knows the person whom Mina gave a key.'

-nun projects a lexical matrix as below. The constructive meaning of [+ EXTEND] signals that an appendix structure will follow which is to extend the current expression. Sometimes, rising tone or the same tone copy can also project this constructive meaning (see Chapter 8).

$$\begin{Bmatrix} \text{Constructive dimension}[+\text{EXTEND}] \\ \text{Mood and emotion dimension} \\ \text{Interpersonal dimension}[+\text{SUBJECTIVE}] \\ \text{Style dimension} \end{Bmatrix}$$

The appendix structure will be unfolded in the following way: at first, a node can be introduced by LINK transition and prepare for the appendix structure. Then, when NP *Jina-nun* is parsed, the lexical action of *-nun* may move the pointer back to the root node, while building a new extended structure as normal. Crucially, the appendix structure needs to have an anaphoric copy of the formula *Jina* to make sure that it is about *Jina*. In that sense, the LINKed structure also provides a context from which the anaphoric value of the expression can be updated (see Figure 7.10).

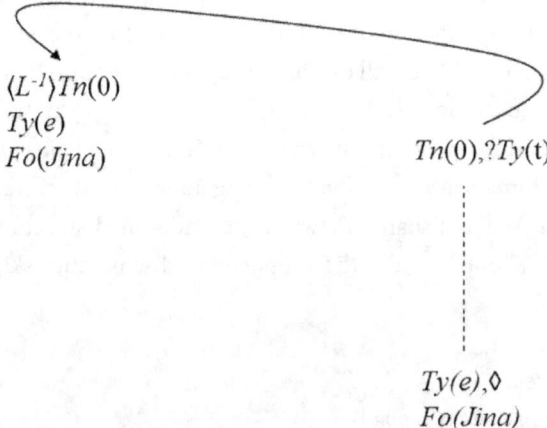

Figure 7.10 Anaphoric copy.

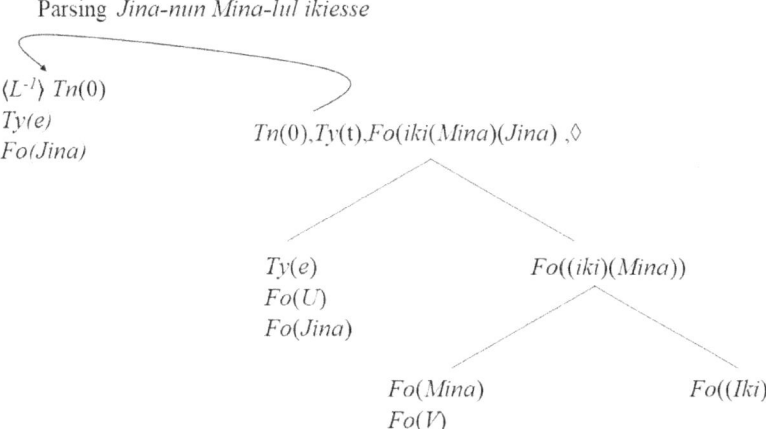

Figure 7.11 Updating the implicit arguments from the context.

After this step, when the accusative NP *Mina-lul* in (20c) is parsed, the tree will be updated as follows. The accusative case particle *-lul* provides a case filter $?\langle\uparrow_1\rangle Ty(e \to t)$ to the node decorated by *Mina-lul*: Now, when the verb *iki* is parsed, a full propositional template will be provided by the verb. As we can see in the following example, meta-variable *Fo(U)* projected by the verb *iki* is updated by the term provided by link adjunction (see Figure 7.11).

LINKed structures will be excellent tools to represent the expressive and attitudinal meanings projected by particles during the structure-building processes. As shown in the previous example, the anaphoric copy from the main lexical item will be kept in the LINKed structure, yet within the LINKed structure the diverse meanings can be added in an incremental manner. We shall come back to this in Chapters 8 and 9.

7.3. Pragmatic syntax hypothesis: Efficiency, expressivity and empathy

Language arises in the life of the individual through an ongoing exchange of meanings with significant others. (Halliday 1978: 2)

In this book, I adopted DS as a logical foundation (i) to encapsulate and explain particles as constructive primitive and also (ii) to show how structural, propositional meanings and speaker-attitudinal meanings are interwoven in tandem. The starting point of this current book is based on the central proposal of pragmatic syntax (Kiaer 2014). In Kiaer (2014), I initially propose that the goal of any linguistic structure building is to optimize syntactic structure building (both production and comprehension) by achieving the meaningful, communicative proposition as quickly as possible with minimal structure-building effort. Simply speaking, people's communication behaviours such as speaking, signing, writing or texting is driven by the desire to make communication efficient (i.e. saving or least effort). Efficiency is an important cause of structural variations as discussed in Chapter 3. It is unconsciously encoded in our brains that we speak in a way that saves any unnecessary cost. I have demonstrated in previous chapters that particle realization is sensitive to the functional load it plays. That is, why particles play more crucial roles in languages where word order is less important in syntactic structure building.

However, this is not the full story. Human decisions are not always geared by efficiency-seeking Ziphian law (Ziph 1949). If efficiency were the only cause, people would communicate as if they were sending a telegram. This is not the case. Apparently inefficient linguistic behaviours are frequently observed in language use. Suppose you are listening to an informal conversation on quite a tricky topic. People use somewhat meaningless filler expressions such as *you know* in English, not once but constantly throughout the conversation.

Kiaer (2014) argued for expressive motivation in syntactic structures. This is also shown in particle behaviours. That said, the choice of particles is sensitive to multiple factors such as the speakers' intention, emotions, attitudes, relation with the audience and the registers where the utterance takes place. With the formal linguistic framework, mostly based on a single written sentence in a strictly formal register, it is almost impossible to understand the rich expressive dimensions of real and literary language use. Altogether this will be considered non-core, peripheral area that does not deserve formalists' attention. Yet, who decides what is core and what is peripheral?[12]

In this book I add empathy as an ever-important driving force in communication. People's linguistic behaviours are influenced by a principle of empathy that is sensitive to socio-pragmatic appropriateness. That is, we speak/write/text/communicate in the ways which are most appropriate in each linguistic situation (e.g. atmospheres, interlocutors, themes) in order to achieve mutual understanding and empathy among a particular language community. As we have seen in Chapter 5, the role of interpersonal relations or the expressive and interpersonal dimension of linguistic behaviours have often been sidelined because the richness of expressions and meanings found in Asian languages is not found in English nor in other European languages. In Asian cultures, the sense of belonging through following the set of social conventions is considered ever crucial. Finding the right particle(s) as well as accompanying prosody and gesture between interlocutors is not just a matter of two individuals' independent negotiation based on their interpersonal relations. Instead, the process is greatly influenced by social factors such as age, social rank and conventions set out by the linguistic community.

The use of the same particles can also create a sense of emotional attachment and empathy. For instance, in Japanese, -*ne* is one of the most popular ending particles in conversations. The function of -*ne* includes requesting confirmation or sympathy and seeking or showing agreement. Cook (1990) further argues that -*ne* is not limited to solicitation of agreement on information content but frequently signals 'affective common ground' between speaker and hearer – requiring the hearer's cooperation (Hasagawa 2014: 299–301). Intonation is also important in this regard. In the online register such as computer-mediated communication (CMC), a set of particles together with different multimodal emojis brings a set of emotions that creates a sense of identity and further belonging as we have seen in Chapter 4.

Based on this observation, I introduce a 3E model in Figure 7.12. I propose that ordinary language users constantly negotiate between these three desires in order to produce the most optimal linguistic behaviours relative to the given communicative environment. This book shows how human parsers labour and interact in order to meet this goal and how such endeavours are captured in the grammar. I also propose that particle behaviours can best be understood when we consider these three driving forces. The linguistic behaviours and patterns we observe in this book are the consequence of human parsers' constant modulation of these three motives. At each occasion, the emphasis and subsequent modulation process may differ, creating room for more diversity in linguistic behaviours (see Figure 7.12).

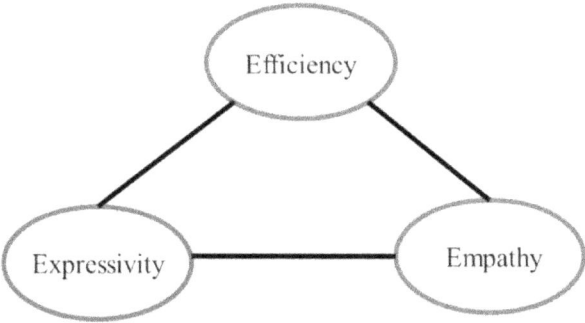

Figure 7.12 Three motives: Efficiency, expressivity and empathy.

So far, I have kept to observations in a monolingual setting. However, in our ever-diversified world, ordinary speakers' daily communication cannot be captured within a single named language. When it comes to the hybrid uses of multiple languages, a monolingual grammar cannot but signal interlocutors' normal forms of communication as 'ungrammatical'. In the next section, I shall revisit the notion of ideal speakers in the initial Chomskian framework.

7.4. Re-considering 'ideal' speakers in the multilingual turn: A remaining puzzle

This notion of ideal speakers and their language use within a vacuum is somewhat false from its conception. The ideal speaker is assumed to speak his/her mother tongue. Yet, notice that the mother tongue is a singular form. The implication is that the ideal speaker is also a monolingual speaker. Monolingualism is indeed an ideology of contemporary theoretical linguistics. However, notice that the majority of, if not all, 'ordinary' speakers in our time interact with each other in a multilingual environment. This is not the case for some people but it is for most people in the world. It seems however that most linguistic theories still have their foundation in the grammaticality judgements of monolingual speakers, mostly in formal, written registers.

Ordinary people in our time, wherever they may be situated, communicate while crossing the borders of languages. Given this, it is worth asking whether the notion of (in)correctness based on the grammar of one single named language should play such a crucial role in the architecture of grammar at all. In the same vein, it is almost too absurd to measure grammaticality or appropriateness based on a one-dimensional understanding of register in one variety of a language without considering the individual's socio-pragmatic situation.

If we really want to observe how people communicate in our time, and to describe and explain the dynamic mechanisms and the underlying architectures of their communication, we need a better manner through which to understand the ways multi- or translingual individuals interact.

García and Wei (2014), among many others, proposed the notion of translanguaging: borderless languaging by ordinary multilingual individuals. Unlike code-switching, *translanguaging* does not require individuals to switch from one language to another, but rather allows a person to choose and assemble semiotic primitives sourced from their entire semiotic repertoire. In this way, the process of *translanguaging* disregards the imposed social and political boundaries between languages. This makes so much sense in understanding Asian languages. Due to a long history of language interaction, multilingualism is a norm in this region. Many semiotic primitives, cultures and values are shared across the borders of languages and nations. Very often, distinguishing one language from another based on respective nation-state statuses is not only difficult but pointless due to their linguistic and cultural commonality.

In translanguaging theory, meanings are not a static, already-established set of semiotic primitives, but rather are recreated in each context by translingual individuals. The core idea of a dynamic lexicon and inter-active meaning making is close to what DS formalism, which I adopt in this book, proposes. Diverse semiotic primitives will be reassembled to create tailor-made meanings suitable for each situation across any named language border. These newly created meanings will together build a multidimensional meaning for the lexical item. As Kiaer (2018) proposed in defining the meanings of each lexical item, etymological meaning is becoming truly borderless as the world becomes much more interwoven than ever before and the English language becomes more visible and impactful worldwide compared to any other period in history. However, the translanguaging method of ordinary, multilingual speakers that is natural to themselves can be understood as inappropriate at best by generativists.

In order to explain the creative, dynamic and transformative meaning making processes, one needs to have a dynamic system that can allow multidimensional meanings composed of a diverse semiotic repertoire, both verbal and non-verbal. The theoretical foundations that can be suitable for multilingual individuals' ordinary language behaviour, or *languaging*, are much needed and long overdue.

I believe that the ultimate grammar formalism should be able to model multilinguals' daily use of language and the underlying interactional competence. Hence, the theory of translanguaging can be an excellent model to provide the conceptual foundation for linguistic modelling. I hope to work on a project of this nature in the near future.[13]

7.5. Summary

In this chapter, I have introduced the DS formalism and also proposed the 3E model. I argue that the desire to make a communication socio-pragmatically appropriate and thus empathetic as well as efficient and expressive is essential in understanding any syntactic variation.

8

Constructive particles and syntactic fluidity

Syntactic structure is built much more flexibly than has generally been assumed in grammar formalisms. Particularly when it comes to spoken syntax, we can also see that context and prosody play a crucial role in its predictability. We also see that languages with flexible word orders have a wide range of particles with combinatory and constructive force. This all shows that it is not verbs alone which contain structural information. In this chapter, I shall show how different mechanisms in DS can be used in explaining incremental structure building in various Asian languages.

8.1. Constructive case particles

Word-order flexibility is typically observed in languages with relatively well-developed morphological case-marking systems (see Erguvanlı 1984, among many others). As Erguvanlı (1984: 5) observes, word order in Turkish has no 'primary' grammatical function, such as signalling grammatical relations (e.g. subject or direct object), or the syntactic form (e.g. question or embedded clause). In our Asian target languages, we find strong correlation between flexible ordering and the availability of constructive particles. If the word order is flexible with SOV preferred ordering, it is much more likely that particles will play the constructive roles rather than verbs. Consider example (1).

(1)   *Mary Bill-la gi-re* [Tibet]
       Mary Bill likes

Due to the flexible word order, this sentence could potentially be ambiguous without *-la*. If *-la* were not present, this would mean that either Mary likes Bill or Bill likes Mary. The *-la* disambiguates the meaning into 'Mary likes Bill'.

As we have seen in Chapters 2 and 3, contemporary linguistic theory, which puts too much emphasis on a fixed word order and the role of verbs, has problems in explaining languages with flexible word order and a rich constructive morphology. From this verb-centred perspective, cross-linguistically common verb-less or nominal structures, particularly in the literary genre or in informal speech, will always be considered exceptional and puzzling.

Indeed, a syntactic fluidity compensated by different socio-pragmatic strategies remains largely unexplained in most contemporary linguistic theories, as I have demonstrated in earlier chapters. In this book, I argue that not only verbs but also morphological case particles or pragmatic pressure-driven principles such as locality are responsible for an incremental structure building together with prosody and context. In particular, particles behave like 'little predicates' by virtue of their structure-unfolding ability. In this chapter, following Kiaer (2007, 2014), I shall propose that case particles project a structural skeleton, which is later to be stored as a lexical macro through routinization. In the following section, I shall show how particle clusters in Korean project a provisional structure.

8.1.1. Particle sequence: Projecting a lexical macro

Kiaer (2007) proposed the constructive role of case particles in Korean, following insight from Nordlinger (1998) (see Figure 8.1). As discussed in Chapter 7, case particles almost automatically project structural anticipation for each nominal expression. This automatic update is routinized in the grammar. In order to capture this frozen, routinized structure-building nature, an alternative stronger characterization for each of the case particles is preferred. Such stronger updates would lead to the partial trees given in Figure 8.1. Bold lines are the structural skeleton projected by a particle cluster annotated.

All macro actions in Figure 8.1 are the updates of the relation triggered by local *adjunction. Additionally, all the relations updated by case particles can be subsumed under $\langle\uparrow_0\rangle\langle\uparrow_1^*\rangle Tn(a)$. For instance, $\langle\uparrow_0\rangle\langle\uparrow_1^*\rangle Tn(a)$ includes $\langle\uparrow_0\rangle Tn(a)$ (=nominative particle -ka update), $\langle\uparrow_0\rangle\langle\uparrow_1\rangle Tn(a)$ (=accusative particle -lul update), $\langle\uparrow_0\rangle\langle\uparrow_1\rangle\langle\uparrow_1\rangle Tn(a)$ (=dative particle -hanthey update).

Given this characterization, a sequence of case-marked NPs can be locally fixed together as one syntactic unit. In each case, the structural relation projected by the case-marked NP can be subsumed as the update of an underspecified structural relation, introduced by local *adjunction. The macro actions proposed in Figure 8.1 can be adjusted and adapted in other languages too as we shall soon return.

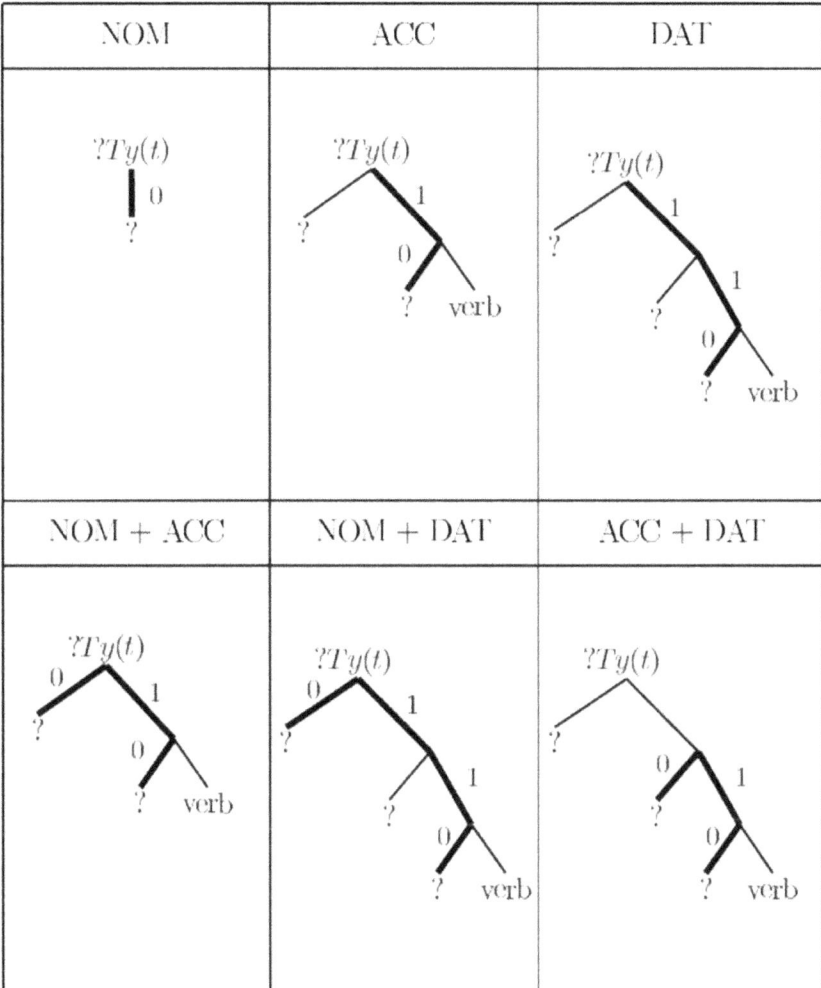

Figure 8.1 Lexical macros via case particles (Kiaer 2007: 124).

8.1.2. Description of constructive case particles

Below, I shall present some key particles, mostly from A-group languages, which exhibit flexible orders with rich case particles and the pragmatic realization of expressions. I shall show examples of particles that play the role of unfolding a simple local structure in these languages. One thing to note is that, just as argument and adjunct distinction in many of these languages is not so straightforward, it is not clear at times whether the particles can be considered constructive or expressive (Chapter 1).

For instance, in Japanese, locative or instrumental particles can be understood as constructive particles yet perhaps not as primary constructive particles. They can specify syntactic as well as semantic and pragmatic meanings (see Table 8.1).

From the tables below with particle repertoires, what we in fact discover is that even if all these languages have constructive case particles, each language has a unique set of constructive particles and the way they are realized differs between languages. Consider again our target languages.

A group: Flexible word orders with rich case particles, pragmatic realization of expressions (i.e. pro-drop), in general particle-rich languages such as Arabic, Korean, Japanese, Tamil, Hindi, Urdu, Bengali, Tibetan, Tagalog, Turkish, Persian, Mongolian, Sanskrit (most of them except Standard Arabic show strong verb-finality).

Table 8.1 Constructive particles in Japanese

Case particle	Example	Usage
Nominative	*Ga*	*sensei ga* 'the teacher'
Accusative	*Wo* (sometimes romanized as *–o*)	*sensei wo* 'the teacher'
Genitive	*No*	*sensei no* 'of the teacher'
Locative (direction/static)	*Ni*	*eki ni* 'to/at the station'
Instrumental	*De*	*densha de* 'by train'
Locative (dynamic)	*De*	*eki de* 'at the station'
Source	*E*	*eki e* 'to the station'
Directional	*Kara*	*eki kara* 'from the station'

Table 8.2 Constructive particles in Bengali

Case particle	Example	Usage
Nominative	Unmarked	*bandhu* 'friend'
Genitive	*-r*	*bandhu-r* 'of the friend'
Accusative	*-ke*	*bandhu-ke* 'friend'
Locative	*-e, -y, -te*	*ghar-e* 'in the room'

Thompson (2010).

Table 8.3 Constructive particles in Hindi

Case particle	Example		Usage
	Singular	Plural	
Nominative	Unmarked	*-e*	*kamraa* 'room', *kamr-e* 'rooms'
Oblique	*-e*	*-ō*	*kamr-e* 'room', *kamr-ō* 'rooms'
Vocative	*-e*	*-o*	*kamr-e*, 'O room!' *kamr-o*, 'O rooms!'

Acc/Dat arguments are in oblique case marking. Context matters to distinguish Agnihotri (2013).

Table 8.4 Constructive particles in Urdu

Case particle	Example		Usage
	Singular	Plural	
Nominative	unmarked	unmarked	*larka*, 'boy'
Oblique	-ē	-ōm	*larkē kā* 'of the boy'
			larkōm kā 'of the boys'
Vocative	-ē	-ō	*larkē* 'O boy!'
			larkō 'O boys!'

Schmidt (1999).

Table 8.5 Constructive particles in Turkish

Case particle	Example	Usage
Absolute	unmarked	*ev*, 'house'
Definite accusative	*-(y)ı-, -(y)i-, -(y)u-, -(y)ü-*	*evi*, 'house'
Dative	*-(y)a-, -(y)e-*	*eve*, 'by the house'
Locative	*-da-, -de-, -ta-, -te-*	*evde*, 'at the house'
Ablative	*-dan-, -den-, -tan-, -ten-*	*evden*, 'from the house'
Genitive	*-(n)ın-, -(n)in-, -(n)un-, -(n)ün-*	*evin*, 'of the house'

Table 8.6 Constructive particles in Persian

Case particle	Example	Usage
Nominative	unmarked	*ketāb* 'the book'
Oblique	*-o*	*ketāb-o* 'the book'

Lazard (1992).

Table 8.7 Constructive particles in Mongolian

Nominative	unmarked	*nom* 'book'
Accusative	*-g/ig*	*nomig* 'book'
Genitive	*-n/in*	*nomin* 'of a book'
Dative/Locative	*-d*	*nomd* 'in a book'
Ablative	long vowel + *-s*	*nomos* 'from a book'
Instrumental	long vowel + *r*	*nomoor* 'with (instr.) a book'
Comitative	*-t-i*, dependent on vowel, for example, *-toi and -tei*	*nomtoi* 'with a book'

A Mongolian Grammar: Outlining the Khalkha Monologian with Notes on the Burlat, Kalamuck, and Ordoss Mongolian (1926). Print.

Table 8.8 Constructive particles in Tagalog

	Common singular	Common plural	Personal singular	Personal plural
Direct	ang, 'yung (iyong)	ang mgá, 'yung mgá (iyong mgá)	si	sina
Indirect	ng, n-ung (niyong)	ng mgá, n'ung mgá (niyong mgá)	ni	nina
Oblique	sa	mgá	kay	kina

Kroeger (1993).

Table 8.9 Constructive particles in Tibet

Absolutive	Unmarked	kekän 'the teacher'
Agentive	Ki'	kekän-ki' 'by the teacher'
Genitive	Ki	kekän-ki 'of the teacher'
Oblique	La	pönpo-la 'to the leader'
Ablative	Nä	lhāsa-nä 'from Lhasa'
Associative	Tang	āma-tang pūkutso 'the mother and the children'

Colloquial Tibetan: A Textbook of the Lhasa Dialect (English and Tibetan Edition) (Tibetan) Bilingual Edition.

B group: Flexible word orders yet no case particles, pragmatic realization of expression (i.e. pro-drop), in general particle-rich languages, mostly SVO order preferred, as in Mandarin Chinese, Thai, Indonesian, Vietnamese, Khmer, Lao, Burmese (SOV preferred).

Compared to A-group languages, B-group languages are often known to have more rigid word orders, yet many argue that there is still no basic word order in these languages. For instance, Li and Thompson (1981: 26) state that 'no basic word order can be established' in Mandarin. In languages like Khmer, SVO word order is used in a relatively predictable way, yet occasionally particles also play the role of constructing the structure. In example (2a and b), *nij* marks the possessive relation, and *nəw* the accusative relation in the structure building.

(2)
    a. *puəʔma : ʔ **nij** kʰɲom*   [Khmer]
        'My friend'
    b. *kʰɲom ʔaoj cru : k **nəw** muəj camnuən*
        'I gave the pig a bunch of bananas.'

In languages such as Burmese, the use of case particles is optional. Although these particles may be considered constructive particles, they may also be understood as expressive particles. As in many other languages, Burmese case particles are simply monosyllabic morphemes. *Ká* expresses source – locative and temporal – and can be translated as 'from'. *Ká* can cover many other meanings as well as the normal subjecthood (e.g. phà-ká 'the frog' as a subject). Likewise, *-ko* indicates direct objecthood (e.g. *phà-ko* 'the frog' as a direct object), but it can also denote movement to a location. *-ko* can easily be dropped if the location is known or frequently mentioned (Jenny and San San Hnin 2017). In languages such as Arabic, particles are often visible in spoken varieties but not in the written register.

Lao is one of the languages showing flexible word order but no reliance on constructive case particles when it comes to unfolding a structure. Enfield (2007) shows that indeed Lao lacks disambiguation in case marking, or, in our terms, constructive case marking. He notes that pragmatics play a more crucial role in disambiguating and building meanings than do lexical particles.

Consider an example from Enfield (2007: 274). Example (3) could potentially be interpreted in three different ways. However, Lao speakers have hardly any problem in establishing interpretation. This is simply because they find the argument or participant for the action from the context.

(3) *tam3 khuaj2 taaj3* [Lao]
crash.into buffalo die
i. (She) crashed into a buffalo and died.
ii. (She) crashed into a buffalo and (it) died.
iii. (She) crashed into a buffalo and (the car) died (it stalled).

Enfield (2007: 276) puts it as follows:

> That this ubiquitous relaxation of the word order patterns coexist with a total lack of morphological marking of semantic roles or grammatical relations might suggest chaos. But in real contexts of usage, Lao speakers have no difficulty in communicating. . . . When core referential information is not symbolically encoded in the grammar, <u>potential ambiguities in role and reference relations are readily resolved by features of context, if indeed they need to be resolved</u>. (underlining mine).

Lao is an example of a language where context plays a crucial role in projecting a structural skeleton and disambiguating it when necessary.

Context-dependent structure building can also be applicable to A-group Asian languages. As discussed in Chapter 7, when a structural pattern is repeated over time and routinized, particles tend to disappear as their functional load becomes low. The repeated use of particles not only is redundant but can decrease the expressivity of the work. This is the case in poetry or songs. That said, particles matter in structure building, yet their distribution and function are decided by contextual information and pragmatic value on each occasion. In the following section, I shall present a case study of Tagalog to show how case particles can be used in constructive way.

8.1.2.1. Case study: Tagalog

In terms of word order, Tagalog is very flexible, thus leading to variable sentence and phrase structures. As such, grammatical relations are realized through particles. For example, there are six different ways of saying 'Bea introduced Jasmine to Angela' using the same markers, holding the same grammatical and propositional meaning but varying in order:

(4)
    a. *Ipinakilala ni Bea si Jasmine kay Angela.*
       Introduced GEN-Bea NOM-Jasmine DAT-Angela
    b. *Ipinakilala ni Bea kay Angela si Jasmine.*
       Introduced GEN-Bea DAT-Angela NOM-Jasmine
    c. *Ipinakilala kay Angela si Jasmine ni Bea.*
       Introduced DAT-Angela NOM-Jasmine GEN-Bea
    d. *Ipinakilala kay Angela ni Bea si Jasmine.*
       Introduced DAT-Angela GEN-Bea NOM-Jasmine
    e. *Ipinakilala si Jasmine kay Angela ni Bea.*
       Introduced NOM-Jasmine DAT-Angela GEN-Bea
    f. *Ipinakilala si Jasmine ni Bea kay Angela.*
       Introduced NOM-Jasmine GEN-Bea DAT-Angela
       'Bea introduced Jasmine to Angela.'

The particles *-ni, -si* and *-kay* are constructive particles, as they are grammatically essential in constructing a structure. Generally, Tagalog follows a VSO structure, with variable ways of ordering the noun-phrase complements that follow, provided that the verb remains in the initial position. This tends to be the more natural structure that is preferred by most Tagalog speakers. However, the inversion marker 'ay' can be used to create an SVO structure. For example:

(5)
    a. *Magaling talaga si Angelica.* [VSO]
       Good really NOM-Angelica.
       'Angelica is really good.'
    b. *Si Angelica ay magaling talaga.* [SVO – with inversion marker '*ay*']
       NOM-Angelica 'AY' good really.
       'Angelica is really good.'

It is important to note that the use of *ay* is often regarded as formal or literary by ordinary Tagalog speakers. In everyday conversation, the *ay* can be dropped and replaced with a pause, thereby making the sentence or phrase less stilted to Tagalog speakers:

(6)   *Si Angelica* PAUSE *magaling talaga.* [SVO – with pause]
       NOM-Angelica good really.
       'Angelica is really good.'

The syntactic function of *ay* or a pause, or intonational break, can be captured by lexical actions in DS. Informally, this can be done by proposing that the pause after the nominal NP projects a verbal structure. The register-sensitive nature of particles can also be stored in a lexical matrix as we have discussed in Chapter 6. We shall return to this in Chapter 9.

8.2. Building a complex structure

Apposition-like mechanisms of extending and enriching structures are particularly popular across languages. In Chapter 7, I introduced the notion of LINKed structures. This mechanism enables us to build an extended complex structure – mainly through subordination or coordination.

Schematically, as in Figure 8.2, all the information built through linked structures are put together incrementally and built at the same time as propositional meaning is being built. Crucially, each piece of information

$$\{L1 + L2 + L3 \ldots\}$$
Left -- ▶ Right

Figure 8.2 Building a sequence of LINKed structures.

projected by each LINKed structure (L) is modulated as structure-building continues, making the meanings of the utterance multidimensional and rich, yet also consistent throughout the utterance unit, in accordance with the MMH proposed in section 5.2.

Each additional structure is conjoined, sometimes through visible particles, pauses or similar intonational patterns. Kiaer (2014) showed that, in the case of Korean, repeated particles are used with similar intonational patterns to ensure the addition and specification of meanings.

(7)   (*Kwail-ul*) ↗ (*sakwa-lul*) ↗ (*fuji-lul*) ↗ *saoseyo.*   [Korean]
      Fruit-ACC   apple-ACC   fuji-ACC   bring.please
      'Please bring fuji apple as/among fruit.'

In (7), the direct object, accusative marker *-lul* is repeated but, at the same time, a similar rising tone (↗) is repeated. In the case of (7), all words are two syllables. It is noticeable often those (sequence of) additional structures share prosodic length. Consider the below example from Persian, where *–ra/-ro* is repeated to update the direct object as is done in Korean.

(8)   *Mive-ro angur-ro dust dar-am*   [Persian]
      Fruit-RA grape-RA like-1SG
      'I like grape among fruit.'

Updating and extending a structure in this manner is prevalent cross-linguistically, particularly in informal speech. Aside from apposition-like structures, there are variable structures where one can also have a mother notion that is further extended on the spot or afterwards as a sort of afterthought. This manner of updating a structure can be explained as applying a sequence of LINKed structures.

Consider the two Lao examples:

(9)   *dtaay laew po han*   [Lao]
      die PRF father TPC.DIST
      '(He)'d be dead, the father.'

(10) *ao mia hao nii*
      take wife 1.FA TPC
      'Took a wife, I (did).'

As we have seen in Chapter 7, according to DS formalism, the pronominal subjects in these examples can remain as a meta-variable U, underspecified at the beginning of the utterance, while an adjunct structure is built. Later, when the specified values are found, these values will update the meta-variables in both main and adjunct or appendix structure: as the father in (9) and the first-person pronoun in (10). This is the basis of understanding topic construction in DS (Kempson, Cann and Kiaer (2006)).

Consider Thai examples (11) and (12). The underlined nominal, following immediately like an afterthought, enriches the meaning of the agent or the subject of the proposition.

(11)
    pɔ̂ɔ <u>kǎo</u> sɯ́ɯ rót [Thai]
    Father, he buy car

(12)
    kruu <u>kǎo</u> mâi maa
    Teacher, he not come

This update however is sensitive to prosody. A quick pause is taken between the words 'father' and 'he', as well as 'teacher' and 'he' to signify that the pronoun is being used with that subject. If, however, the words are said in rapid succession, the listener will assume possession, that is, 'His father bought a car' and 'His teacher didn't come.' It could also be possible that the speaker is getting attention of his/her father or a teacher and saying that someone else bought a car or didn't come. This is determined from the social context. Furthermore, the words ค่ะ (ka) or ครับ (kráp) would likely be used after addressing them, since these are titles that deserve respect.

In (12), the host noun, in this case, an address term (the teacher), is updated with clausal information. This update can also be explained via the LINK operation. Note that the essence of building a LINKed structure from the main structure is the shared lexical item. This requirement is met in the earlier examples of Lao and Thai – from the immediately following context. Indeed, various forms of enriching mechanisms are available in all our target languages. For instance, well-known Persian *ezafe* structures can also be understood as a way of updating the information in the base structure.

(13)
    ketab-<u>e</u>   *man*   *ru-y<u>e</u>*   *miz*   *ast*   [Persian]
    book-ez   I (my)   on-ez   table   is
    'My book is on the table.'

In this Persian example, the underlined *-e* vowel ensures that the repeated expressions are all linked together in one structure. Expressions put together via *ezafe* structures often have a head and complement relation. In this case, we can understand the repeated use of *-e* vowel and the subsequent prosody project LINKed structures in a sequential manner.

8.3. Summary

In this chapter, we have discussed the roles of constructive particles in flexible syntax, presenting examples from both A- and B-group languages. I also showed how the LINK operation in DS can be used in explaining building an extended clause. There are numerous other structures that allow for the flexible building of diverse, multiple pieces of information in an extended structure. The repeated uses of particles or prosodic triggers ensure that the given expressions are to be construed in the same utterance domain rather than in different, independent domains. This rule of locality has been stored as universal structure-building routines across human languages, particularly effective in spoken communication. Simply put, unless otherwise indicated, human parsers put together fragmentary information in the same local domain to build and enrich the existing meanings rather than initiating independent structures. It is mainly a prosodic break or contextual factors that encourage parsers to stop this process of enriching and updating a term or a structure and move on to the next. The dynamic interaction between these devices ensures that syntactic structure builds seamlessly and predictably across users. I believe that this reflects the innate syntactic competence of the human parser and must be modelled as part of any linguistic theory.

9

Expressive and attitudinal particles

Particles express a range of speakers' emotions and attitudes and add multiple levels of meaning derived from expressivity and empathy. As we shall explore in this chapter, particles contain a rich repertoire of emotional and attitudinal meanings and are able to express encouragement, enthusiasm, endearment, friendliness, affection, (dis)agreement, surprise, (dis)belief, doubt or certainty, hesitation and many more. Some particles can make an utterance sound feminine, while others add a masculine nuance. Crucially, many particles are used to reflect interpersonal relations. Furthermore, particles can strengthen or soften an utterance, and make it casual, assertive, emphatic, or formal. So-called topic and focus particles are well known, but the array of functions and meanings that these particles contribute to the utterance exceed the topic/focus discussion in the literature; they are better described as perspective and attitudinal particles, as we discussed in Chapter 6.

Particles can also have a performative function and they are used in making mild or strong requests; they are also used to realize different modalities such as deontic, epistemic, evidential and volitional modalities. This process is much more fine-grained than previously thought and is hard to generalize simply through features such as politeness and honorifics/humilifics. This chapter aims to show the repertoire of diverse expressive and attitudinal meanings which particles in Asian languages exhibit.

9.1. Socio-pragmatic attributes of particles

In this section, I shall discuss the attributes of particles which contain expressive and attitudinal meanings, using the classification of socio-pragmatic meanings I proposed in section 6.3.

(1) Socio-pragmatic dimension

(i)   *Social hierarchy*: a particle can reveal the speaker-hearer dynamic. That is, it can refer to a relationship where the speaker is senior (S > H), equal (S = H) or junior to the hearer (S < H).
(ii) *Interpersonal relations*: a particle reveals a close/intimate and benevolent or respectful relationship between the speaker and hearer.
(iii) *Mood and emotions*: a particle can express the speaker's attitudes, emotions and moods in the utterance.
(iv) *Style*: a particle can reveal whether an utterance is used in monologue, dialogue or a genre such as poetry or prose. It can also show whether it has a masculine or feminine voice.
(v)   *Perspective and attitude*: a particle can express the speaker's attitude and perspective.

First, I shall show the attributes of particles which can reflect social hierarchy and interpersonal relations. These particles are prevalent in Northeast, South and Southeast Asian languages. As briefly discussed in Chapter 4, languages which have been influenced by Buddhism tend to have a fine-grained, complex system for interpersonal relations.

9.1.1. Interpersonal attributes

HON	This is a simple honorific attribute which contains the S < H feature.
HON+++	This is often called super- or ultra-honorific. This attribute is found in particles from Southeast Asian languages such as Thai and Burmese.
HUM	(humbling/humilific) This is an attribute which contains S < H features yet also contains the feature of lowering oneself. Sometimes, the extreme form of humbleness is only expressed non-verbally.
DIST	Distal.
ORD	This attribute shows that the person under description is ordinary.
ROY	This attribute shows that the person under description is royal. For instance, in Burmese, the royal suffix -tɔ/dɔ indicates that an object or person is associated with royalty or high religious status.
HOLY	This particle is used for religious objects.

Expressive and Attitudinal Particles 179

	For instance, in Burmese, the classifier *shu/zu* is generally used with holy objects, such as Buddha images and pagodas, but, in some contexts, may be used to refer to highly respected teachers and saints.
MALE/FEMALE	These attributes reflect gender. In languages which develop detailed kinship and address terms, those terms are often gender sensitive.
FAMILARITY/ INTIMACY	This attribute reflects a familiar and intimate relation between speaker and hearer.

To my understanding, Lao grammar has much more fine-grained attributes for interpersonal relations than any other language. The Lao language encodes even the following relations in the grammar: e = elder, E = spouse, Br = brother, C = child, G = sibling, Fa = father, Mo = mother, Pa = parent.

9.1.2. Mood and emotion-related attributes

Emotion-related particles are diverse and complex. Often, the exclamation mood particle or vocative particle is only functionally glossed as [EXCL] or [VOC]. However, these attributes need to be glossed in more detail than they currently are to be able to capture the complex meanings of emotion-related particles found in these Asian languages. Exclamation often conveys different emotions. Note that most of the moods are realized through different word orders in European languages, yet they are mainly expressed through particles in Asian languages.

EXCL (++)	This attribute reflects exclamation and surprise about a situation. Some particles show weaker exclamation, whereas others show stronger exclamation.
INTR	This attribute reflects a questioning mood.
DECL	This attribute reflects a declarative mood.
PROPOS	This attribute reflects a propositive mood.

Again, in Lao, we see a more sophisticated system of mood. A mood attribute factive is further divided in the following way based on the added meaning attributes. See Enfield's (2007) glossing notations.

FAC. EMPH	factive, emphatic
FAC. EXPLIC	factive, explicating
FAC. FILLIN	factive, filling in presupposed information
FAC. ONRCD	factive, putting on record
FAC. NEWS	factive, proposition is news
FAC. RESIST	factive, resists current stance
FAC. SURPR	factive, proposition is surprising
FAC. WEAK	factive, weakens commitment

The imperative in Lao can be further divided based on added attitudinal meanings such as pleasing, rushing and softening.

IMP. PLEAD	imperative, pleading
IMP. RUSH	imperative, rushing
IMP. SOFT	imperative, softening
IMP. SUGG	imperative, suggesting
IMP. UNIMPD	imperative, states that the addressee is unimpeded

There are two types of obligative mood in Lao based on the strength it imposes to the addressee.

OBLIG. STR	strong obligative
OBLIG. WEAK	weak obligative

Moreover, there are attributes which show complex emotions such as encouragement, enthusiasm, endearment, friendliness, affection, (dis)agreement and surprise. In Burmese, the particles *kwa*, *kwá* and *kwɛ* can intensify the emotion, indicate intimacy or at times express dismay and frustration. The form *kwɛ* is often used to soften the utterance or add a personal note. The utterance to which these particles are added can be a statement, command or question.

9.1.3. Style-related attributes

A particle can reveal whether it is used in monologue, dialogue or a genre such as poetry or prose. It can also represent a masculine or feminine voice. The following attributes are found in Asian languages.

CASUAL	This attribute reflects casualness.
ASSERTIVE	This attribute reflects assertiveness.

(IN)FORMAL	This attribute reflects (in)formality.
FEMINITY	This attribute reflects the feminine voice.
MASCULINTY	This attribute reflects the masculine voice.
POETIC	This attribute reflects a poetic style.
ARCHAIC	This attribute reflects an archaic style.

For instance, in the case of Persian, if the objective suffix particle is added, it adds a poetic or an archaic style. If the particle is not used, it makes the style colloquial.

9.1.4. Perspective and attitude-related attributes

As discussed in Chapter 6, topic or focus particles reflect complex meaning which is hard to be narrowed down as topicality or focality. Perspective- and attitude-related attributes can be summed up as follows.

9.1.4.1. Perspective particles

SUBJECTIVE	This attribute reflects a subjective perspective.
OBJECTIVE	This attribute reflects an objective perspective.
EMPHASIS/ FOCUS/IMPORT	This attribute reflects emphasis, focus or importance.
FORG	This attribute reflects a foregrounding nature.
TOP	This attribute marks the referent as topical, in the centre of interest.

9.1.4.2. Attitudinal particles

SOFTENING	This attribute reflects softening of the utterance.
HEDGE	This attribute reflects signalling caution or probability.
HES	This attribute reflects hesitation.
DOUBT	This attribute reflects doubt.
BELIEF	This attribute reflects belief.
CERTAINTY	This attribute reflects certainty.

Asian languages have a rich repertoire of hedging and softening expressions realized through particles, prosody and non-verbal expressions. The semiotic repertoire presented earlier appears across Asian languages in daily communication. Whether to use the particle or not depends on the speaker's subjective decision. The essence of meanings projected by particles is expressive in nature. That is, as discussed in Chapter 4, they meet the criteria for expressives, repeated as follows.

1. **Independence:** particle meaning contributes a dimension of meaning that is separate from the regular descriptive content.
2. **Non-displaceability:** particle predicates something specific of the utterance situation.
3. **Perspective dependence:** particle content is evaluated from a particular perspective. In general, the perspective is the speaker's, but there can be deviations if conditions are right.
4. **Descriptive ineffability:** speakers are never fully satisfied when they paraphrase particle meanings.
5. **Immediacy:** particles achieve their intended act simply by being uttered; they do not offer much other content.
6. **Repeatability:** if a speaker repeatedly uses particles, the effect is generally one of strengthening the emotive content, rather than one of redundancy.

9.1.5. Asian languages: Rich with socio-pragmatic meanings

As I set out in this book, particles provide important clues to finding and recognizing the interpersonal and socio-pragmatic meanings of utterances in Asian languages. Wymann (1996: 204) notes that languages like Korean could be classified as epistemic modality-prominent languages. This is also the case for most of the Asian languages discussed in this book, which have rich repertoires of modalities. In fact, the modal meanings represented by English auxiliaries evolve to be relatively restricted and limited, compared to the fine-grained, rich meanings which particles in Asian languages can represent. Nevertheless, most of the observation and formal description of modal meanings in contemporary linguistics are based on English auxiliaries. Hence, socio-pragmatically and socioculturally prominent modal meanings which particles in these languages reflect have thus far been inevitably sidelined in the literature. Even in most detailed glossing conventions, the attributes discussed earlier are often ignored and unsaid.[1] Because of this, the complex and dynamic nature of particles in Asian languages has been left untouched in linguistic research.

Wymann also proposed that interpersonal agreement could replace grammatical agreements such as number and gender. This concept is very close to the MMH that I proposed in Chapter 5.

In the following section, I shall present examples of how particles convey different emotional and attitudinal meanings cross-linguistically. Most of the particles which carry socio-pragmatic attributes occur at the end of the utterance (9.2), but some can appear even in the beginning or in the middle of the utterance (9.3). In the following section, I shall present case studies on some key particles from Thai, Tagalog, Burmese, Chinese and Japanese. For other languages, I shall provide a brief description and tables. The goal of this chapter is not to provide a comprehensive survey of particles in Asian languages, but instead to help readers understand the diverse and complex meanings that particles can represent. I shall also briefly discuss how non-verbal expressions play an important role in expressing emotions and attitude (9.4). Finally, I shall show some showcases using the LINK operation in DS to explain how expressive and attitudinal meanings can be integrated in ongoing proposition building.

9.2. Cross-linguistic evidence: Sentence/utterance-final particles (SFP/UFP)

In the following section, I shall explore cross-linguistic evidence demonstrating how SFP/UFP exhibit both expressive and attitudinal meanings.

SFP/UFP normally express different emotional/attitudinal meanings together with the accompanying intonation. In this sense, intonation plays an important role.

9.2.1. Thai: Case study 1

In Thai, particles are placed at the end of a phrase, sentence or discourse. Many are abstract in their meaning and functionality and as such cannot be precisely translated into a single English word.

9.2.1.1. Ka *and* Khrap

ค่ะ (*ka*) and ครับ (*khrap*) are used to show respect and formality to elders, superiors and people with whom the speaker is unfamiliar. *Ka* is the feminine form, meaning that it is only used by women when speaking with both men and other women. *Khrap* is the masculine form.

(2)

ยินดี	ที	ได้รู้จัก	ครับ/ค่ะ
Yindee	*tee*	*dairuujak*	*khrap/ka*
Nice	to	have met (you)	KHRAP/KA

'Nice to meet you.'

The tone of *ka* is different when used in an interrogative sentence rather than a statement, as seen below. There is no tone marker (the vertical line above the first consonant) when *ka* is used as a question. This creates a rising tone rather than a falling tone (Thai has five tones).

(3)

ไป	ไหน	คะ
Bpai	*nai*	*kaa*
Go	where	KAA

'Where are you going?' [polite]

Ka and *khrap* can accomplish a variety of peripheral objectives including, but not limited to, displaying masculinity or femininity, conveying sarcasm, exaggerating a statement and even acting flirtatiously. The greater difference in age, social status and closeness, the more frequently these particles should be inserted into dialogue. A lack of these particles is noticeable and can come across as disrespectful. This confirms that particle can reflect complex sociopragmatic meanings.

9.2.1.2. Ja/Jaa

จ๊ะ (*ja*) or จ๋า (*jaa*) is an informal conversational particle used by older people speaking to younger people. It conveys an intimate tone. This particle can be described as having [S > H], [+ INIMATE] attributes. Although not exclusive to women, *ja* is generally a feminine particle. For example, grandparents, especially grandmothers, will use this particle with their grandchildren, and mothers with their children.

(4)

สวัสดี	จ๊ะ	ลูก
Sawadee	*ja*	*loog*
Hello	JA	children

'Hey kids!'

Also note that the speaker may place added emphasis on the direct object, or hearer of the sentence by referencing them after the particle. This can be the case of *ja* and other particles including *ka, khrap, si* and *na*. Unlike most particles in Thai, this particle can appear sentence-medially.

9.2.1.3. Na

นะ (*na*) is a particle used to make a command, request or statement more firm or emphatic. It is used among familiars, including friends and family. Unlike *ka*, *khrap* and *ja, na* is not gender-specific and is narrower in its usage. For example:

(5)

อย่า	กิน	นะ
Yaa	*gin*	*na*
Don't	eat	NA

'Don't eat that!' [firm particle]

(6)

รอ	ก่อน	นะ
Ro	*gon*	*na*
Wait	before	NA

'Hold on!' [firm particle]

(7)

รัก	นะ
Rag	*na*
Love	NA

'Love you!' [firm particle]

Na can also be used in conjunction with other particles, including *ka, khrap* and *ja/jaa*. This simply makes the statement increasingly emphatic. For example:

(8)

ขอบคุณ	นะ	ค่ะ
Khobkun	*na*	*ka*
Thank you	[NA-KA particle combination, emphatic]	

'Thank you so much!'

9.2.1.4. Si

สิ (*si*) is used specifically for commands. Because of the urgent and forceful tone it conveys, it is typically used by familiars, especially if the speaker is older (i.e. parent to child). The written form is สิ (*si*), which has the same pronunciation.

(9)

เอา	ขนม	มา	กิน	หน่อย	ซิ
Ao	*kanom*	*ma*	*gin*	*noy*	*si*
Take	snack	come	eat	little	SI

'Go grab some snacks for us to eat.' [command particle]

(10)

มา	ซิ	ลูก
Ma	*si*	*loog*
Come	SI	child!

'Come here, kid!' [urgent particle],

(11)

ดู	นี่	ซิ
Du	*ni*	*si*
Look	this	SI

'Look at this!' [command particle]

9.2.1.5. La

ล่ะ (*la*) is a particle similar to *na* and *si* in that it can be used with commands. In addition, *la* is often associated with questions. It serves two main functions: (i) When the speaker needs to know something, *la* is added to the end of a question to emphasize the need for an answer and (ii) *la* can also be used to revert a question back to someone, similar to 'And you?' in English. Like *ja*, *na* and *si*, it is used primarily in casual contexts.

(12)

ทำไม	เขา	ไม่	มา	ล่ะ
Thammai	*khaw*	*mai*	*maa*	*la*
Why	he/she	not	come	LA

'How come he/she didn't come?' [rhetorical particle]

(13)

สบายดี	คุณ	ล่ะ
Sabaydee	*Khun*	*la*
(I'm) well.	You	LA

'I'm well. And you?' [question particle]

A slightly different form, ละ (*la*) (similar pronunciation but with a different tone) can be used when the speaker is telling the listener something he/she anticipates they do not know.

(14)

ฉัน	ไม่	ไป	ละ
Chan	*mai*	*bpai*	*la*
I	not	go	LA

'I'm not going anymore.'

9.2.1.6. Rog

หรอก (*rog*) is used to soften a negative statement. As with other particles discussed, *rog* is casual and tends to be used among familiars. *Rog* is one of the only particles that is not often used in conjunction with other particles. Examples include the following:

(15)

ไม่เป็นไร	หรอก
Maibpenrai	*rog*
It doesn't matter	ROG

'It doesn't really matter.' [softener]

(16)

เขา	ไม่	รู้	หรอก
Khaw	*mai*	*ruu*	*rog*
He/she	doesn't	know	ROG

'He probably doesn't know.' [softener]

9.2.2. Tagalog: Case study 2

In Tagalog, *a* is used in sentences that express an event or situation that is contrary to expectation: either the speaker's own expectation or that of the person addressed. Consider the following example:

(17)

Maganda	*pala*	*ito,*	*a!*
pretty	pala	this,	A

'Oh, but this is pretty!'

Ha is used only in informal contexts, in utterances directed towards people with whom one uses the second-person singular pronoun. *Ha* may be added to a question, a command, or request, or one of several types of social formulae, and it expresses importunity.

(18)

Hintayin	*mo*	*nga*	*ako,*	*ha?*
wait	you	please	me,	HA

'Please wait for me, won't you?'

It can also show sarcasm or challenge an assertion made by the person addressed. Consider:

(19)

Marunong	*ka,*	*ha?*
smart	you,	HA

'You think you're smart, don't you?'

In addition, several enclitic particles in Tagalog play prominent roles in conveying expressive or attitudinal meaning, and are used in daily conversation and informal settings. Examples include *na* and *pa*. These markers function in specific grammatical contexts and each of them have seemingly opposite uses; the former most often expresses a recent change or expected action/event, whereas the latter tends to express an ongoing state/action or a tone of unexpectedness. What the exact nuance is, however, depends on the wider context of when the phrase or sentence is said. Consider the following examples. In (20a), no particle is used, indicating a neutral situation or objective perspective. In (20b) and (20c) particles are used to convey other shades of emotion and meaning.

(20)
   a. *Dumating   si Jenny.* [Neutral]
      Came   NOM-Jenny
      'Jenny came.'
   b. *Dumating   na   si Jenny.* [Expressing confirmation of an expected
                                     action/event]
      Came   NA   NOM-Jenny
      'Jenny has arrived.'
   c. *Dumating   pa   si Jenny.* [Expressing unexpectedness to an action/
                                     event]
      Came   PA   NOM-Jenny
      'Jenny came as well.'

The particles *pala* and *yata* are also used for expression; they each function to alter the nuances of a phrase or sentence in the language. In (20a), the speaker expresses sudden realization through the enclitic particle *pala* and in (21b), uncertainty is expressed through *yata*.

(21)
    a. *Dumating*   *pala*   *si Jenny.* [surprised]
       Came   PALA   NOM-Jenny
    b. *Dumating*   *yata*   *si Jenny.* [uncertain]
       Came   YATA   NOM-Jenny
       'Jenny came.'

The presence of the particle *po* or *ho* is used to indicate politeness in more formal settings, most notably when a younger person is speaking to an elder.

(22)
    a. *Umuulan*   *sa labas.* [standard]
       Raining   LOC-outside.
       'It is raining outside.'
    b. *Umuulan*   *po*   *sa labas.* [polite]
       Raining   PO   LOC-outside.
       'It is raining outside.'

Both the Thai and Tagalog case studies show the multidimensional, expressive nature of particles. The same set of particles can carry different socio-pragmatic meanings depending on the context. Particle absence is not simply arbitrary particle drop, but often reflects the speaker's intention to remain neutral to the situation. Together with prosody, particles create a subtle bundle of socio-pragmatic meanings specific to each situation. These aspects of particles in Asian languages are among the hardest challenges when translating into English and other European languages.

9.2.3. Japanese: Case study 3

As was touched upon in Chapter 6, Japanese sentence-final particles *ne* and *yo* are 'involvement particles' that serve not to change the information content of a sentence, but instead to invite the listener's involvement in the discourse. Consider example (23). In Lee's (2002) view, *ne* is indicative of an accordance of information between two interlocutors while *yo* is indicative of a nonconformity of information between two interlocutors. Both particles invite the partner's involvement. Involvement particles also serve to strengthen the interpersonal relationship between the speaker and other participants.

(23)

    a. *Eiga,*   *omoshirokatta.*
    b. movie   was.interesting
    c. 'The movie was interesting.'

    d. *Eiga,*   *omoshirokatta*   *ne.*
    e. movie   was.interesting   NE
    f. 'The movie was interesting.'

    g. *Eiga,*   *omoshirokatta*   *yo.*
    h. movie   was.interesting   YO
    i. 'The movie was interesting.'

Example (23a) shows an interactively neutral statement, in which the speaker does not involve the listener in their opinion or feeling. Example (23b) makes use of the incorporative marker *ne*, inviting the listener's alignment with the speaker's opinion that the movie was interesting. The use of *ne* also indicates that the listener has seen the movie, with the speaker seeking the listener's confirmation that the movie was indeed interesting. Example (23c) demonstrates that *yo* enhances the speaker's interlocutionary position as the deliverer of the utterance content. The use of *yo* indicates either that the listener has not seen the movie, or that the listener has seen the movie but holds the opinion that it was not interesting.

Ogi (2014) provides a sociolinguistic account for the sentence-final particle *ne/na* alternation in Japanese. *Ne* and *na* have the same function as an involvement particle that invites the listener's alignment with – or confirmation of – the speaker's utterance content or feelings. While *ne* can be used by a speaker of any age and gender, Ogi points out that *na* appears only to be used by males that are socially higher than the listener. In addition to this, the use of *na* with predicates in the *desu/masu* register (formal) is restricted to aged males. Ogi notes that this combination is not used by males between their twenties and forties, suggesting that they are still too young to be qualified for this. Ogi supports the view that *na* has a separate function of sharing 'camaraderie' with the hearer, which *ne* does not possess.

(24)

    Ii   *tenki*   *desu*   *na/ne.*
    good   weather   BE   NA/NE
    'It's a fine day-NA/NE.'

The utterance in (24), when used with *ne*, serves simply as a way for the listener to align with the contents of the utterance. *Na*, on the other hand, indicates the offering of camaraderie on the part of the speaker to the listener. The reason for this may be that the speaker is indexing a higher sociocultural status of him/herself over the listener. The use of the incorporative marker asking for the listener's involvement, then, is a friendly gesture of a socially superior interlocutor to a socially inferior one. Such an act can only be performed in such an interlocutory relationship.

It is natural for the particle *na* to be used with the *da/ru* form (informal) as the predicate presupposes an intimate relationship between two interlocutors, or a socially superior speaker with a socially inferior listener. This means that *na* does not index speaker age, but instead simply holds the function of bestowing camaraderie onto the listener. Ogi states that 'the camaraderie expressed by the particle implies that the speaker treats the hearer as a person who is close to him so that he can share camaraderie with the hearer, which in turn reinforces friendliness that is already conveyed in the utterance'.

(25)

> *Iyaa,   jitsuni   migotona   hoomuran   deshita   na.*
> well   truly   spectacular   home.run   BE-past   NA
> 'Well, it was a really spectacular homerun-NA.'

In this example, the listener has caused damage to the speaker's car with the homerun that they hit during a baseball match. The use of *na* on the part of the speaker bestows camaraderie to the listener, pointing to the futility and humour of the situation.

In terms of gender, Ogi argues that *na* is not used by female speakers because it does not match well with *onna-rashisa* 'womanliness'. The argument follows that women's speech in Japanese society is conditioned to be passive and polite, requiring a certain social distance. The positive performative act of offering camaraderie is unfit for this, and such an act is afforded only to men.

In addition to the particles discussed here, the following SFPs/UFPs are commonly found in Japanese. They show how different attitudes and socio-pragmatic meanings are projected through particles in Japanese.

a) か *ka*: This particle modifies a declarative statement into an interrogative question. For example: おいしいですか。 (*oishii desu ka*), 'Is it delicious?'

b) っけ *kke*: This is used when one is unsure of something and expresses feelings of doubt. For example: 昨日だったっけ？ (*kinō datta kke*), 'Was it yesterday?' It is often used when talking to oneself.

c) な *na*: This is used when one wants to express a personal feeling. It may be used to state a fact in which one has emotional investment, to express one's admiration or emotional excitement, to soften an imperative, or to encourage agreement, as a mild imperative. For example: ちょう楽しいな。 (*chou tanoshii na*), 'It's really fun, isn't it?'

d) なあ *nā*: This particle is simply an elongated form of the previous particle and expresses strong emotion, either to encourage agreement, as above, or to express one's desires. For examples: 寿司を食べたいなぁ。 (*sushi wo tabetai naa*), 'I want to eat sushi (so badly right now!)'

e) ね *ne*: This is used when the speaker wants to verify a statement or otherwise show agreement, reach consensus, or build solidarity with the listener. For example: 残念ですね。 (*zan'nen desu ne*), 'It's a pity, isn't it?'

f) の *no*: This may be used to form informal questions or to give some sort of emphasis to one's statement. Depending on intonation and context, it may soften a statement (particularly in women's language), or be used to strongly assert one's belief in something. In this sense, it may also act as an indirect imperative, by indicating what the speaker believes should happen and, thus, what the listener is expected to do. For example: 誰なの？ (*dare na no?*), 'Who is it?'

g) さ *sa*: This particle contrasts with *ne* in the sense that where *ne* helps build solidarity and agreement, *sa* is used to assert the speaker's own ideas or opinions. It is often used repeatedly in conversation to retain a listener's attention. For example: これさ。 (*kore sa*), 'This is the one!'

h) わ *wa*: This is used primarily by women, and has a meaning similar to *yo*, but is softer and less assertive. For example: 私がやりますわ。 (*watashi ga yarimasu wa*), 'I'll do it.'

i) よ *yo*: This is used by a speaker who is asserting that the information preceding the particle is information he/she is confident in, particularly when supplying information that the listener is believed not to know. For example: 今日暑いですよ。 (*kyou atsui desu yo*), 'It's hot today!'

j) ぜ *ze*: This is used to push a listener to do something, or to remind them of something. In certain contexts, it can carry a threatening overtone. For example, 踊ろうぜ。 (*odorous ze*), 'Let's dance.'

k) ぞ *zo*: This is used to strongly assert the speaker's decisions and opinions, and serves to discourage dissent or protest. For example, お前のせいだぞ。 (*omae no sei da zo*), 'It's your fault!'

9.2.4. Chinese: Case study 4

In Mandarin Chinese, attitudinal particles generally appear at the end of an utterance, yet some can also appear at the end of phrases within larger sentences and can have both grammatical and expressive functions. As SFPs/UFPs largely appear in spoken language, not all of them have a standardized written representation in the form of a character.[2] In contemporary Chinese, an important factor in the expression of particles in written language is the internet, which has popularized the rendering of colloquial spoken language into written form, but has also increased the variation in written expressions of individual particles across geographic and virtual spaces.[3] In Mandarin Chinese too, the meaning expressed by particles is highly context-dependent. Nevertheless, Wu (2004) concludes that they do, for the most part, 'convey consistent indexical meanings across different usages'. Chu (2009) has since argued that while many uses of particles work in individual contexts, they do not necessarily cross over into other linguistically similar examples. In addition to being impacted by context, the meanings of particles can also depend on the tone of utterance. For example, Chu argues that the particle *a* 啊 includes an interpersonal orientation; a high tone indicates that the meaning is oriented towards the hearer, and a low tone means that it is oriented towards the speaker him/herself.[4] Chu refers to a particle's 'modality function' and 'discourse function' while acknowledging that they can nonetheless be used to express a variety of meanings.

Shei (2014) lists some of the most frequently used particles – *a* 啊, *ba* 吧, *bei* 呗, *ne* 呢, *o* 哦, *o* 喔, *ou* 噢, *ma* 嘛, *ye* 耶, *la* 啦, *le* 了 – and indicates their primary function. The following is a summary of each of the most common expressive uses of the most common particles. More expressive meanings can be added in different context. That is, for all the particles given, there are numerous additional meanings that could arise depending on the specific context in which the utterance is located. The particles discussed are primarily modal, in that their primary function is to indicate the speaker's opinion or emotion regarding what is being discussed. Other particles are primarily grammatical but can be said to have expressive functions as well.

a) *a* 啊: The particle *a* 啊 is one of the most frequently used particles in Mandarin Chinese and can have many different meanings depending on context. Shei notes that this particle's primary function is to convey emotion or conviction, but it can also be used to mark a question or a series of nouns or phrases.[5] That said, the same particle can have both constructive and expressive meanings at the same time.

b) *ba* 吧 and *bei* 呗: The particles *ba* 吧 and *bei* 呗 are variants used in much the same way to express uncertainty, suggestion or invitation. They can often be translated as 'perhaps' or 'let's' in English. For example, '走吧!' (*zou ba!*, 'let's go!') They may also have a humorous or mocking function by making a suggestion that the speaker knows would likely embarrass the target. Shei notes that *bei* 呗 in particular is used in a humorous function as its intonation is considered to be more lively.[6] In the following example, *ba* 吧 is used rhetorically to tease the hearer:

(26)

ni	*kan*	*houhui*	*le ba!*	*yizhen*[7]
you	look	regret	SFP/UFP	Yizhen

'See? Do you regret it now, Yizhen?'

c) *ne* 呢: The particle *ne* 呢 can be used to indicate contrast or to request information, and can often be translated into English as 'as for . . .' or 'what about . . .?' Chu notes that *ne* 呢 does not have a strong expressive function, but has the interpersonal function of directing the hearer to 'look in previous context for something that contrasts with what is in the current utterance' ('as for . . .') or 'pick up and continue the current discourse' (what about . . .?).[8] Furthermore, when intonation is taken into account, an utterance using *ne* 呢 could have strong expressive connotations, for example '而我呢?' (*er wo ne?*, 'what about me?') may indicate that the speaker finds a situation unfair and is directing the hearer to consider their point of view. In a sense, this particle can be glossed in the spirit of contemporary linguistics as a simple topic marker/particle (TOC). Yet, with this simple glossing, one may not be able to include all the diverse and complex meanings this particle projects as in the case of other languages observed in Chapter 6.

d) *o* 哦: This particle functions as a warning or reminder. It can be positive or negative, and can convey a tone of affectionate concern or even humour, depending on intonation. For example:

(27)

buyao	*gaosu*	*mama*	*o*
not-want	tell	mother	SFP/UFP

'Do not tell your mother!'[9]

e) *ma* 嘛: This particle assumes a shared understanding of the contents of the sentence, and can be translated into English as 'as we know . . .', '. . . isn't it?' or '. . . right?'

f) *de* 的: The *shi... de* 是... 的 construction in Mandarin is used to express factual judgements; through this the particle *de* 的 has gained an expressive meaning indicating emphatic conviction akin to the English statement 'It is a fact that . . . .'. This can manifest as assurance or emphatic disagreement, both of which are usually expressed in English through intonation (Yang 2009). For example:

(28)
    a. *ta hui mai* 'He will buy [it]'
    b. *ta hui mai de* 'He **will** buy [it]'

9.2.5. Lao: Case study 5

Lao also has a rich repertoire of SFP/UFPs. Let's consider some of the key particles. In Lao, ເດີ້ (*der*) is an informal spoken particle that makes statements, sentiments and well-wishes, warnings, announcements and commands sound more soft, pleasant or friendly. Consider the examples and how this particle can reflect various emotions and attitudes depending on the context. It is used across various age groups; for example, children can use it with adults and vice-versa.

(30)

ຂອບໃຈ ເດີ້
Khobjai	*der*
Thank you	DER

'Thank you' [sentiment – friendly]

(31)

ເຮົາ ສິ ໄປ ຕອນ ຫ້າ ໂມງ ເດີ້
Hao	*si*	*bpai*	*dton*	*ha*	*mong*	*der*
We	will	go	at	5	o'clock	DER

'We're going at 5 o'clock' [announcement – pleasant]

(32)

ເຈົ້າ ຕ້ອງ ເຮັດ ວຽກບ້ານ ໃຫ້ແລ້ວ ມື້ນີ້ ເດີ້
Jao	*dtong*	*het*	*wiagban*	*hai*	*laew*	*meuni*	*der*
You	must	do	housework	cause	finish	today	DER

'You need to finish the housework today.' [command – softening]

ເດີ້ can also be used with ແດ່ (*daae*) or ແນ່ (*naae*) to soften a request. For example:

(33)

    ເຈົ້າ ເຮັດ ອັນນີ້ໃຫ້ ຂ້ອຍ ແດ່ເດີ
    Jao   het   anni   hai   khoi   daae   der
    You   do   this   for   me   DAAE   DER
    'Please do this for me.' [softening]

Sometimes people spell it with a tone marker, perhaps in repetitions, or to add emphasis. Consider (34) and (35).

(34)

    ເຈົ້າ ເຮັດ ຫຍັງ
    Jao   het   nyang
    You   do   what?
    'What do you do?'

(35)

    ເຈົ້າເຮັດຫຍັງແດ່
    Jao   het   nyang   daae?
    You   do   what   DAAE?
    'What things do you do?'

Particles like ແດ່ (*daae*), in addition to being used in requests, can be used for a different function: asking questions invoking a multifaceted answer. As in (35), they transform the question of 'what do you do?' (invoking a simple, one-answer response) into something along the lines of 'what things do you do?' (invoking an answer with multiple parts). Again, ແດ່ (*daae*) is more polite and formal, while ແນ່ (*naae*) is more casual.

9.2.6. Tibetan: Case study 6

Tibetan also has a rich repertoire of SFP/UFPs.

    a) *ta*: This implies that the speaker is not in agreement with the person to whom he is speaking, or is emphasizing the surprising or threatening nature of the situation in question. Consider the following:

(36)

    hā   shora   sōnga   ta
    Horse   escape   PFCT   TA
    'Watch out, the horse has escaped!' [surprise, warning]

b) *pa/ka/nga*: These particles are used when the speaker is trying to elicit agreement with what he is saying. These particles correspond to tag questions, as follows:

(37)

thatā	chīpō	rētha	pa
now	late	be	PA

'It's late now, isn't it?'

9.3. Cross-linguistic evidence: SIP/UIP

Vocative particles and interjection particles are, in some sense, similar in that they open a proposition and set the tone for the proposition.[10] According to the MMH, the emotional and attitudinal values of the opening and wrapping-up particles in the same local domain of an utterance should not be contradictory. If they are contradictory, the resulting effect may be sarcastic or pun-like or may make the utterance less reliable.

For instance, in Hebrew, interjections in biblical Hebrew are most likely 'natural sounds', that is, vocal gestures or sounds that a person utters when experiencing certain emotions. Interjections can be used to express both positive and negative emotions. Examples of interjections in the Hebrew Bible normally indicate despondency. If the interjection signals sadness, but the sentence or the utterance ends with the contradictory emotion such as joy or happiness within the same local domain, the audience will be perplexed. Similarly, the following interjections are used in Tibet. The expressions that appear after them should have emotional meanings consistent with these interjections.

(38)

ō 'Oh!'
ātsi 'Darn!'
āro 'Ow!'
ācu 'Ooh, that's cold!'
ātsa 'Ouch, that's hot!'
ākha 'What a shame!'
āma 'Oh Lordy!'

The interpersonal relations and the register information that are expressed at the initial position of the utterance need to be carried throughout the utterance.

In literary and poetic Persian, ای (*ey*, similar to 'hey!') is used as an honorific vocative, whereas آی (*āy*) can be used in colloquial Persian to address juniors. Once interpersonal relation and register information are set, at least within the single unit of utterance, it needs to be maintained.

Tables 9.1–9.7 show how particles deliver expressive and attitudinal meanings at different positions of an utterance in different Asian languages. SMP/UMP refers to sentence-medial particle/utterance-medial particle.

Table 9.1 Expressive particles in Bengali

Particle	Example	Meanings
ta – used at the start of sentence to indicate hesitation, as if looking for the right word. **SIP/UIP**	*Ta kotota bhaat debo bolo?*	So tell me, how much rice should I serve you?
ba – used with question words adding doubt or helplessness. It can follow or precede the interrogative directly or appear elsewhere. **SMP/UMP**	*Cholei jokhon jabe thik korecho, tokhon ki ba bolte pari?*	If you've already decided to leave, what else can I say?
ki – filler word or 'what do I know', 'what more?', 'you don't say'. **SFP/UFP**	*Amake to ar kichu bolena, ki jani ki korche?*	Well, he doesn't tell me anything these days, how can I say what he is doing?
	Bhalobasha chara ar ki ba dite pari tomay?	Apart from love, what else can I give you?

Table 9.2 Expressive particles in Hindi

Particle	Example	Meanings
hii – means 'only' and is a focus particle. **SMP/UMP**	*raam seb hii khaataa hai*	Ram eats only apples.
hii – can also emphasize the meaning of what the listener should do in the given circumstances. **SMP/UMP**	*aap ab mohan kii shaadii kar hii diijiye*	You should now get Mohan married off.
bhii – means 'too' and is a focus particle. **SMP/UMP**	*raam seb bhii khaataa hai*	Ram eats apples too.
to – is used to open a sentence, like 'so' in English.	*to kaun aa rahaa hai*	So, who is coming?

Expressive and Attitudinal Particles

Table 9.3 Expressive particles in Urdu

Particle	Example	Meanings
tō – emphasizes the preceding noun or verb and contrasts it with something else. **SMP/UMP**	vo tō urdū parhē gā	*He* will study Urdu (contrast: the other students may not).
hī – emphasizes the preceding word and excludes something else (which may not be expressed). **SMP/UMP**	ahmad qila hī dēkhnā cāhtā thā, bādśāhī masjid nahīm	Ahmad wanted to see *the fort*, not the royal mosque.
bhī – occurs as an emphatic particle following a noun, emphasizing the comprehensiveness of the idea expressed in the sentence, and is usually translated as 'even'. **SMP/UMP**	baccā bhī ye jāntā hai	Even a child knows this.
bhī – following a verb, it emphasizes and expresses the speaker's impatience or exasperation. **SMP/UMP**	ab cup karō bhī!	Now just keep quiet!
tak – is sometimes used as a particle meaning 'even'. It is more emphatic than bhī. **SMP/UMP**	naujavān kyā, būrhē tak xuśī manā rahē haim	Even the elders are celebrating, not to mention the young people.

Table 9.4 Expressive particles in Vietnamese

Particle	Example	Meanings
ạ – a particle used at the end of a sentence to express formal politeness, especially to seniors. **SFP/UFP**	Chào cụ ạ.	How do you do? (*to an older person*)
nhé – emphatic particle. **SFP/UFP**	Tôi muốn ăn quả táo nhé	I want to eat an apple (slightly added assertiveness).
à – expresses mild surprise. **SFP/UFP**	Chị quên rồi à?	You forget already (I'm surprised).
kia – expresses 'preference'. **SFP/UFP**	Nó thích sơ-mi màu xanh kia!	He likes a blue shirt instead [of white, for instance].

Table 9.5 Expressive particles in Lao

Particle	Example	Meanings
tii4 – presumptive. **SFP/UFP**	saam3 khon2 taaj3 tii4	Surely I'm correct in thinking that three people died?
vaa3 – inferential particle, inferring information. **SFP/UFP**	saam3 khon2 taaj3 vaa3	Do I rightly infer that three people died?
naa3 – explication particle, explaining a point with sureness. **SFP/UFP**	qanø-nii4 kheej2 het1 ˆ do moˋo3-lam2 ˋnaa3	This one has been a Lam artist, you must understand.
veej4 – emphatic particle, speaker saying that the sentence is definitely the case.	maø tat2-sin3-caj3 maj1 vaa1 boøˋ paj3 laø veej4	I decided anew, 'Heck, I won't go!'

Table 9.6 Expressive particles in Burmese

Particle	Example	Meanings
kwa1 – enthusiastic **SFP/UFP**	cha1 kwa1	fight!
ha1 – exclamative **SFP/UFP**	na2 deare2 ha1	It's painful.
kwa2 – frustration **SFP/UFP**	thwa3 meare2 kwa2	I am leaving!
pa1 – demonstration of agreement **SFP/UFP**	hote pa1	Absolutely!
nau2 – expresses warmth **SFP/UFP**	thwa3 meare2 nau2	Good-bye.

Table 9.7 Expressive particles in Khmer

Particle	Example	Meanings
phɔɔɲ – means 'too' or surprise	cɲaɲ phɔɔɲ	It is unexpectedly delicious!
dae – hesitation and softening	cɲaɲ dae	It is not so delicious.

9.4. Beyond verbal particles

Particles project a wide range of expressive and attitudinal meanings. Not only morphological particles, but also non-verbal expressions like prosody and gesture play an important role in making an utterance socio-pragmatically rich. This is clearly visible across Asian languages, as we discussed in Chapter 5. For instance, in India, reading head and chin movements matters greatly in figuring out the speaker's intention and attitude.

Sometimes, non-verbal expressions play more important roles than verbal expressions in communication (see Chapter 5). Asian languages also contain a full

Figure 9.1 Greeting in Thai and Lao.

range of hedging and softening devices; these attitudinal aspects are more effective when expressed in conjunction with prosody and gestures (see Figure 9.1).

Thai and Lao people show respect through a greeting called the *wai*. In order to *wai* properly, one's palms are placed together and held up to the face in a bowing position. Similar to the five registers of spoken Thai, there are five levels of respect used in the *wai*. The higher hands are raised the more respectful. The highest level of respect is for monks. In this position, one's thumbs are placed between eyebrows. The next four levels of respect are reserved for parents, teachers, elders and equals, respectively. To *wai* those equal in status (the lowest form of *wai*), palms are placed together in front of the chest. Other Asian languages also contain a broad and fine-grained repertoire of gestures which can be indicative of the nature of different interpersonal relations.

The meaning of prosody is hard to generalize – though it is important both in terms of building a structure and revealing speakers' attitudes and emotions.

For instance, in Burmese, the end of an utterance is marked by a down-drift, irrespective of the lexical tone of the final syllable, while an up-drift frequently marks an unfinished utterance and often appears at the end of a subordinate clause. The down-drift at the end of an utterance also appears in questions, both yes/no and content questions. For emphasis or other pragmatic reasons, the final syllable of an utterance may also be delivered with a high pitch. This is also common in more formalized language, such as news reports (Jenny and Hnin Tun 2017: 22). Reading this prosodic information is important in order to achieve harmonious communication. In the following section, I present two cases in Korean and Chinese studies which explore the role of prosody in the formation of social meanings.

9.4.1. Prosody and social meaning: The case of Korean

Prosody and social meaning are clearly related, although their relation is difficult to characterize or prove. Jun (2000) proposed the IP boundary tones and their meaning potential in reference to the Korean language. Table 9.8 shows some examples.

Jun (2005, 2014) also presented similar systematic relations from a prosodic typological perspective, including evidence from Asian languages such as Korean, Japanese, pan-Mandarin, Cantonese, Standard Bengali and Mongolian.

Table 9.8 Meanings of boundary tones

L%	This tone is the most common in stating facts, and in declaratives in reading.
H%	This tone is the most common in seeking information as in yes/no questions.
LH%	This is commonly used for questions, continuation rises, and explanatory ending.
HL%	This tone is most common in declaratives and wh-questions. It is also commonly used in news broadcasting.
LHL%	This tone sometimes intensifies the meaning of HL%, but like LH%, it also delivers the meanings of 'being persuasive, insisting, and confirmative'. It is also used to show annoyance or irritation.
HLH%	This tone is used when a speaker is confident and expecting listeners' agreement.
LHLH%	This tone is less common than others, and has a meaning of intensifying some of the LH%'s meanings, that is, 'annoyance, irritation or disbelief'.
HLHL%	This tone is more common than LHLH%, but not as common as single, bi- or tritonal boundary tones. It sometimes intensifies the meaning of HL%, confirming and insisting on one's opinion, and sometimes, like LHL%, it delivers nagging or persuading meanings.
LHLHL%	This tone is rare and its meaning is similar to that of LHL%, but has a more intense meaning of being annoyed.

9.4.2. Emotional intonation: Evidence from Chinese

Li et al. (2011) aim to answer the question of how lexical tones interplay with the intonation in a tonal language by specifically examining the emotional intonations in Mandarin Chinese. It focuses on emotional intonation by analysing the fundamental frequency (F0).[11] The results show that the tone patterns vary greatly among these emotions when compared to neutral emotion in the aspects of tonal range, tonal register and tonal contours, and in some of the emotion intonations the successive addition intonation can be detected. When compared to neutral emotion, 'fear' features an obvious tremor voice, higher F0, and narrower pitch range; 'sad' has a lower F0 and a reduced pitch range; 'disgust' is very similar to 'sad', with a successive addition falling offset tone; both 'happy' and 'surprise' have a successive additional rising tone, and both of them have higher pitch range, but 'surprise' has a higher bottom pitch and narrower range than 'happy' and is expressed with a slightly greater speed than 'happy'; 'anger' also has a higher pitch and faster speech patterns, and a falling successive addition tone. This is an interesting experiment. Yet, in order to show how prosody and emotions are linked and find the general pattern, big data analysis across gender and age group in different registers will be essential.

9.5. Formal analysis of expressive particles

In this section, I shall demonstrate how different expressive and attitudinal meanings can be added and modulated in the course of building linguistic representation using the LINK mechanisms adopted in DS.[12] The basic intuition of adding and extending meaning is explained in Cann et al. (2005, chapter 8; see also Chapter 7 of this book). Yet, how particles in Asian languages project expressive meanings and how various meanings from different dimensions can interact have not been properly discussed.

The beauty of DS formalism is that it is easily applicable across languages and linguistic phenomena without adding any abstract or non-intuitive complexity.[13] The purpose of this section is not to go through every example I have shown in the previous chapters and provide an analysis, but instead to provide some exemplary cases, hoping that other researchers and educators in the region are able to develop their own versions of a multimodal, multidimensional grammar to capture and explain the socio-pragmatically rich nature of Asian languages.

Particles have a dual nature: constructive and expressive. As we have seen in Chapter 8, some particles project a lexical macro which can unfold a structural skeleton for the upcoming structure. Other particles are responsible in realizing multimodal, multidimensional meanings. Sometimes, the same particle(s) can assume both roles. For instance, so-called sentence/utterance-final particles signal the near end of a local structure (playing a constructive role) yet at the same time they reflect a wide range of emotions and attitudes (playing an expressive and attitudinal role), as we have observed in this chapter. I propose that a particle projects an appendix-like LINKed structure where these newly added meanings can be stored and processed.

Within DS literature, Yamanaka (2008) used a LINK relation to add honorific meaning to a currently unfolding linguistic representation. Consider the Japanese sentence (39), taken from Yamanaka (2008).

(39) Masa: *O-isogi-dat-ta.* [Japanese]
 POL-hurry-COP-PST
 '(He) was in hurry.'

Yamanaka showed that in saying *oisogidatta* ('(He) was in hurry') as in (39), the predicate *isogi* invokes honorific meaning which shows Masa's respect for Yamada sensei ('Teacher Yamada'). Here, the core idea behind is to treat the socially added meanings (here, honorific) as information added to the propositional meaning using a LINK relation. My proposal shares this intuition with Yamanaka's work.

In section 9.1, I have introduced the following attributes as a part of socio-pragmatic meanings.

(i) Interpersonal attributes
(ii) Mood and emotion-related attributes
(iii) Style-related attributes
(iv) Perspective and attitude-related attributes

Meanings in each of these dimensions can be added by using an independent LINKed structure. Each attribute (e.g. HON, RESPECT, EXCL, POETIC, SUBJECTIVE) can be used as a functor in the actual LINKed structure.

While the mother, propositional structure in the communication grows, the adjunct structures via a LINK operation can be initiated at different points in the utterance. This process can be motivated by different linguistic mechanisms. Some languages use explicit lexical items such as relative clause pronouns to indicate such a transition and other languages have more subtle devices such as particles and prosody. As discussed in Chapter 8, Kiaer (2014) shows the role of repeated rising tone as a trigger for the sequence of adjunct structures.

The trigger for the adjunct LINKed structure can be verbal expressions but also non-verbal expressions. Though diverse meanings are added and displayed, crucially, the meanings projected in the adjunct structure are incrementally checked and modulated to see whether it is consistent and harmonious with the meaning of the mother structure as well as with the meanings projected by other adjunct structures (see section 8.2).

(40) Multiple applications of LINK operation

Real-time line of structure-building

 a) Propositional structure grows ---------------------------------
 b) Multidimensional meanings are added via LINK operations
-------$A(L_1..L_n)$------------$B(L_1..L_n)$-------$C(L_1..L_n)$------------

Schematically, at point A, a number of LINKed structures can be initiated. The meanings projected by these structures should be consistent with the meanings in the mother propositional structure. Likewise, at point B, a number of LINKed structures can be initiated. The meanings projected by these structures should be consistent with the meanings in the mother propositional structure as well as with the meanings built by adjunct structures at point A. The same process will be repeated at point C and so on.

Suppose that at point A, a relatively initial point in structure building, the LINKed structure has S < H interpersonal meaning, yet at a later point B or C, the LINKed structure projects an S > H interpersonal meaning. Or suppose that at point A the style attribute has the value of informal, yet the style attribute at point C is formal. Although the degree of unnaturalness may differ in each case, either the structure-building will continue aborting the particular adjunct structure or the whole process will collapse and finish.[14]

The idea of this adjunct structure building 'linked' to the main propositional structure can successfully incorporate multimodal, multidimensional, on-spot meanings that are added in the process of overall structure building. In this book I proposed the MMH should be kept in a single unit of utterance.

Consider a simple illustration from English example:

(41) ??? *I hate John, whom you know, whom I so much like.*

The speaker can have different attitudes towards John, of course, but if that happens in the same unit of utterance as in (41), it may cause pragmatic unnaturalness. In Chapter 5, we observed various examples which violate MMH. The solution to repair an utterance such as this will be either to abolish the proposition altogether or to abort the contradicting clause. In this way, we can explain correction-type afterthought examples within incremental schemata.

Consider the Hindi examples again. (42) is natural, yet (43) is unnatural due to socio-pragmatic inappropriateness caused by a mismatch of honorifics, violating MMH.

(42)
    a. *tu* (intimate) *a*   'you come'   [Hindi]
    b. *tum* (informal) *ao*   'you come'
    c. *aap* (polite) *aiye*   'you come'

(43)
    a. ??? *tu* (intimate) *ao*   'you come'   [Hindi]
    b. ??? *tum* (informal) *aiye*   'you come'
    c. ??? *aap* (polite) *a*   'you come'

In the DS formalism, we can explain that each second-person pronoun has the same structural expectation – that is to wait for the verb to compete the ongoing structure. However, besides this requirement, each pronoun yields the socio-pragmatic expectation that is to be coded in the LINKed structure. Hence, the LINKed structure projected by *tu* will carry the intimate relational meaning, whereas *tum* will carry the informal relational meaning and *aap* will carry the polite meaning within the LINKed structure.

Then, the verb will come. The stem part of the verb will project the structural skeleton and the underlying ending particles will project a LINKed structure with attitudinal meaning. Structurally speaking, (43a–c) are all grammatical sentences. Yet, the oddity comes because the LINKed structure projected by the subject and the verb, when put together and modulated, becomes inconsistent. For instance, in (43b) *tum* contains [+ S > H or S = H] and [+INFORMAL] features, whereas *aiye* contains [S < H] and [+ POLITE] features. LINKed structures built by these two expressions will form inconsistent pragmatic message. This is why the examples in (43) are structurally acceptable but socio-pragmatically unacceptable.

To demonstrate how LINKed structures are built in a sequence, in the following example, I shall showcase how multiple LINKs are projected in the particle clusters through showcasing a Thai example in (44). In this example, the underlined particles enhance interpersonal meaning, namely, respect.

Expressive and Attitudinal Particles 207

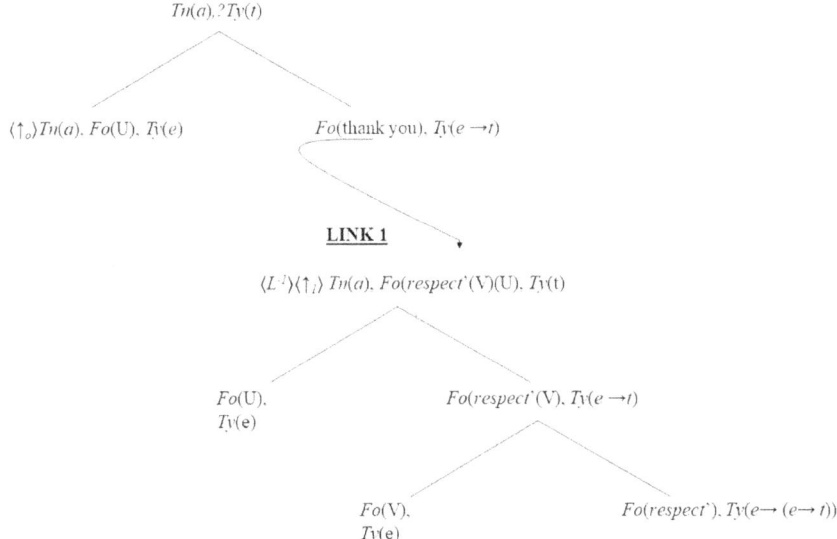

Figure 9.2 Single LINK application.

(44) 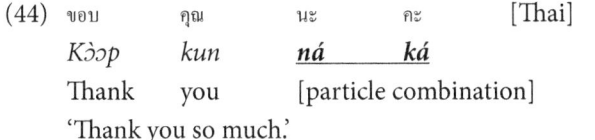 [Thai]
    Kɔ̀ɔp   kun   **ná**   **ká**
    Thank   you   [particle combination]
    'Thank you so much.'

Step 1: Parsing honorific particle -*na'*

Initial structure is unfolded by the verb and the speaker-and-hearer value – that is annotated with a meta-variables U and V, respectively as *Fo(U)* and *Fo(V)*, and is found from the context (Figure 9.2).

This step shows the LINK operation introducing a new node through the honorific particle -*na'*. As addressed earlier, in the LINKed structure we can see that the substructure unfolds under the predicate *respect*. This is one way of dealing with a multidimensional lexical matrix. An attribute in the lexical matrix can play a role as a functor. In the case of -*na'*, I propose the functor *respect* (Figure 9.3).

Step 2: Parsing honorific particle *ká*

Step 1 shows how the LINKed structure is introduced by the second honorific particle -*ká*. In the LINKed structure, we can see that the substructure is

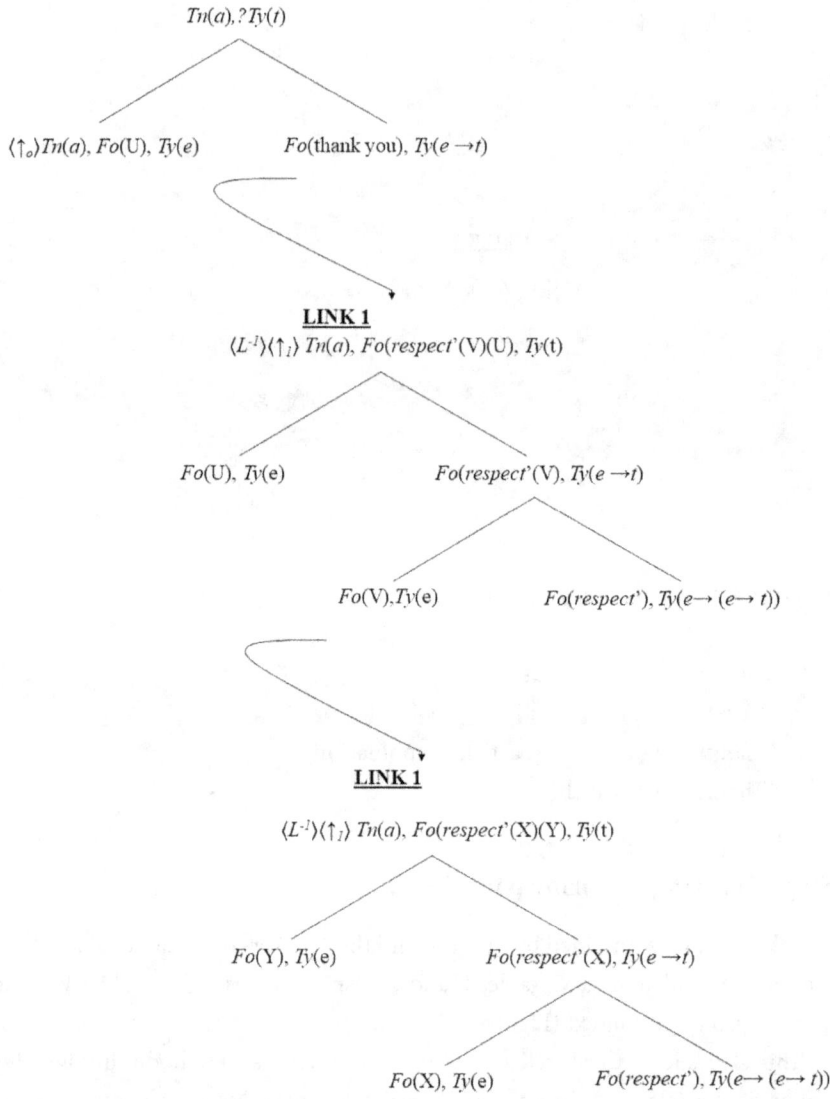

Figure 9.3 Multiple LINK application.

unfolded under the same predicate *respect*. The two LINKed structures reflect the accumulated, hence enhanced, meanings for a respect dimension. In the examples in step 1, the *Fo(X)* and *Fo(Y)* will be updated with the same formulaic values in three structures. Particle clusters also often reflect different dimensions of meanings. In this case, the new predicate will be used for that LINKed relation. When a sequence of particles respect multidimensional meanings of respect, intimacy, formality, masculinity, for instance, the utterance can have a sequence of an adjunct, LINKed structures combined with L(respect) (i.e. whether the factor is respect), L(intimacy), L(formality) and L(masculinity). Sometimes, one particle can express different meanings. See Lao example in (45) which we discussed in Chapter 4.

(45)
    a. *Saam3 khon2 taaj3* **bàà3** [Lao]
       Three person die   QPLR.
       'Is it the case that three people died?'
    b. *Saam3 khon2 taaj3* **tii4**
       Three person die   QPLR.PRESM
       'Surely I'm correct in thinking that three people died?'
    c. *Saam3 khon2 taaj3* **vaa3**
       Three person die   QPLR.INFER
       'Do I rightly infer that three people died?'

Each interrogative particle underlined will commonly share a predication for the interrogative mood. Yet, at the same time, each particle will project additional, distinct attitudinal meaning that can be annotated in the independent LINK structure. By using LINK operations in DS, we have formal ways to encode fine-grained meaning differences and show how multidimensional meanings are interwoven as the structure unfolds.

The meanings added through various particles are inseparable from the propositional meaning and make the linguistic representation socio-pragmatically rich and valid. As in the syntactic structure building, the meanings are evaluated in an incremental way as the structure grows. The multiple application of LINK operations is possible but, as discussed, it needs to be consistent and should not violate MMH.

In this book, I have limited the discussion to a single utterance unit. Yet, in order to model real communication, the target of linguistic observation and description should be extended into a spontaneous, multimodal dialogue. In principle, the multiple uses of LINK operations, as I have shown in this book, can be extended in the modelling of dialogue. Indeed, this is what DS researchers have concentrated on, working in collaboration with dialogue scholars in psychology and computer science in recent years. Kempson et al. (2019) among others demonstrate how DS can be used as a mechanism for interaction. In particular, it is fascinating to see how structure-building efforts are coordinated and modulated by multiple participants with different goals. A dynamic process such as this however, is achieved effortlessly and seamlessly in communication, generating a multitude of expressive and dimensional meanings.

Modelling a dialogue, particularly in Asian languages, where understanding and interpretation of much of the implicit expressions depend on the context, often embedded in its unique culture, will bring a real challenge to language modelling. This is certainly a direction in which I aim to pursue future research.

9.6. Summary

This chapter explores diverse expressive and attitudinal particles in Asian languages. I proposed the socio-pragmatic attributes of particles and presented evidence from different Asian languages, demonstrating four case studies using Thai, Tagalog, Chinese and Japanese.

There are many utterance-final particles cross-linguistically, although there are many utterance-initial and middle particles. The meanings expressed by these different particles must be modulated and remain consistent throughout an utterance. Continuing on from Chapter 5, I also argued that prosody and non-verbal expressions play an important role in expressing emotions and attitude, though little so far has been done by means of study in this field and much more is needed. Finally, I have provided some showcases using the LINK operation in DS to explain how expressive and attitudinal meanings can be integrated in ongoing proposition building. In addition, I have explained the usage of LINK operations in modelling the multimodal, multidimensional meanings projected by particles.

Epilogue

Towards a sensible grammar: Multimodal interactional instinct and beyond

Wouldn't it be sensible to have a grammar that can explain *why* we say *what* we say in our day-to-day communication with each other in much simpler terms? A grammar that makes sense to us all without imposing overly abstract and theoretical assumptions? Wouldn't it be sensible to have a grammar that is built on the shared platform of description and observation; that is empirically reliable and agreeable across the disciplines of linguistics? Wouldn't it then also be sensible to look beyond English-like languages and crystalize our understanding of what constitutes a language universal from a cross-linguistic perspective? These were the questions which helped me to *un-think* the basic attributes and dynamics of the human language, and which pushed me to embark on the journey which ultimately resulted in this book.

By showcasing Asian languages, I have aimed to demonstrate the syntactic fluidity and semantic/pragmatic diversity that are particularly visible in socio-pragmatic meaning constructions. These aspects of Asian languages have been something of a sticking point in contemporary linguistics. This is because contemporary linguistics and its empirical foundations are mostly based on Western European languages; hence, many of the core characteristics of Asian languages have been understood as exceptional, at best. Even highly advanced theoretical investigations could not explicate the aforementioned characteristics in simple and sensible terms.

In this book, I proposed that the foundational problem contributing to this gap in knowledge cannot be found in a particular formal toolkit but is rooted in the basic foundations of modern linguistics, that is, their Anglo- or Euro-centricism. What has emerged from this Anglo- or Euro-centric view is a syntactic rigidity which has been at the centre of theoretical modelling, often leaving fluid structures in a somewhat grey area of information structure. In addition, within this Anglo- and Euro-centric view, the fine-grained, multidimensional meanings that Asian languages are able to reflect are often oversimplified or under-represented. For instance, balancing and negotiating intimacy and respect is perhaps the most important aspect in the acquisition of Asian languages; yet most language teaching concentrates on grammar alone, without tying in essential socio-pragmatic knowledge.

Contemporary theoretical linguistics is flawed from its conception as it attempts to pursue logical foundations in a vacuum. The basic input under discussion is often presented as a contextless, single, isolated, verbal sentence often from a very formal written register. However, the linguistic process of meaning making is dynamic, interactive and context sensitive; and it never happens in a vacuum. The way we interact with each other on a daily basis is highly register-sensitive and is multimodal by definition. For instance, the socio-pragmatic meaning of respect or intimacy is composed through both verbal and non-verbal channels arising from the cultural context, and is transferred through multimodal interaction.

I argued that the essence of 'interactional instinct' in human communication lies in the ability to orchestrate and modulate multidimensional meanings. By incorporating multimodal meanings, emotional and attitudinal meanings in each communication become fully enriched and embodied. However, there is clear limit in this study. My proposal in this book does not cover the full range of dialogue data. Multimodal modulation across speakers is much more complex and dynamic than in a single utterance. This is certainly what I aim to pursue in future study.

The 'ideal' sentence in the mindset of contemporary linguistics is undoubtedly made up of one single named language. Indeed, contemporary linguistic theory is rooted in monolingual ideology. The majority of – if not all – 'ordinary' speakers in our time interact with each other in a multilingual environment. Monolingual ideology has never thoroughly penetrated any place at any time in human history, yet this view is often implicitly accepted in the Anglophone world. It seems that most linguistic theories still have their foundation in the grammaticality judgements of monolingual native speakers. For decades, the notion of native speakerism has been almost obsolete and proven to be invalid in applied linguistics (see Paikeday 1985). However, this finding has never been incorporated into theoretical linguistics. This is not surprising given the chasm between theoretical and applied linguistics and the lack of meaningful interaction and feedback between them.

From the perspective of a monolingual ideology, ordinary speakers' methods of communicating by mixing semiotic primitives from different languages (i.e. translanguaging) can be unanimously labelled as wrong, incorrect or 'hard-to-judge', at best. To my knowledge, no formal theory thus far has aimed to provide an explanation for the diverse multilingual communication that is increasingly becoming a norm in our time. In this book, I have introduced the notion of translanguaging and hinted at the possibility of using it as the conceptual foundation for linguistic modelling.

If we really want to observe how people communicate in our time, and to describe and explain their communication, we need a better method of understanding the ways in which multi- or translingual individuals interact. Theoretical foundations that can be suitable for explaining multilingual individuals' ordinary language behaviour – or *languaging* – are much needed and long overdue.

This book presented diverse data from Asian languages and aimed to show how multimodal information can contribute to the building of complex and multidimensional meanings. I proposed the revised pragmatic syntax hypothesis in which *efficiency, expressivity* and *empathy* are understood as the real drive behind any communicative behaviours. I also adopted the dynamic syntax framework to formalize these ideas, and presented some examples which show how formalism can indeed explain the enrichment process of structures and meanings. I did not want to overwhelm readers with too much logical formalism. Hence, I chose not to present formal analysis for each language and example. Rather, I leave that task for readers and researchers: to observe, describe and explain.

Notes

Abbreviations and conventions

1 To avoid confusion, I have put the local orthography in brackets after the romanized form. This is intended to elucidate understanding for target languages in which romanization is less straightforward.
2 For example: https://www.eva.mpg.de/lingua/pdf/Glossing-Rules.pdf; http://www.llf.cnrs.fr/sites/llf.cnrs.fr/files/statiques/Abbreviation_gloses-eng.pdf
3 Asian languages on the whole present major problems for traditional romanization systems; these issues are still largely unresolved. This is the case for many Asian languages.

Chapter 1

1 'There is a rich English-language material in some of these languages as catalogued in Huffman's *Bibliography and Index of Mainland Southeast Asian Languages and Linguistics* (1986), but most of this literature is in the form of unpublished doctoral theses written in American university linguistics departments during the 1970s and 1980s and therefore not readily available' (Smyth 2002: 5).
2 During interviews I conducted with UK primary school pupils in 2018 as part of a project aimed at increasing the general awareness of Asian languages and culture, many students believed that the language spoken in India is 'Indian'.
3 https://www.state.gov/foreign-language-training/ Foreign Service Institute 2019

   A) Category III languages
      'Hard languages' – Languages with significant linguistic and/or cultural differences from English.
      E.g. Persian Farsi, Hebrew, Hindi, Russian, Serbian/Croatian, Tagalog, Thai, Turkish, Uzbek, Urdu
   B) Category IV languages
      'Super-hard languages' – Languages which are exceptionally difficult for native English speakers.
      E.g. Arabic, Chinese, Japanese, Korean, Pashto
4 Clitics are morphemes that have the syntactic characteristics of a word yet are morphologically bound to other words.

5 It is noticeable that Kuno did not gloss the endings with DECL but left them as they were.
6 In this book, I assume the basic unit to be an utterance rather than a sentence. Sentence-centred linguistics is a strong example, demonstrating the limits of theoretical linguistics, which is primarily grounded in the formal written register.
7 Chomsky (1965) distinguished three levels of empirical adequacy that a formal linguistic analysis can meet. They are observational, descriptive and explanatory adequacy. Chomsky (1965: 63) put emphasis on explanatory adequacy as the following quote shows:

> A linguistic theory that aims for explanatory adequacy is concerned with the internal structure of the device [i.e. grammar]; that is, it aims to provide a principled basis, independent of any particular language, for the selection of the descriptively adequate grammar of each language.

8 In the nineteenth-century colonial period, a great effort was made to impart the language of the colony onto the colonized peoples. Little effort was made to investigate the colonized peoples' languages. For example, little is known in the UK with regard to Indian languages. Exceptionally, in the early twentieth century, Japanese scholar Ogura Shinpei's research made an enormous impact in the research and linguistic understanding of the Korean language.
9 In a sample of 568 sentences of Caesar's writings containing all three elements examined by Pinkster (1990), the proportions were SOV ordering (63 per cent), OSV ordering (21 per cent), OVS ordering (6 per cent), VOS (5 per cent), SVO (4 per cent) and VSO (1 per cent).
10 https://wals.info/feature/81A#2/18.0/152.9
11 Sorbian and Basque exhibit OV ordering. German and Dutch in the generative grammar framework are considered OV ordering – although the OV orderings observed in these languages are significantly different from what we observe in Asian languages.
12 Arabic is interesting, in that according to WALS, Egyptian, Gulf, Kuwait and Iraqi Arabic show SVO order as a preferred order, whereas Modern Standard Arabic prefers VSO order, and Syrian Arabic prefers no dominant order.
13 Data for this section is taken from https://www.ethnologue.com/.
14 It is interesting to note that while Indian languages belong to the Indo-European language family in terms of etymology, when it comes to particle behaviours, Indian languages behave just like other Asian languages, rather than mirroring Western European languages. The etymological link does not reproduce similarity in the morphosyntactic and pragmatic behaviours of European and Indian languages.

Chapter 2

1. This chapter is modified and extended from Kiaer (2007).
2. Any discontinuity between an expression and some associated expression at the right periphery of some clausal sequence can only be local: there is no long-distance dependency between some position of construal ('the gap') and some right-place constituent.
3. This book strongly features Korean as it has been developed from Kiaer (2007, 2014). However, I have tried to show patterns and examples from various Asian languages throughout.
4. For syntactic explanations, I use Yale romanization, and elsewhere I strive for intuitive phonetic romanization.
5. Karimi reports that there is some restriction between two dislocated *wh*-expressions (Karimi 2018: 167).
6. The subjacency condition forbids movement across more than one bounding node, to adopt movement terminology.
7. These criteria are: (i) movement; (ii) coordination; (iii) deletion (i.e. ellipsis); (iv) reciprocal binding and weak cross-over and (v) symmetry of scope construal. All discussion of these criteria will make reference to assumptions which are standard within movement analysis (e.g. c-command, binding principles, deletion) (see Phillips 1996, 2003).
8. Chomsky (1986) and Lasnik and Saito (1992) argued that application of more than one long-distance movement from within the same clause necessarily yields a subjacency violation.
9. Nordlinger's generalization on case morphology is as follows:

   - **Generalization A:**
     Case morphology can construct grammatical relations on a par with, and independently from phrase structure.
   - **Generalization B:**
     Case morphology can construct larger syntactic context, including providing complex information about the clause.

10. There are two functions in LFG which are as follows.

    a. f SUBJ: outside in
    b. f: [SUBJ f:[ ]]: inside out

    In the regular designator (f SUBJ), f denotes the outer f-structure. It states that f-structure from which one can follow a path *inwards* through SUBJ to the f-structure is denoted by the whole designator. Hence, functional application works from the outside in. *Inside-out* functional application is exactly the opposite.

11 Karamanis (2001) modified Baldridge's version of CCG and specified the argument's syntactic position in the lexicon. For instance, the value + FRO denotes that there is a fronted argument involved.

Chapter 3

1. 'I have no explanation as to why anyone thinks that a reaction time experiment tells you more about psychological reality than a fact about synonymy' Chomsky (2011: 52).
2. Often information beyond 'syntax' is required for even grammaticality judgements as we have discussed earlier.
3. Psycholinguists are understandably sensitive to appropriate control technique to ensure no interfering factors, for example, by using a sufficient number of filler sentences.
4. The reaction of a speaker to a sentence has traditionally been considered as a grammaticality judgement. However, as grammar is a mental construct not accessible to conscious awareness, speakers do not link the status of a sentence to the grammar. Instead, speakers judge sentences based on how 'good' or 'bad' it sounds to them. An acceptability judgement, in this framework, is an immediate, spontaneous response of the native speaker to strings of words, where acceptability is a percept that exists only within a participant's mind. As precepts are in nature difficult to measure, one common method is to ask participants to report their perceptions along a devised scale. In this way, an acceptability judgement is in fact a reported perception of acceptability (Chomsky 1965, Schütze 1996).
5. Kiaer and Shin (ms) shows that the interpersonal mismatch is more easily observed when the length between the subject and verb becomes longer. Simply put, one cannot remember everything and one of the most efficient ways to build a structure is to lower the burden of memory load.
6. Global checking may be possible and done in reading and writing, but not in speaking and hearing. In speaking and hearing – which reflects the spontaneous use of language – checking is only done locally.
7. Thanks to Professor Jiyoung Shin for insightful discussion on this topic.
8. Aoshima et al. (2004: 42) noted, 'By unforced reanalysis, we mean a revision that is not licensed by any incompatibility of the initial analysis of the parse with subsequent material.' Simply, there is no morphosyntactic motivation to revise a structure and thus, structural revision as such is not compulsory.
9. Aoshima et al (2003a) assumed that the *Wh*- phrase has two features, namely, a *wh*-feature and θ-feature. Yet, at the point of the first gap, neither of these features

is satisfied, because no verb has yet been seen. Furthermore, since the gap is not pronounced, positing a new gap doesn't entail any phonological commitment. When readers encounter the Q-particle on the embedded verb as in (20), both the *wh*-feature and the θ-feature will be checked. The *wh*-feature is checked because the Q-particle is a scope marker and the θ-feature is also to be checked because it can be recognized as an argument of the verb. On the other hand, in (20), when readers encounter the first verb without a Q-particle, the θ-feature can be checked, but the *wh*-feature cannot be checked.

10 This can also be observed in other language syntax textbooks. For instance, Pica and Rooryck (1994) have observed tensions within French linguistics:

> It is not entirely surprising that, on the one hand, the majority of French intellectuals have tended to disregard generative grammar as soon as they realized that it was moving from a system of syntactic rules towards a theory based on a small amount of general constraints and principles.

> On the other hand, the descriptive data on French which was collected by more traditional approaches has not always been taken into account by the French generativist school. French generativists have sometimes disregarded the amazing amount of data which had been accumulated by the European structuralist tradition, since this tradition was considered to be entirely hostile. As we have tried to show, this assumption was based on a partial misunderstanding.

Chapter 4

1 The *OED* defines *benevolence* as disposition to do good, desire to promote the happiness of others, kindness, generosity, charitable feeling (as a general state or disposition towards humankind at large) or favourable feeling or disposition, as an emotion manifested towards another; affection; goodwill (towards a particular person or on a particular occasion).
2 I think glossing this example is too complicated and it is unnecessary for the discussion. So I will leave out glossing for this example.
3 This phrase, appearing here in its Korean pronunciation, can alternatively be pronounced *Zhǎng yòu yǒu xù* in Mandarin Chinese, and in various other pronunciations in Cantonese Chinese, Vietnamese and so on. Commonly thought of as a Chinese philosophy (and indeed it did originate in ancient China), Confucianism has had an enormous impact on the cultural traditions of countries all over East Asia, Korea and Vietnam in particular.

4   Buddhism and Hinduism must have had great influence on Southeast Asian languages and culture. For instance, Caryāgīti, a collection of Buddhist mystical songs of realization (eighth to twelfth centuries), greatly *influenced* the development of the Bengali language and literature. Vaishnavism (a major Hindu tradition) also contributed to the development and enrichment of Bengali language and literature throughout the Middle Ages (Ranjamrittika Bhowmik, p.c.). However, more research is needed to prove how these religions influenced Southeast Asian languages.

Chapter 5

1 Intimacy matters even in the choice of language varieties. People do not automatically choose to speak in dialect simply because they are from the same region as their companion. Speaking in dialect or initiating dialect use reflects the intimacy between interlocutors.
2 It is important to note that age is calculated differently in Korea than in other parts of the world. Koreans count the time in the womb as the first year of life; each child is a year old at birth. Additionally, one's age changes not on one's birthday in Korean culture, but on the first day of the new year. This means that everyone changes age on the same day and that all people born in the same year are the same age, regardless of the date of birth. By this system, a child born on 1 January of this year and a child born on 31 December of this year will both turn two years old on 1 January of next year. Age is such an important factor in Korean society and culture that even a difference in one month of age could change relational dynamics.
3 There is interesting difference between languages too. For instance, seniority seems to be less clear in the case of nodding in Japanese compared to Korean (Sotaro Kita, p.c.). Bowing is common in Korean and Japanese cultures but not in Chinese.
4 While this can be said to generally be the case across Asian countries and cultures, each individual culture naturally has a different tolerance to politeness and certain behaviours in different situations.
5 Thanks to Professor Zhu Hua and Li Wei for inspiring comments which helped me to develop this part.
6 The particular wording 'orchestrating' is from Li Wei's talk (p.c.).
7 An interesting point is that, because address terms are so important in Korean culture, even heritage speakers, while speaking in another language like English, strongly feel that they should use address terms and never refer to anyone older than themselves with their first names. The following comments are from

interviews with a Korean American professor in the United States and a Korean woman living in the United Kingdom:

> 'I have lived in the US for 40 years but I can't call Professor Song's first name although we speak mainly in English. I need to call him Professor Song. Otherwise, he will be seriously offended.' (John, Professor, Korean American, sixty years old)

> 'I couldn't call my father-in-law's first name for a long time. I had to call him 'David's Dad' for a while. They thought it was weird and felt distant. So I finally called him 'Paul'. But, it was very difficult at first.' (Korean woman living in London, married to an Englishman)

8 One can consider such a relation to be both intimate and benevolent, but in some cases the combination of intimacy and social hierarchy can produce suppressive social dynamics.
9 One may regard that swear words have only expressive functions, that is, they only reflect one's emotions. Yet, the use of such words can also reflect interpersonal dimensions. People consider when and where to use them very carefully. In a sense, the fact that one feels comfortable using swear words is a sign of feelings of intimacy and confidence towards others.
10 Half-talk (*panmal*) is an informal speech style in Korean used between friends.
11 There is no 'polite particle following at the end' here. The polite meaning in this example is not signifying a particle, but rather the tone of the sentence, which is set off by the word '*dooy*' alone, not a particle. Lao doesn't really have a universal polite particle like Thai does with *krap* and *ka*.
12 See Agnihotri (2013).
13 It is used for people of higher status, older in age, strangers and non-intimates. For example, in primary and middle school students use the pronoun 'vous' when talking to their teachers, while the teachers use the second-person singular pronoun 'tu'. It is not until the last few years of high school that teachers started using the pronoun 'vous' when addressing their students as a sign of mutual respect. When talking to strangers, whether asking for directions in the street or ordering food in a restaurant, the pronoun 'vous' is used and it would be considered incredibly rude to use the pronoun 'tu' (Nathalie Pascaru, p.c.).
14 'Many Bengali women go through their whole adult lives addressing their parents-in-law as apni even if, as is usually the case, they live with them. The second person familiar tumi is used between husband and wife, friends, and relatives, although it is not unusual for younger members of the family to address their elders as apni and be themselves addressed as tumi. It is unusual for adult Bengalis in Bangladesh to change from apni to tumi amongst themselves or to address foreigners with tumi, but in West Bengal a more informal attitude prevails and the use of tumi among colleagues and acquaintants is more common.' (Thomson 2012: 68)

15 This phenomenon of calling the elderly or other older people using kinship terms seems to be quite prevalent across Asia, particularly in Northeast Asia and Southeast Asia.

Chapter 6

1. https://glossary.sil.org/term/plural-number
2. See Dryer (2013).
3. 'The adverbial topic, including a postpositional one, is basically a stylistic topic. It exploits the basic separating function of the true topic . . . the so-called topic construction in Japanese is, in fact, of two kinds: one that reflects experiential judgment, and another that is a stylistic variant of a simple sentence. . . . The genuine topic construction is correlated with one mode of human judgment, while the other, the stylistic topic, is only a superficial device similar to scrambling.' (Shibatani 1990: 277)
4. This would mean 'The elephant has a long nose' (some specific one).
5. Source: https://halshs.archives-ouvertes.fr/halshs-00945897/document
6. This is another way of glossing the particle. Transliteration is another glossing strategy.
7. Saying nothing does not necessarily mean expressing nothing. For example, the lack of emojiing while texting may indicate indifference.

Chapter 7

1. Classical Arabic and Modern Standard Arabic (MSA) exhibit VSO languages. Yet, other spoken Arabic dialects including colloquial Jordanian Arabic follows a SVO order. Yet, even in 'standard' language, the use of certain particles and stylistic choices can make fronted nominal subjects (Nadia Jamil, p.c.).
2. Here, 'left-to-right' doesn't mean writing order (cf. Arabic is written in right to left), it just means that the linguistic structure is built in a 'time-linear' manner. Leftmost structure is what's been built first, right-most structure is what's been built at the latest.
3. I aimed to simplify the formalisms of dynamic syntax (DS) as much as possible for the purpose of reader accessibility. For a detailed formalism, see Cann et al. (2005) and Kempson et al. (2001).
4. Case is a system of marking dependent nouns for the type of relationship they bear to their heads. Traditionally the term refers to inflectional marking, and, typically, case marks the relationship of a noun to a verb at the clause level or of a noun to a preposition, postposition or another noun at the phrase level (Blake 2001: 1).

5   In this book, parsing and structure-building refer to the same process. Parser, structure-builder and ordinary speaker also all have the same meaning.
6   Recent studies in theoretical syntax showed the necessity to define syntactic operations as sensitive to phonological factors to explain somewhat (neglected) syntactic phenomena (e.g. Kitagawa and Fodor 2003).
7   See further Gregoromichelaki and Kempson (2019), 'Procedural Syntax'. 10.1017/9781108290593.017.
8   Thanks to Nadia Christopher for data consultation.
9   Languages of this kind are 'without distinct construction-specific semantic rules, compositional semantics relying instead on the association operator, which says that the meaning of a composite expression is associated with the meanings of its constituents in an underspecified fashion' (Gil 2005a: 1).
10 The formal DS definition of locality is as following:
$$\langle\uparrow_0\rangle\langle\uparrow_1\rangle X \equiv \langle\uparrow_0\rangle X \ \vee\ \langle\uparrow_0\rangle\langle\uparrow_1\rangle X \ \vee\ \langle\uparrow_0\rangle\langle\uparrow_1\rangle\langle\uparrow_1\rangle \cdots.$$
11 Notice that the application of local *adjunction yields a locally underspecified tree-node address $\langle\uparrow_0\rangle\langle\uparrow_1\rangle Tn(a)$. If there are two local. ly unfixed nodes with the same address as this, based on LOFT, it simply means that they are the same node, and with the case specification given, this will be just one node with two inconsistent decorations such as $\langle\uparrow_0\rangle\langle\uparrow_1\rangle Tn(a)$ (=object) and $\langle\uparrow_0\rangle Tn(a)$ (=subject).
12 'But how are we to know which phenomena belong to the core and which to the periphery? The literature offers no principled criteria for distinguishing the two, … the distinction seems both arbitrary and subjective.' (Sag 2010: 486–545)
13 I am very grateful to Prof Li Wei and Prof Zhu Hua for insightful conversation.

Chapter 9

1   This becomes a real challenge in Asian linguistics. Descriptions in Asian linguistics, such as romanization and glossing are often found to be inconsistent. The problem lies in the system, which takes little consideration of the way that language is actually used by native speakers in daily life.
2   Shei (2014: 206).
3   Thanks to Alexandra Kimmons for this observation and comments.
4   Chu (2009: 284).
5   Shei (2014: 207–8).
6   Shei (2014: 232).
7   Example from Shei (2014: 225).
8   Chu (2009: 298).

9. Example from Shei (2014: 256).
10. There are great similarities between particles and interjections, but there are significant differences too. For simplicity's sake, particles can be understood as an interjection attached to a word which expresses strong emotion.
11. Fundamental frequency (F0) is a physical property of sound (in the case of speech, the number of glottal pulses in a second). It is measured in Hz.
12. I believe that the term 'LINK' structure itself well captures the intuition of enriching and extending a structure by 'LINKING' an appendix structure with the main ongoing structure.
13. It is true, however, that the formalism presented in the literature so far does not appear particularly simple, despite the intention of the original authors. Therefore, in this book I tried to demonstrate the essence of the formalism without too much logical outlook.
14. Note that the degree of unnaturalness is also sensitive to the register, communication environment, culture and individual tastes/choices.

Bibliography

Agnihotri, R. K. (2013). *Hindi: An Essential Grammar*. London: Routledge.
Alfonso, A. (1971). 'On the \"adversative\" passive'. *The Journal-Newsletter of the Association of Teachers of Japanese*, 7(1), 1–7.
Aoshima, S. Phillips, C. & Weinberg, A. (2004). 'Processing filler-gap dependencies in a head-final language'. *Journal of Memory and Language 51*, 23–54.
Aoshima, S. Phillips, C. & Yoshida, M. (2005). 'The source of the bias for longer filler-gap dependencies in Japanese'. Paper presented at the 18th Annual CUNY Conference on Human Sentence Processing, University of Arizona, Tucson.
Asudeh, A. (2011). 'Local grammaticality in syntactic production'. In Emily M. Bender & Jennifer E. Arnold (eds), *Language from a Cognitive Perspective: Grammar, Usage, and Processing. Studies in Honor of Thomas Wasow*, pp. 51–79. Stanford: CSLI Publications.
Badhe, P. & Kulkarni, V. (2015). 'Indian sign language translator using gesture recognition algorithm'. *2015 IEEE International Conference on Computer Graphics, Vision and Information Security (CGVIS)*, 195–200.
Baldridge, J. (2002). 'Lexically Specified Derivational Control in Combinatory Categorial Grammar'. Unpublished doctoral dissertation, University of Edinburgh, Edinburgh.
Ball, P. (2011). *Patterns in Nature: Why the Natural World Looks the Way It Does*. Chicago: University of Chicago Press.
Bhatia, T. & Ritchie, W. (2004). *The Handbook of Bilingualism* (Blackwell Handbooks in Linguistics). Oxford: Blackwell.
Bickel, B. & Nichols, J. (2013). 'Inflectional Synthesis of the Verb'. In Matthew S. Dryer & Martin Haspelmath (eds), *The World Atlas of Language Structures Online*. Leipzig: Max Planck Institute for Evolutionary Anthropology. Retrieved online at http://wals.info/chapter/22. Accessed on 11 November 2019.
Birdwhistell, R. L. (1970). *Kinesics and Context: Essays on Body Motion Communication*. Philadelphia: University of Pennsylvania Press
Blackburn, P. & Meyer-Viol, W. (1994). 'Linguistics, logic, and finite trees'. *Bulletin of Interest Group of Pure and Applied Logics 2*, 2–39.
Blake, B. (2001). *Case*. Cambridge: Cambridge University Press.
Bolinger, D. (1961). 'Verbal evocation'. *Lingua*, 10, 113–27.
Bošković, Ź. & Takahashi, D. (1998). 'Scrambling and last resort'. *Linguistic Inquiry* 29, 347–66.
Braun, F. (1984). 'Rumänische Anredeform'. In W. Winter (ed.), *Anredeverhalten*, 151–89. Tübingen: G. Narr Verlag.
Bresnan, J. (1982). 'Control and complementation'. *Linguistic Inquiry*, 13(3), 343–434.

Bresnan, J. (2001). *Lexical Functional Syntax*. Oxford: Blackwell.
Brown, L. (2015). 'Revisiting "polite" –yo and "deferential" –supnita speech style shifting in Korean from the viewpoint of indexicality'. *Journal of Pragmatics*, 79, 43–59.
Brown, P. & Levinson, S. (1978). 'Universals in language use: Politeness phenomena'. In E. N. Goody (ed.), *Questions and Politeness: Strategies in Social Interaction*, pp. 56–289. New York: Cambridge University.
Brown, P. & Levinson, S. (1987). *Politeness: Some Universals in Language Usage (Studies in Interactional Sociolinguistics; 4)*. Cambridge: Cambridge University Press.
Cann, R., Kempson, R. & Marten, L. (2005). *The Dynamics of Language*. Oxford: Elsevier.
Cho, M. (2011). 'Study on the Finalizing Function of Connective Endings and the Role of Intonation'. Unpublished PhD thesis, Korea University, Seoul.
Chomsky, N. (1957). *Syntactic Structures*. The Hague: Mouton.
Chomsky, N. (1965). *Aspects of the Theory of Syntax*. Cambridge, MA: MIT Press.
Chomsky, N. (1981). *Lectures on Government and Binding*. Dordrecht: Foris.
Chomsky, N. A. (1986). *Knowledge of Language: Its Nature, Origin and Use*. New York: Praeger.
Chomsky, N. (1995). *The Minimalist Program*. Cambridge, MA: MIT Press.
Chomsky, N. (1998). *Minimalist Inquiries: The Framework*. Cambridge, MA: MIT Press.
Chomsky, N. (2011). *The Generative Enterprise Revisited: Discussions with Riny Huybregts, Henk van Riemsdijk, Naoki Fukui and Mihoko Zushi*. Mouton: De Gruyeter.
Chen, M. & Chung, J. (2002). 'Seniority and superiority: A case analysis of decision Making in a Taiwanese Religious Group', *Intercultural Communication Studies XI-1*.
Christopher, N. (2018). 'Aspects of Information Structure in Kazakh – The Dynamic Syntax Approach'. Unpublished doctoral dissertation, University of London, London, UK.
Chu, C. (2009). 'Relevance and the discourse functions of Mandarin utterance-final modality'. *Language and Linguistics*, 3(1), 282–99.
Cook, H. (1990). 'The sentence-final particle ne as a tool for cooperation in Japanese conversation'. In H. Hoji (ed.), *Japanese Korean Linguistics*, pp. 29–44. Stanford: CSLI.
Dalrymple, M. (2001). *Lexical Functional Grammar*. New York: Academic Press.
Dryer, Matthew S. (2013a). *Coding of Nominal Plurality*. In M. S. Dryer & M. Haspelmath (eds), *The World Atlas of Language Structures Online*. Leipzig: Max Planck Institute for Evolutionary Anthropology. Available online at http://wals.info/chapter/s6. Accessed on 7 November 2019.
Dryer, Matthew S. (2013b). *Determining dominant word order*. In M. S. Dryer & M. Haspelmath (eds), *The World Atlas of Language Structures Online*. Leipzig: Max Planck Institute for Evolutionary Anthropology. Available online at http://wals.info/chapter/s6, Accessed on 7 November 2019.

Dyson, T. (2001). 'The preliminary demography of the 2001 census of India'. *Population and Development Review*, *27*(2), 341–56.

Eelen, G. (2001). *A Critique of Politeness Theories*. Manchester: St. Jerome Publishing.

Enfield, N. J. (2007). *A Grammar of Lao* (Vol. 38). New York: Walter de Gruyter.

Erguvanli, E (1984). *The Function of Word Order in Turkish Grammar*. Berkeley: University of California Press.

Ferguson, C. (1991). 'South Asia as a sociolinguistic area'. In E. Dimock, B. Kachru & Bh. Kririshnamurti (eds), *Dimensions of South Asia as a Sociolinguistic Area: Papers and Memory of Gerald Kelly*, pp. 25–36. New Delhi, Oxford.

Fitt, C. (2017). *Non-typical wa in the Corpus of Spontaneous Japanese and expressive semantics: at the pragmatics-syntax interface*. Mst thesis, University of Oxford, Oxford.

Fodor, J. D. (2002). 'Prosodic disambiguation in silent reading'. *Proceedings of the North East Linguistic Society*, *32*, 113–32.

Futane, P. & Dharaskar, R. (2011). '"Hasta Mudra": An interpretation of Indian sign hand gestures'. *2011 3rd International Conference on Electronics Computer Technology, 2*, 377–80.

Garcia, O. & Wei, L. (2014). *Translanguaging: Language, Bilingualism and Education*. New York: Palgrave Macmillian.

Gick, B., Wilson, I. & Derrick, D. (2012). *Articulatory Phonetics*. Oxford: John Wiley & Sons.

Goddard, C. (2005). *The Languages of East and Southeast Asia: An Introduction*. Oxford: Oxford University Press.

Göksel, A. & Kerslake, C. (2005). *Turkish: A Comprehensive Grammar*. New York: Routledge.

Grewendorf, G. (2001). 'Multiple wh-fronting'. *Linguistic Inquiry*, *32*, 87–122.

Grewendorf, G. & Sabel, J. (1999). 'Scrambling in German and Japanese: Adjunction versus multiple specifiers'. *Natural Language & Linguistic Theory*, *17*, 1–65.

Gregoromichelaki, E. & Kempson, R. (2019). 'Procedural syntax'. In K. Scott, B. Clark & R. Carston (eds), *Relevance, Pragmatics and Interpretation*, pp. 187–202. Cambridge: Cambridge University Press, . doi: 10.1017/9781108290593.017

Grice, H. P. (1975). 'Logic and conversation'. In P. Cole and J. Morgan (eds), *Studies in Syntax and Semantics III: Speech Acts*, pp. 183–98. New York: Academic Press.

Gungordu, Z. (1997). 'Incremental constraint-based parsing: An efficient approach for head-final languages'. Unpublished doctoral dissertation, Centre for Cognitive Science, University of Edinburgh, Edinburgh.

Gutman, A. & Beatriz, A. (2013). *Mongolian*. Retrieved from http://www.languagesgulper.com/eng/Mongolian.html

Halliday, M. (1967). *Intonation and Grammar in British English*. The Hague: Mouton.

Halliday, M. (1978). *Language as Social Semiotic: The Social Interpretation of Language and Meaning*. London: Edward Arnold.

Harada, S. I. (1976). 'Honorifics'. In Masayoshi Shibatani (ed.), *Syntax and Semantics: Japanese Generative Grammar*. New York: Academic Press, 499–561.

Hasegawa, Y. (2014). *Japanese: A Linguistic Introduction.* Cambridge: Cambridge University Press.

Hawkins, J. (1994). *A Performance Theory of Order and Constituency.* Cambridge: Cambridge University Press.

Hawkins, J. (2004). *Efficiency and Complexity in Grammars.* Oxford: Oxford University Press.

Hawkins, J. (2014). *Cross-Linguistic Variation and Efficiency.* Oxford: Oxford University Press.

Hejmadi, A., Davidson, R. & Rozin, P. (2000). 'Exploring Hindu Indian emotion expressions: Evidence for Accurate Recognition by Americans and Indians'. *Psychological Science, 11*(3), 183–7.

Hoffman, B. (1995). 'Integrating "free" word order syntax and information structure'. In *Proceedings of the Seventh Conference of the European Chapter of the Association for Computational Linguistics.* Association for Computational Linguistics.

Huffman, Franklin E. (1986). *Bibliography and Index of Mainland Southeast Asian Languages and Linguistics.* New Haven: Yale University Press.

Hua Z., Li, W. & Jankowicz-Pytel, D. (2019). 'Whose karate? Language and cultural learning in a multilingual karate club in London', *Applied Linguistics*, amz014, https://doi.org/10.1093/applin/amz014

Ide, S. (1982). 'Japanese sociolinguistics: Politeness and women's language'. *Lingua, 57*, 357–85.

Ide, S. (1989). 'Formal forms and discernment: Two neglected aspects of universals of linguistic politeness'. *Multilingua, 8*(2/3), 223–48.

Inoue, A. & Fodor, J. (1995). 'Information-based parsing of Japanese'. In R. Mazuka & N. Nagai (eds), *Japanese Sentence Processing,* 9–64. Hillsdale, NJ: Lawrence Erlbaum.

Jain, D. & Cardona, G. (2007). *The Indo-Aryan Languages.* London and New York: Routledge.

Jenkins, J. (2007). 'English as a Lingua Franca: Attitude and identity'. *English World-Wide, 30*(3), 327–31.

Jenny, M. & Tun, H. (2017). *Burmese: A Comprehensive Grammar.* London: Routledge.

Jun, S. (1993). 'The Phonetics and Phonology of Korea Prosody'. Unpublished doctoral dissertation, The Ohio State University, Columbus, OH.

Jun, S. (2000). K-ToBI (Korean ToBI). Labelling conventions: Version 3. *Speech Sciences 7*, 143–69.

Jun, S. (2005). 'Prosodic typology'. In S. Jun (ed.), *Prosodic Typology,* pp. 430–58. Oxford: Oxford University Press.

Jun, S. (2014). *Prosodic Typology II: The Phonology of Intonation and Phrasing.* Oxford: Oxford University Press.

Kachru, B. B. (1985). 'Standards, codification, and sociolinguistic realism: The English language in the outer circle'. In R. Quirk and H. Widdowson (eds), *English in the World: Teaching and Learning the Language and the Literature.* Cambridge: Cambridge University Press.

Kaplan, D. (1989). 'Demonstratives: An essay on the semantics, logic, metaphysics, and epistemology of demonstratives and other indexicals'. In J. Almog, J. Perry & Howard Wettstein (eds), *Themes from Kaplan: Constancy and Change in China's Social and Economic History, 1550-1949*, pp. 481–614. Oxford: Oxford University Press.

Kaplan, R. & Zaenen, A. (1989). 'Long-distance dependencies, constituent structure, and functional uncertainty'. In M. Baltin & A. Kroch (eds), *Alternative Conceptions of Phrase Structure*, pp. 17–42. Chicago: University of Chicago Press.

Karamanis, N. (2001). 'A categorial grammar for Greek'. In *Proceedings of the 15th International Symposium on Theoretical and Applied Linguistics.* Aristotle University of Thessaloniki.

Karimi, S. (ed.) (2003). *Word Order and Scrambling.* Oxford: Blackwell.

Karimi, S. (2018) 'Generative approaches to syntax'. In A. Sedighi & P. Shabani-Jadidi (eds), *The Oxford Handbook of Persian Linguistics.* Oxford: Oxford University Press.

Kathol, A. (1995). 'Verb-movement in German and topological fields'. In *Papers from the 31st Regional Meeting*, Chicago Linguistic Society, pp. 231–45. Chicago: Chicago Linguistic Society.

Kathol, A. & Pollard, C. (1995). 'Extraposition via complex domain formation'. In *Proceedings of the 31st Annual Meeting of the ACL.* Cambridge, MA: Association of Computational Linguistics.

Kempson, R., Cann, R. & Kiaer, J. (2006). 'Topic, focus and the structural dynamics of language'. *The Architecture of Focus*, 59, 82.

Kempson, R. & Kiaer, J. (2010). 'Multiple long-distance scrambling: Syntax as reflections of processing 1'. *Journal of Linguistics*, 46(1), 127–92.

Kempson, R., Meyer-Viol, W. & Gabbay, D. (2001). *Dynamic Syntax: The Flow of Language Understanding.* Oxford: Blackwell.

Kempson, R., Gregoromichelaki, E. & Howes, C. (2019). 'Language as mechanisms for interaction: Towards an evolutionary tale'. In A. Silva, S. Staton, P. Sutton & C. Umbach (eds), *Language, Logic, and Computation.* TbiLLC 2018. Lecture Notes in Computer Science, vol. 11456. Berlin and Heidelberg: Springer.

Kendon, A. (1988). 'How gestures can become like words'. In Fernando Poyatos (ed.), *Cross Cultural Perspectives in Nonverbal Communication,* pp. 131–41. Toronto: C.J. Hugrele.

Kendon, A. (2004). *Gesture: Visible Action as Utterance.* Cambridge: Cambridge University Press.

Keresztes, László. (1992). *Praktische ungarische Grammatik.* Debrecen: Debreceni Nyári Egyetem.

Kiaer, J. (2007). 'Processing and Interfaces in Syntactic Theory: The Case of Korean'. Unpublished doctoral dissertation, University of London, London.

Kiaer, J. (2010). 'On the Meaning and Distribution of TUL in Korean: Evidence from Corpora'. *Language Research*, 46(2), 257–72.

Kiaer, J. (2014). *Pragmatic Syntax (Bloomsbury Studies in Theoretical Linguistics)*. London: Bloomsbury.

Kiaer, J. (2017a). *Does a Language Have to Be European to Be Modern?* Retrieved from https://www.languageonthemove.com/does-a-language-have-to-be-european-to-be-modern/

Kiaer, J. (2017b). 'Korean drama and variety shows in teaching pragmatics and intercultural communicative competence: A case study from KFL learners' interviews'. *Journal of International Korean Education*, 3(1), 113–45.

Kiaer, J. (2018). *Translingual Words: An East Asian Lexical Encounter with English*. 1st edn. London: Routledge.

Kiaer, J. & Shin, J. (2012). 'Prosodic interpretation of object particle omission in Korean (Mokjeokgyeokjosa saengryak hyeonsange daehan unyuljeok haeseok)'. *Korean Linguistics (Hangugeohak)*, 57, 331–55.

Kiaer, J. & Shin, J. (ms) *Prosodic Length and Grammaticality Judgements: The Case of Korean*. Korea Uniersity.

Kiaer, J., Park, M. J., Choi, N. & Driggs, D. (2019). 'The roles of age, gender and Settingin Korean Half-talk Shift (2019)'. *Discourse and Cognition*, 26(3), 279–308.

Kim, A. H. (2011). 'Politeness in Korea'. In D. Z. Kádár, & S. Mills (eds), *Politeness in East Asia*, pp. 176–207. Cambridge: Cambridge University Press.

Kim, S. (2010). *Hwupochwung kwumwunuy wunyulkwu hyengseng yangsang*, 'A Prosodic Analysis on Post-verbal Expressions in Korean'. Master's thesis, Korea University, Seoul.

Kim, J. B., Sells, P. & Yang, J. (2007). 'Parsing two types of multiple nominative constructions: A Constructional approach'. *Language and Information*, 11(1), 25–37.

Kitagawa, Y. & Fodor (2003). 'Default prosody explains neglected syntactic analyses of Japanese.' In W. McClure (ed.), *Japanese/Korean Linguistics*, vol. 12, pp. 267–79. Stanford, CA: CSLI Publication.

Knapp, M. L. & Hall, J. A. (2005). *Nonverbal Communication in Human Interaction*. 6th edn. Belmont, CA: Wadsworth.

Knapp, M. L., Hall, J. A. & Horgan, T. G. (2014). *Nonverbal Communication in Human Interaction*. Belmont: Wadsworth/Cengage learning.

Ko, S. (1997). 'The resolution of the dative NP ambiguity in Korean'. *Journal of Psycholinguistic Research*, 26(2), 265–73.

Koh, H. (2002). *A Cross-Cultural Study of Address Terms in Korean and English*. PhD dissertation, University of Hawaii, Hawaii.

Koizumi, M. (2000). 'String vacuous overt verb raising'. *Journal of East Asian Linguistics*, 9, 227–85.

Kratzer, A. (1999). 'Beyond ouch and oops: How descriptive and expressive meaning interact'. http://semanticsarchive.net/Archive/WEwNGUyO/. A comment on David Kaplan's paper, Cornell Conference on Theories of Context Dependency.

Kroeger, P. (1993). *Phrase Structure and Grammatical Relations in Tagalog*. Center for the Study of Language (CSLI).

Kuno, S. (1973). *The Structure of the Japanese Language (Current Studies in Linguistics Series; 3)*. Cambridge, MA and London: MIT Press.

Kurosawa, A. (2003). 'A Dynamic Syntax Account of the Syntactic and Pragmatic Properties of Japanese Relative Clauses'. Unpublished doctoral dissertation, King's College London.

Larson, R. (1988). 'On the double object construction'. *Linguistic Inquiry*, 9(1), 335–91.

Lasnik, H. and M. Saito. (1992). *Move Alpha: Conditions on Its Application and Output*. Cambridge, MA: MIT Press.

Lazard, G. (1992). *A Grammar of Contemporary Persian*. Costa Mesa, CA: Mazda Publishers.

Lee, D. (2002). 'The function of the zero particle with special reference to spoken Japanese'. *Journal of Pragmatics*, 34, 645–82.

Lee, E., Madigan, S. & Park, M.-J. (2016). *An Introduction to Korean Linguistics*. London: Routledge.

Lee, H. (2003). 'Parallel optimization in case systems'. In M. Butt & T. H. King (eds), *Nominals: Inside and Out*, pp. 15–58. Stanford: CSLI Publications.

Lee, H. (2006). 'Effects of focus and markedness hierarchies on object case ellipsis in Korean'. *Discouse and Cognition* 13(2), 205–31.

Lee, S. (2001). 'Argument composition and linearization'. *OSUWPL* 56, 53–78.

Lee, S. (2006). 'A pragmatic analysis of accusative case-marker deletion'. *Discourse and Cognition*, 13(3), 69–89.

Li, A., Fang, Q. & Dang, J. (2011). 'Emotional intonation in a tone language: Experimental evidence from Chinese'. In *ICPhS*, pp. 1198–201. Retrieved from: https://www.internationalphoneticassociation.org/icphs-proceedings/ICPhS2011/OnlineProceedings/RegularSession/Li,%20Aijun/Li,%20Aijun.pdf

Li, C. & Thompson, S. (1981). *Mandarin Chinese: A Functional Reference Grammar*. Berkeley: University of California Press.

Lyons, J. (1977). *Semantics*. 2 vols. Cambridge: Cambridge University Press.

Masunaga, K. (1988). 'Case deletion and discourse context'. In *Papers from the Second International Workshop on Japanese Syntax*, pp. 145–56. Stanford, CA: SCLI Stanford.

Matsumoto, Yoshiko (1988). 'Reexaminations of the universality of face'. *Journal of Pragmatics*, 12(4), 403–26.

Mazuka, R. & Itoh, K. (1995). 'Can Japanese speakers be led down the garden path?' In R. Mazuka & N. Nagai (eds), *Japanese Sentence Processing*, pp. 295–329. Hillsdale: Lawrence Erlbaum Associates.

McClure, W. (ed.), *Japanese/Korean Linguistics*, vol. 12, pp. 267–79. Stanford, CA: CSLI Publication.

McConville, M. (2001). *Incremental Natural Language Understanding with Combinatory Categorial Grammar*, Mst. thesis, University of Edinburgh.

McNeill, D. (1992). *Hand and Mind: What Gestures Reveal About Thought*. Chicago: University of Chicago Press.

Mehrabian, A. (1972). *Nonverbal Communication*. Aldine-Atherton, Illinois: Chicago.

Mehrabian, A. (1981). *Silent Messages: Implicit Communication of Emotions and Attitudes*. Belmont, CA: Wadsworth.

Michaud, A. & Brunelle, M. (2016). 'Information structure in Asia: Yongning Na (Sino-Tibetan) and Vietnamese (Austroasiatic)'. In C. Féry & S. Ishihara (eds), *The Oxford Handbook of Information Structure*, Chapter 38. Oxford: Oxford University Press.

Miyagawa, S. (2001). 'The EPP, scrambling, and wh-in-situ'. *Current Studies in Linguistics Series*, 36, 293–338.

Miyagawa, S. (2003). 'A-movement scrambling and options without optionality'. In S. Karimi (ed.), *Word Order and Scrambling*, pp. 177–200. Oxford: Blackwell.

Miyagawa, S. (2005). 'EPP and semantically vacuous scrambling'. In J. Sabel & M. Saito (eds), *The Free Word Order Phenomenon: Its Syntactic Sources and Diversity*, pp. 181–220. Berlin: Mouton de Gruyter.

Miyamoto, E. (2002). 'Case markers as clause boundary inducers in Japanese'. *Journal of Psycholinguistic Research*, 31, 307–47.

Moore, N., Hickson, M. & Stacks, D. W. (2014). *Nonverbal Communication: Studies and Applications*. New York: Oxford University Press.

Muhamedowa, R. (2015). *Kazakh: Routledge Comprehensive Grammars*. London and New York: Routledge.

Neeleman, Ad (1994). 'Scrambling as a D-structure phenomenon'. In N. Corver and H. van Riemsdijk (eds), *Studies on Scrambling*, pp. 387–429. Berlin: Mouton.

Newmeyer, F. (2005). *Possible and probable languages*. Oxford: Oxford University Press.

Nemoto, N. (1993). 'Chains and case positions: A study from scrambling in Japanese'. Unpublished doctoral dissertation, University of Connecticut.

Nordlinger, R. (1998). *Constructive Case*. Stanford: CSLI.

Nordlinger, R. & Lousia, S. (2006). 'Apposition as coordination: Evidence from Australian languages'. In *Proceedings of the LFG06 Conference*, Universität Konstanz, Germany.

Ogi, N. (2014). 'Language and an expression of identities: Japanese sentence-final particles ne and na'. *Journal of Pragmatics*, 64, 72–84.

Otero, C. (1994). *Noam Chomsky: Critical Assessments (Critical Assessments of Leading Linguists)*. London: Routledge.

Özge, D., Marinis, T. & Zeyrek, D. (2015). 'Incremental processing in head-final child language: online comprehension of relative clauses in Turkish-speaking children and adults'. *Language and Cognitive Processes*, 30(9), 1230–43.

Paikeday, T. M. (1985). 'May I kill the native speaker?' *TESOL Quarterly*, 19(2), 390–5.

Palmer, H. (1986). 'Words and terms'. *Philosophy*, 61(235), 71–82.

Pica, Pierre, Johan Rooryck. 'On the development and current status of generative grammar in France: A personal point of view', ms CNRS, UQAM, Indiana University.

Philips, C. (1996). 'Order and Structure'. Unpublished doctoral dissertation, MIT.
Philips, C. (2003). 'Linear order and constituency'. *Linguistic Inquiry*, 34, 37–90.
Phillips, C. (2009). 'Should we impeach armchair linguists?' In S. Iwasaki, H. Hoji, P. M. Clancy & S.-O. Sohn (eds), *Japanese/Korean Linguistics, vol 17*, pp. 49–64. Stanford, CA: CSLI Publications, University of Chicago Press.
Phillips, C. & Schütze, M. (2006). 'Relating structure and time in linguistics and psycholinguistics'. G. Gaskell (ed.), *Oxford Handbook of Psycholinguistics*. Oxford: Oxford University Press.
Phillips, C. & Wagers, M. (2007). 'Relating structure and time in linguistics and psycholinguistics'. In *Oxford Handbook of Psycholinguistics*, pp. 739–56. Oxford: Oxford University Press.
Pica, P. & Rooryck, J. (1994). 'On the development and current status of generative grammar in France: A personal point of view'. In C. Otero & N. Chomsky (eds), *Critical Assessments*. London: Routledge, 1994.
Pinkster, H. (1990). 'Evidence for SVO in Latin?' In R. Wright (ed.), *Latin and the Romance Languages in the Early Middle Ages*, pp. 69–82. London: Routledge.
Potts, C. (2005). *The Logic of Conventional Implicatures*. Oxford: Oxford University Press.
Potts, C. (2007). 'The expressive dimension'. *Theoretical Linguistics*, 33(2), 165–97.
Potts, C. & Kawahara, S. (2004). 'Japanese honorifics as emotive definite descriptions'. *Semantics and Linguistic Theory*, 14, 253–70.
Pritchett, B. (1992). *Grammatical Competence and Parsing Performance*. Chicago and London: University of Chicago Press.
Reape, M. (1994). 'Domain union and word order variation in German'. In J. Nerbonne, K. Netter and C. Pollard (eds), *German in Head-Driven Phrase Structure Grammar*, pp. 151–98. Stanford: CSLI.
Rizzi, L. (1997). 'The fine structure of the left periphery'. In L. Haegeman (ed.), *Elements of Grammar: A Handbook of Generative Syntax*, pp. 281–337. Dordrecht: Kluwer.
Ross, J. R. (1967). *Constraints on Variables in Syntax*. Doctoral dissertation, MIT. Published as Ross, J. R. (1986). *Infinite Syntax!* Norwood, NJ: ABLEX.
Sadler, L. & Nordlinger, R. (2006). 'Case stacking in realizational morphology'. *Linguistics*, 44(3), 459–87.
Sag, I. A. (2010). 'English filler-gap constructions'. *Language*, 86(3), 486–545.
Sag, I., Wasow, T. & Bender, E. (2003). *Introduction to Formal Syntax*. Chicago: Chicago University Press.
Saito, M. (1985). 'Some Asymmetries in Japanese and Their Theoretical Implications'. Unpublished doctoral dissertation, MIT.
Saito, M. (1989). 'Scrambling as semantically vacuous A-movement'. In M. Baltin & A. Krock (eds), *Alternative Conceptions of Phrase Structure*, 192–200. Chicago: University of Chicago Press.
Schmidt, R. L. (1999). *Urdu: An Essential Grammar*. London: Routledge.

Schütze, Carson T. (1996). *The Empirical Base of Linguistics: Grammaticality Judgments and Linguistic Methodology.* Chicago and London: University of Chicago.

Schütze, C. T. & Sprouse, J. (2014). 'Judgment data'. In R. Podesva & D. Sharma (eds), *Research Methods in Linguistics*, 27–50. Cambridge: Cambridge University Press. doi:10.1017/CBO9781139013734.004

Schwartzberg, J. & Bajpai, S. (1992). *A Historical Atlas of South Asia* (2nd impression, with additional material ed., The Association for Asian studies. Reference series; no. 2). New York and Oxford: Oxford University Press.

Sedighi, A., Shabani-Jadidi, P. & Karimi, S. (2018). 'Generative approaches to syntax'. *The Oxford Handbook of Persian Linguistics.* Oxford: Karimi.

Selkirk, E. (1984). *Phonology and Syntax: The Relation Between Sound and Structure.* Chicago: MIT Press.

Sharma, D. (2003). 'Nominal clitics and constructive morphology in Hindi'. In M. Butt & T. H. King (eds), *Nominals: Inside and Out*, pp. 59–84. Stanford, CA: CSLI.

Shei, C. (2014). *Understanding the Chinese Language: A Comprehensive Linguistic Introduction.* London: Routledge

Sherr-Ziarko, E. & Kiaer, J. (2019). 'A prosodic analysis of intervening objects in English phrasal verbs using the British National Corpus'. In S. Calhoun, P. Escudero, M. Tabain & Paul Warren (eds), *Proceedings of the 19th International Congress of Phonetic Sciences. Melbourne, Australia 2019*, pp. 275–9. Canberra, Australia: Australasian Speech Science and Technology Association Inc.

Shibatani, M. (1990). *The Languages of Japan.* Cambridge: Cambridge University Press.

Shimojo, M. (2005). *Argument Encoding in Japanese Conversation.* Basingstoke: Palgrave Macmillan.

Simpson, J. (1991). 'Warlpiri morphosyntax: A lexicalist approach'. *Studies in Natural Language and Linguistic Theory.* Dordrecht: Kluwer.

Smyth, D. (2002). *Thai: An Essential Grammar.* London and New York: Routledge.

Sohn, H. (1999). *The Korean Language* (Cambridge Language Surveys). Cambridge: Cambridge University Press.

Song, J. J. (2012). *Word Order.* Cambridge: Cambridge University Press.

Spear, F. S. (1995). 'Metamorphic phase equilibria and pressure-temperature-time paths'. Retrieved from www.minsocam.org/MSA/Monographs/Mono01.html

Sperber, D. & Wilson, D. (1986, 1995, 2005). *Relevance: Communication and Cognition.* Oxford: Basil Blackwell.

Staal, J. F. (1967). *Word Order in Sanskrit and Universal Grammar.* Dordrecht: D. Reidel Publishing Company.

Steedman, M. (2000). *The Syntactic Process.* Cambridge, MA: MIT Press.

Stowe, L. (1986). 'Evidence for on-line gap-location'. *Language and Cognitive Processes*, 1, 227–45.

Sun, C. (2006). *Chinese: A Linguistic Introduction.* Cambridge: Cambridge University Press.

Tabor, W., Galantucci, B. & Richardson, D. (2004). 'Effects of merely local syntactic coherence on sentence processing'. *Journal of Memory & Language*, 50(4), 355–70.

Takano, Y. (2002). 'Surprising constituents'. *Journal of East Asian Linguistics*, 11, 243–301.

Takubo, Y. & Kinsui, S. (1997). 'Discourse management in terms of mental spaces'. *Journal of Pragmatics*, 28(6), 741–58.

Thompson, H. R. (2010). *Bengali: A Comprehensive Grammar*. London and New York: Routledge.

Thompson, H. R. (2012). *Bengali* (Vol. 18). Amsterdam: John Benjamins Publishing.

Thomson, L. (1965). *A Vietnamese Grammar*. Seattle: University of Washington Press.

Tsujimura, N. (2005, 2013). *An Introduction to Japanese Linguistics*. Oxford: John Wiley & Sons.

Tsutsui, M. (1984). *Particle Ellipses in Japanese*. ProQuest Dissertations and Theses, University of Illinois at Urbana-Champaign.

Vermuelen, R. (2007). 'Japanese *wa* phrases that aren't topics'. In R. Breheny & Nikolaos Velegrakis (eds), *UCL Working Papers in Linguistics* 19, 183–201.

Vetter, H., Volovecky, J. & Howell, J. (1979). 'Judgments of grammaticalness: A partial replication and extension'. *Journal of Psycholinguistic Research*, 8(6), 567–83.

Wasow, T. (2002). *Postverbal Behavior*. Stanford: CSLI.

Wasow, T. (2007). 'Gradient data and gradient grammars'. In *Proceedings from the Annual Meeting of the Chicago Linguistic Society*, 43(1), 255–71. Chicago Linguistic Society.

Wharton, T. (2009). *Pragmatics and Non-Verbal Communication*. Cambridge: Cambridge University Press.

Wu, R. (2004). *Stance in Talk: A Conversation Analysis of Mandarin Final Particles*. Amsterdam: John Benjamins Publishing Company.

Wymann, A. T. (1996). *The Expression of Modality in Korean*. Doctoral dissertation, Universität Bern, Switzerland.

Yamanaka, A. (2008). *Utterance Interpretation, Group-Defining Practices and Linguistic Meaning: Japanese a Case Study*. PhD dissertation, King's College, London.

Yang, C. 杨才英 (2009). 'The interpersonal meaning of chinese modal particles'. (论汉语语气词的人际意义), *Foreign Language and Literature* 外国语言文学 (6), 26–32.

Yatabe, S. (1996). 'Long-distance scrambling via partial compaction'. *In Formal Approaches to Japanese Linguistics, 2*, pp. 303–17. MIT Working Papers in Linguistics.

Yeon J. & Brown, L. (2011). *Korean: A Comprehensive Grammar*. London and New York: Routledge.

Yoshimoto, K. (2000). 'A bistratal approach to the prosody-syntax interface in Japanese'. In R. Cann, R. Cann, C. Grover & P. Miller (eds), *Grammatical Interfaces in HPSG*, pp. 267–82. Stanford: CSLI Publications.

Yousef, S. (2018). *Persian: A Comprehensive Grammar*. London and New York: Routledge.

Zebrowitz, L. A., Montepare, J. M. & Lee, H. K. (1993). 'They don't all look alike: Individual impressions of other racial groups'. *Journal of Personality and Social Psychology*, 65(1), 85–101. doi:10.1037/0022-3514.65.1.85

Zipf, G. (1949). *Human Behavior and the Principle of Least Effort*. Cambridge, MA: Addison-Wesley.

Zwicky, A. (1986). 'German adjective agreement'. *Linguistics*, 24(5), 957–90.

Index

acceptability   43, 48–9, 218
adjunction   36, 37, 146–50, 159, 166, 223
affection   65, 67–8, 89, 110, 177, 180, 194, 219
age   80–6, 103, 105, 107–11, 161, 184, 190–1, 195, 203, 220–1
(dis)agreement   65, 177, 180, 195
agreement   4, 65, 70, 93, 114, 161, 177, 180, 183, 192, 196–7, 200, 202
Anglo-centric   ix, 2, 5–6, 9, 23, 42, 57, 211
Anglophone   2, 24, 212
Arabic   2, 10, 16–17, 134, 168, 215–16, 222
Asia   2, 10–11, 15, 17–20, 80–1, 83, 85, 89, 91, 111, 219, 222
Asian   ix, 1–4, 7, 9–18, 20–1, 23–7, 31, 33, 36, 39, 42, 46, 51–2, 61, 63–4, 65–6, 72, 78–6, 88–9, 92–4, 102–4, 111, 113–14, 116–17, 119, 122–3, 127, 129, 132, 139–40, 157, 160, 163, 165, 171, 177–83, 189, 198, 200–3, 210, 211–13, 215–17, 220, 223
at-issue meaning   66–7
attitudinal   x, 5, 65, 67–9, 75, 82, 85, 113, 117, 122–3, 159, 177, 180–81, 183, 188, 193, 197–8, 200–1, 203–10, 212
attitudinal modality   82
auxiliaries   ix, 4, 39, 66, 68, 72, 182

(un)belief   65, 123, 177, 181, 192
Bengali   2, 8, 10, 16–18, 98, 101–2, 104, 114, 125, 134, 168, 198, 202, 220–1
Brown and Levinson   77–9, 88
Burmese   10, 19, 53, 85, 104, 107, 116, 120–1, 123, 134, 170–1, 178–80, 183, 200, 202

Cann, Ronnie   14, 134, 138, 140, 146, 150, 156, 175, 203, 222
certainty   39–40, 59, 65, 123, 146, 177, 181, 189, 194

Chomsky   1, 8–9, 13, 32, 34, 37, 43–4, 216–18
combinatory categorial grammar (CCG)   23, 37, 40–2, 54, 136, 138
combinatory force   42, 64, 137, 165
commitment meaning   66–7
competence   4, 20, 43–4, 46, 54, 56, 65, 77, 79, 82, 139, 163, 176
computer-mediated communication (CMC)   69, 71, 90–1, 161
constituent recognition domain (CRD)   55–6
constructive   ix–x, 5–6, 10, 20–1, 25, 40, 113, 129, 132, 133, 135, 147, 149, 152–3, 158–9, 165–76, 193, 204

dis-affectionate   68
diverse   7, 14, 17, 19, 64–5, 80, 88, 94, 103, 119, 122, 151, 159, 163, 176–7, 179, 183, 194, 205, 210, 213
doubt   65, 123, 177, 181, 192, 198
dynamic syntax (DS)   x, 134–42, 144, 146, 148, 150, 154–6, 159, 163, 165, 173–6, 183, 203–4, 206, 209–10, 213, 222, 223

efficiency   5, 43, 45–6, 55, 64, 134, 150, 159–61, 213
emoji   69, 71–2, 90–1, 161, 222
emoticon   69–72, 80
emotion   67, 72, 130–2, 158, 179–80, 188, 192–3, 197, 203–4, 219, 224
emotive   67, 73, 182, 233
empathy   5, 79, 91, 133–4, 159–61, 177, 213
emphatic   71, 121, 177, 180, 185, 195, 199–200
encouragement   65, 177, 180
endearment   65, 177, 180
enthusiasm   65, 177, 180
Euro-centric   ix, 5–10, 23, 42, 57, 88, 211

expressive   x, 5–6, 10–11, 14, 21, 65–77, 82, 113, 117, 124–5, 159–60, 163, 167, 171, 177, 179, 181–3, 185, 187–9, 193–5, 198–200, 203–10, 221
expressive semantics   x, 14, 65–6, 82
expressivity   5, 134, 159, 172, 177, 213

face-threatening act (FTA)   77–9, 82
Filled-Gap Effect   45–6
first person pronoun   96, 101–2, 105, 107, 175
flexible word order   11, 15, 17, 19, 25, 141, 144, 165, 166, 171
formal   13, 48, 65, 68–9, 76, 81, 83, 85, 89, 94, 96–7, 99, 101–2, 105, 106–8, 126, 128, 130–1, 133, 160, 162, 173, 177, 181, 183, 189–90, 192, 196, 199, 202, 205, 212, 216
formula   139–40, 143, 156–8
friendliness   65, 78, 177, 180, 191
functor   140–3, 146–7, 204, 207

gender   84, 101, 105, 107, 117, 179, 183, 185, 190–1, 203
grammaticality   7, 27–8, 33, 35–6, 43–4, 46–50, 162, 212, 218
Grice, Herbert Paul   66

Hawkins, John   15, 49–50, 55–6, 61, 64, 150
Hebrew   16–17, 54, 197, 215
Hindi   2, 10, 16–18, 24, 73–4, 93, 100–1, 119–20, 134, 168, 198, 206, 215
honorific   4, 48, 75–6, 79, 83–4, 87, 90, 93, 96, 100–2, 104–7, 110–11, 117, 177–8, 198, 204, 206–7
humble   77, 83, 90, 106, 178

immediate constituent   55
Indonesian   11, 105, 109–10, 134, 144, 170
informal   13, 68, 73–4, 76, 86, 94–5, 97, 99, 101, 107–10, 126–8, 130–3, 141, 148, 160, 166, 174, 184, 188, 191–2, 195, 205–6, 221
instant messaging (IM)   71–2
interactional   ix, 117, 128, 163, 211–12
interpersonal   x, 4–5, 7, 9, 13–14, 21, 65, 68, 72–4, 79, 80, 82, 83–8, 94–6, 103–4, 111, 117, 123, 129–32, 158, 160–1, 177–9, 182–3, 189, 193–4, 197–8, 201, 204–6, 218, 221
intimacy   x, 48, 78, 80–1, 84–6, 84–90, 94–6, 103, 105, 108, 110, 130–2, 148, 179–80, 209, 212, 220–1
IP boundary tone   151–2, 202

Japanese   2, 5–6, 9–10, 12–3, 15–6, 18–20, 24, 34, 36–8, 52, 57–8, 61–2, 75–6, 78–80, 87, 102, 105, 108–9, 116–20, 123–4, 127, 135, 161, 168, 183, 189–91, 202, 204, 210, 215–16, 220, 222

Kaplan, Ronald   66, 146
Kazakh   53–4, 115, 144, 151
Kempson, Ruth   14, 134, 138, 140, 146, 156, 175, 209, 223
Kendon   88
Khmer   2, 20, 105–6, 114, 134, 170, 200
kinship   x, 103, 105, 109–11, 179, 222
Korean   2, 5, 9–10, 12–13, 15–16, 18–20, 24–31, 33, 38, 48, 53, 58, 62, 68, 70–6, 80–1, 85–8, 90–1, 94–5, 98, 105, 108–10, 116–21, 123–32, 134–5, 137, 141, 147–8, 150–2, 154, 157, 166, 168, 174, 182, 202, 215–7, 219–21

languaging   162–3, 213
Lao   2, 8, 16, 20, 69–70, 92, 96–7, 114, 121, 123, 134–5, 141, 144–5, 170–1, 174–5, 179–90, 195, 200–1, 209, 221
left-right asymmetry   24, 41, 134
lexical-functional grammar (LFG)   13, 23, 37, 39–40, 54, 136–7, 146, 217
lexical macro   144, 149, 166, 204
lexical matrix   83–4, 99, 111, 113, 129, 131–2, 157–8, 173, 207
linguistic structure building   136–7, 160
  *adjunction   146, 149, 150
  general update   146
  local *adjunction   146–50, 166, 223
  local/immediate update   146
  non-local/non-immediate update   146
LINK
  LINK(ed) structure   14, 157–9, 174–5, 204–7, 209

LINK operation   157, 175–6, 183, 204–5, 207, 210
LINK relation   156–7, 204
locality   24, 46, 64, 147, 149–50, 166, 176, 223
long-distance dependency   37, 40, 138, 147, 217

Mandarin Chinese   2, 10, 16, 19, 53, 99, 134–5, 170, 193, 202–3, 219
Mazuka and Itoh   52–3
meta-variable   141–3, 145, 169, 174–5, 207
minimized domains (MiD)   50–1, 56
Miyamoto, Edson   54, 59
modal   ix, 124, 143, 147, 152, 182, 193
Mongolian   10, 16, 19, 121, 134–5, 168–9, 202
mood   8, 69, 84, 128–32, 158, 178–80, 204
morphosyntactic   ix, 2, 4, 10, 13–14, 37–8, 42, 44, 113, 135, 216, 218
multidimensional   14, 65–7, 69, 71, 73, 75, 77, 79, 81–3, 98, 113, 124, 128, 132, 156–7, 163, 174, 189, 203–5, 207–10, 212–13
multifaceted   ix, 85, 113, 196
multimodal modulation hypothesis (MMH)   14, 83, 92–5, 97, 111, 132, 174, 183, 197, 205–6, 209
multiple long-distance scrambling   27, 35, 37, 40

oblique movement   36–7
order   6, 9, 11–12, 15–20, 23–8, 31–2, 35, 37–42, 54–6, 61, 64, 80–1, 134–7, 139–41, 144, 150, 154–6, 160, 165–6, 170–2, 216, 222

partial compaction   38
particle
   case particle   ix, 5–6, 11, 15–17, 19–20, 25–6, 32, 39–40, 61–2, 64, 115, 125, 134–7, 147–50, 159, 165–72, 222
   enclitic   4, 188–9
   focus particle   117, 119–23, 125–6, 177, 181, 198

interrogative particle   69–70, 191, 198, 209
proclitic   4
topic particle   25, 117–20, 122–3, 125, 177, 181, 194
performance   7, 20, 43–4, 46, 150
Persian   10, 16–18, 27–8, 31, 33, 97–8, 114, 134–5, 143–4, 168–9, 174–6, 181, 198, 215
perspective   ix, 2–5, 9, 23–4, 32, 64, 72–4, 84, 88, 121–4, 127–9, 131, 133, 153, 166, 177, 178, 181–2, 188, 202, 204, 211–12
Phillips, Colin   7, 46–8, 57, 61, 64, 139, 217
plurality   75, 103, 113–17, 127, 168–70, 222
politeness   48, 69, 73–9, 82–8, 90, 92–3, 95–8, 100–5, 108–11, 117, 130–32, 177, 184, 189, 191, 196, 199, 206, 220–1
Potts, Christopher   x, 14, 65–7, 72, 74, 82
pragmatic syntax   133–4, 136, 159–63, 213
pragmatic syntax hypothesis   134, 136, 159, 213
preference asymmetry   43–5, 154
procedural   42, 46, 49, 64, 133, 137, 223
pro-drop   13, 16, 134, 141, 145, 168, 170
prosody   11–13, 21, 30, 38, 40, 42, 51, 64, 80, 87–8, 91, 93, 96, 125, 127–8, 133–4, 137, 149, 151–4, 156, 161, 165–6, 175–6, 181, 189, 200–3, 205, 210

remnant movement   34–5, 37
respect   75, 78, 81, 83–9, 94, 96–9, 103, 107, 109, 110–11, 175, 183, 201, 204, 206–9, 212, 221
Right Roof Constraint   24
routinization   136, 149–1, 153, 166
royal   105, 106, 178, 199

Saito, Mamoru   24, 26, 32
Sanskrit   1, 8, 11, 15, 16, 134, 168
Schütze, Carlson   47, 218
scrambling   12–13, 26–7, 31–2, 35, 37–8, 40–1, 138, 222

second person pronoun 13, 74, 83, 85, 86, 93, 96–8, 100–11, 143, 188, 206, 221
self-paced reading 45, 152
sentence/utterance-final particle (SFP) 53, 183, 194–6, 198–200
sentence/utterance initial particle (SIP) 197–8
sentence/utterance medial particle (SMP) 198–9
slowdown 45–6, 52, 58
social hierarchy 73, 80, 84, 94, 100–3, 117, 129–30, 178, 221
social status 84–6, 105–6, 111, 184
sociocultural x, 4, 14, 79, 81, 85, 104, 182, 191
socio-pragmatic ix, 3, 5, 9–10, 14–15, 21, 47–9, 65, 74, 79, 81–2, 83–111, 117, 123, 129, 134, 150, 160, 162–3, 166, 177–8, 182–3, 189, 206, 210, 212
speaker-commitment meaning 67
sticker 72
structural routine 64, 134–6, 149–51, 153
style 20, 84–6, 96, 99, 102, 117, 127, 129–32, 145, 158, 178, 180–81, 204–5, 221
surprise 52, 58, 65, 73, 162, 177, 179–80, 189, 196, 199, 200, 203
surprising constituents 23–4, 32–4, 36–7, 40, 134, 151, 153

Tagalog 2, 10, 16, 19, 41, 69, 76, 115, 134, 138, 168, 170, 172–3, 183, 187–9, 210, 215
Tamil 2, 16–17, 134, 168
Thai 2, 11, 16, 20, 76, 85, 96–7, 105–6, 114, 123, 134–5, 151, 170, 175, 178, 183–5, 189, 201, 206–7, 210, 215, 221
3E model 161, 163
Tibetan 10, 15–16, 19, 115, 134, 168, 170, 196
translanguaging 162–3, 213
Tsujimura, Natsuko 6, 61
Turkish 10, 12–13, 16–17, 24, 40, 53, 115, 134–5, 139, 165, 168–9, 215
type 40, 42, 138, 140, 142–3, 206

under-represented 2, 4, 7, 10, 23, 212
underspecification 69, 135–8
un-forced revision 57–9, 61
Urdu 10, 16–18, 74, 98–101, 119–20, 134, 168–9, 199, 215
utterance-final particle (UFP) 183, 194, 198–200
utterance initial particle (UIP) 197–8
utterance medial particle (UMP) 198–9

verb 8–10, 13, 15–16, 19, 23, 25, 28–30, 32, 34–7, 40, 45–6, 49, 52–61, 64, 74, 92, 98, 100–2, 114, 121, 133–6, 139, 141–5, 148–9, 152–4, 159, 166, 168, 172, 199, 206–7, 218–19, 222
Vietnamese 2, 10–11, 16, 20, 110–11, 121, 134, 170, 199, 205, 219

Western European 3, 8, 10, 13–14, 20, 65–75, 81, 83, 103–4, 111, 113–14, 117, 211, 216
wh-feature 58, 218–19
World Atlas of Language Structures (WALS) 9, 13, 15, 103–4, 216

Ziphian law 160